The Mossad Messiah

A novel of Israel

by

Leigh Lerner

Counterflow Press

MONTREAL, QUEBEC, CANADA

Counterflow Press
Montréal, Québec, Canada
www.mossadmessiah.com

Publisher's Note: This is a work of fiction. Names, characters, places, and incidents are a product of the author's imagination. Locales and public names are sometimes used for atmospheric purposes. Any resemblance to actual people, living or dead, or to businesses, companies, events, institutions, or locales is completely coincidental.

Book Layout © 2017 BookDesignTemplates.com

The Mossad Messiah/ Leigh Lerner. – 1st ed.
ISBN, paperback edition: ISBN 978-1-7750690-0-3

Dedicated to Loren,

who urged it to be done

and helped bring it to fruition.

אם תרצו אין זו אגדה
If you will it, this is no fantasy.

–THEODOR HERZL

CONTENTS

PROLOGUE

Rabbi Levi ben David v'Yehudit used to say, "Who could be the Messiah? Virtually any Jew might descend from King David and receive that charge, as it is written, All Israel came together to David at Hebron and said, 'We are your own flesh and blood'." (I Chronicles 11:1)

13 Tishri 5734 – 9 October 1973

Three bloody days into the Yom Kippur War, beleaguered by dwindling materiel and too many dead among the Children of Israel, Defense Minister Moshe Dayan confided to *Rosh HaMemshalah* Golda Meir, "Madam Prime Minister, this is the end of the Third Temple."[1]

Despite it all, the Third Temple survived, and to this day no nation has destroyed it, though many are those ready to rejoice in its demise.

Has the ineffable mind of God another plan for the downfall of the Third Temple, or instead, for its survival? According to Jewish tradition, the future of the Third Temple belongs to the Jews, their decisions, their actions and their reactions. Day by day they write the story of what will come to pass.

BOOK I

בראשית

Genesis / "In the beginning"

CHAPTER ONE

12 Heshvan 5756 – Saturday evening, 4 November 1995
Tel Aviv, Israel

B o BaYom,[2] on that day, late in the night after Yigal Amir assassinated Prime Minister Yitzhak Rabin, the new and acting *Rosh HaMemshalah*, Shimon Peres, son of Yitzhak and Sarah, called together his security advisors, a meeting set in conference rooms enshrouded in secrecy at Israeli Army Intelligence. Seated around a small table were Shabtai Haneshri, director of the Mossad foreign intelligence office; Major General Moshe Ben-David, director of Aman military intelligence; Commissioner Assaf, head of the Israeli National Police; and Carmi Bar-Orcheidin, director of Shin Bet internal security.

These sages of stealth, men accustomed to leverage the wide powers of their office, men schooled in crisis management and covert operations, also knew each other as friends. Usually they traded barbs and compared their families' progress as they waited, but because of the disturbing and unprecedented nature of the moment, they sat silently shuffling papers in their file folders until the expected entrance of Acting *Rosh HaMemshalah* Peres.

Carmi Bar-Orcheidin took a second look at the table and burst the bubble of restraint that enclosed the room. "There's an extra chair here – for whom?"

More silence followed, now filled with shrugs, questioning faces, and dismissive hand motions, only to be halted by the clicks of an opening lock. Seeing Peres at the open door, all arose from their seats. The Acting Prime Minster entered leading a short, slender woman.

Her tight, concentrated face, her pursed lips, her eyes darting from person to person around the table gave the appearance of a hardened tax agent for the Israel Revenue Authority, but her statistical interests went farther afield. Mona Tsofen directed Israel's Central Bureau of Statistics.

"Gentlemen," Peres said, nodding to the group, "do you all know Mona Tsofen, head of our national statistical bureau? In light of tonight's events, I asked her to join us." Those around the table greeted her and looked quizzically at each other.

When all were seated, Peres began. "We mourn the loss of Yitzhak Rabin. We have his assassin, Yigal Amir, in lock-up. Tell me what you know about him. Let's start with motive. Where did this Amir get the idea to kill Rabin?"

Shabtai Haneshri gave a dismissive cluck. "Mossad has no report on him from outside our borders."

Major General Ben-David said, "He went to Yeshivat Kerem B'Yavneh, the first Hesder yeshiva. Students from Hesder yeshivas serve in the army. Our records show that Amir studied Talmud and served well in the Golani Brigade. His yeshiva takes a religious Zionist position that sees Israel as the forerunner of the messiah, but even Amir's fellow soldiers considered him a fanatic."

Commissioner Assaf took a deep breath, exhaled audibly, and shook his head. "He had a clean record with the National Police, though now it appears he prepared two other attempts on Rabin's life."

Carmi Bar-Orcheidin shuffled a file in front of him. "Here are Shin Bet's facts on Amir: because he uttered threats to kill Rabin for two years, we set up a man to follow his moves. Instead, we were set up by our operative. I'm certain our man was himself untrustworthy and misled us. We admit to a profound failure in our protective work."

Peres replied, "We'll discuss this failure privately at a later time. I'd still like to know, what incited Amir to assassinate Rabin? With all his Jewish studies, what could have permitted him to murder?"

Carmi Bar-Orcheidin continued, "Believe it or not, Amir relied on Jewish law, the law of the pursuer, the *Din Rodef*, which gives leave to kill a person in blood pursuit of his neighbor in order to keep the potential murderer from a grave sin.[3] Some say he learned to hate Rabin in classes at Bar Ilan University with his yeshiva rabbis, but these same rabbis deny any malignant teaching. Despite their denials, we have report of their incitement against Rabin in classes that Amir attended. To Yigal Amir, the Oslo Peace Accords proved Yitzhak Rabin was a pursuer of the entire nation of Israel, out to destroy our people."

Peres, thinking of his Nobel Peace Prize, looked up, read the faces of his council, and remarked, "Oslo? So I, too, am one of Amir's 'pursuers'?"

"You haven't noticed the increase in your bodyguard?" the Shin Bet director responded.

"No, but given Amir's overzealous religiosity, I'll tell you what I have noticed. I've noticed growing problems from ultra-Orthodox streams of Judaism, and that's why I asked Mona Tsofen from Central Statistics, to join us. I'll let her explain."

Unlike the others, Mona Tsofen arose to speak, seeking to gain the power of height over her imposing colleagues.

"Only a few months ago Dr. Baruch Goldstein was buried. His religious roots stem from American ultra-Orthodoxy. After he murdered 29 Muslims at prayer and wounded 125 others at the Cave of Machpelah in Hebron, where the Patriarchs and Matriarchs are buried, Goldstein should have been a pariah. To ultra-Orthodox nationalists, he is a hero, and a thousand people attended his funeral. Amir is of his ilk.

"Lest you think the Goldsteins and Amirs are exceptional lunatics, I admonish you to take them seriously. They're a branch of the ultra-Orthodox stock, a branch bearing poisonous fruit, a persistent threat to the State of Israel. In fact, ultra-Orthodoxy itself may become our most significant domestic problem.

"We have up-to-the-minute figures for 1995. Right now the ultra-Orthodox, the Haredim, and Hasidim are 350,000 of us. In twenty years, by 2015, 750,000. At their 5% annual growth rate, they will reach roughly between 3-6 million by 2060, at the high-end figure, more than half of Israel's Jews. Some groups think the State of Israel is illegitimate because the messiah did not bring it about. Others are extremist nationalists, little different from Haredi in their religious practice. How many in the future will consider the whole government a 'pursuer'?

"Many think their settlements beyond the Green Line will restore ancient lands to our State and cause the messiah to come. Some terrorize Palestinians in pursuit of their 'holy' cause. A good many believe their interpretation of halacha, Jewish traditional law, overrides Knesset law and Supreme Court judgments.

"Central Statistics estimates that 30% of the students in elementary schools will be Haredi by 2015. What do they learn about Israel, about democracy, about human rights, about love of neighbor – non-Orthodox neighbor, non-Jewish neighbor? Ultimately, most want Israel governed by halacha, not our democratic tradition of positive law. They vote *en bloc* as their rabbis' demand and therefore could control our parliament before they reach majority status.

"*We* created the assassin Amir because the government underwrote his yeshiva studies but paid insufficient attention when he began walking a path antithetical to our society's well-being, a path perhaps encouraged by his rabbinic masters.

"Now let's add to that individual case the wider demographic threat to our welfare and safety. When the Haredi population explodes into a near-majority, how will Israel finance the Talmud studies of a quarter million men or more, not the tens of thousands the law requires us to subsidize today at the cost of a billion US dollars? How can the country afford the cost of welfare benefits to a huge population unemployed at a rate of 45%? Who will defend Israel when half exempt themselves to study Talmud?

"The murder of Rabin is more than a wake-up call. It cuts to the core of the Jewish soul like the shofar blast at the end of Yom Kippur. We created this explosive threat, and we must now defuse it, or demography will irreparably blow us apart. Demography cries out that tomorrow belongs to the ultra-Orthodox. When tomorrow comes, it will be too late for the secular, the modern Orthodox, and the liberal Jews, and especially too late for the government of the State of Israel to alter our history. We must act soon."

Mona Tsofen sat down. Carmi Bar-Orcheidin took up her theme. "Mona Tsofen is right. Since the Baruch Goldstein debacle, Shin Bet has closely followed the fanatically ultra-Orthodox. Amir believes with perfect faith that certain rabbis wear the mantle of Moses, with the right to enforce their Torah, no matter what Knesset legislates. Amir and his ultra-Orthodox compatriots believe this with perfect faith, and in one more thing: they believe in the coming of the messiah.

"I see your faces. I see eyes rolling upward with incredulity. Don't sneer at this, their dearly held credo. Already one powerful sect of Hasidim in America is ripping itself in two, with half believing their dead rebbe will return as the messiah.

"When the messiah at last arrives, they're convinced that restrictive fences around Torah law will fall away. Nearly 200 years ago Moses Sofer of Bratislava set the stage for ultra-Orthodoxy by adding new rigidity. In his day Jews, enraptured by the modern and yearning to belong to it, inclined their hearts to Western liberal insights and reform. This rabbi reacted with fury by quoting the Mishnah, 'The Torah forbids what is new.'[4]

"The Mishnah forbade Temple gifts of 'new grain,' but Sofer himself innovated. He twisted the phrase to mean that nothing new could be added, and only the old was sacred. With that Mishnah he fenced out champions of change, but also fenced in the faithful with a high stockade of constraints, so that the pure and righteous Haredi live their lives immured by the old law and its new strictures, yet blessing God for their confinement a hundred times a day.

"Ah, but in the days of the messiah, all Jews, some say all humanity, will voluntarily, with a good heart and a new spirit, keep the Torah law. In the days of the messiah, fences around the law will collapse. People will have no propensity to evil, and the words of the prophet will prevail, '. . . I will put My law in their minds and write it on their hearts for they shall all know Me, from the least to the greatest of them' (Jeremiah 31:33). I'm telling you, they believe this with perfect certainty.

"Mona Tsofen is correct. The Land will not be able to contain their numbers, nor our people accept the denial of rights, the rigid rules, and unseemly behavior they may seek to foist upon us as their numbers grow toward majority status. Even now they deface posters of women candidates at election time. They hack advertisements for women's bathing suits from bus stops. They segregate sidewalks and buses, men here, women there. They heave filthy diapers at Shabbat motorists who happen to pass by their areas. They attack people at the Western Wall who practice differently from them. On and on it has gone, until finally it has come to murder. Their burgeoning strictures and violence will eventually cause an unstoppable exodus of our most productive citizens.

"There is only one way to stand this situation on its head. We must bring them their messiah. Bring the messiah and you change the rules of their game. The law will not be gone, but the halacha of mutual mistrust and Haredi superiority should disappear. The right messiah can change their laws and lives."

Peres interjected, "You're as crazy as they are. Bring a messiah, and with him comes chaos."

Carmi Bar-Orcheidin responded, "Chaos for them, perhaps, but that kind of chaos can also be liberating. Mr. Prime Minister, Mossad and Shin Bet have found the man who could be the messiah. We have a plan to bring about his rise, but not now, maybe not for a couple of decades. The day may come when Israel will need the changes he could unleash, and we think he'll mature and become ready to bring them about."

Peres said, "He might also liberate the demons hiding in every shadow. Nevertheless, it's so long-range, you might as well watch him, and yes, develop your plan. Some day we may need it. For now, let's get down to business. We must find and prosecute all involved in promoting and causing the murder of Yitzhak Rabin, and expose the teachers of violence to public disdain."

Rabbi Shimon taught: 'The fast on the ninth of Av mourns the loss of the Temple. The fast on the third of Tishri is the fast of Gedaliah. On that day, the man appointed by the Babylonians to govern Judah, Gedaliah the son of Ahikam, was murdered. Who killed him? A Jew, Ishmael the son of Nethaniah, killed him. The third of Tishri became a fast day to show that the murder of the righteous is equal to the burning of the Temple on the 9th of Av. [5]
Rabbi Levi ben David v'Yehudit asked, should there not be a fast day on the 12th of Heshvan? On that day Yitzhak Rabin son of Nehemiah and Rosa was murdered. Who killed him? A Jew, Yigal Amir son of Shlomo and Geula killed him. If you can argue that the fast of Gedaliah is linked to the destruction of the First Temple because his murder occurred shortly thereafter, then let me argue that the assassination of Rabin presages a future fall of the Third Temple. Unless.

CHAPTER TWO

12 Heshvan 5756, 9:00 PM Saturday night, 4 November 1995
Brooklyn, New York

The doorbell of the Borisover Rebbe's home in Borough Park sounded more like the ringing of an alarm system than a simple summons to the entryway of the multi-story brick house. The valet answered and called the Rebbe. "Rabbi Silverman here to see you."

Emanuel Davidson tightened his robe around his pajamas as he walked into the elevator and pushed "1" to descend from the second floor. Extreme age seemed not to touch his agile mind, but it had wracked his knees to the point that he required the installation of a lift to remain in the Rebbe's manse.

Emanuel invited his visitor, Rabbi Chaim Silverman, majordomo and spiritual business manager of the widespread world of the Borisover Hasidim, into the parlor. The problem had to be pressing for Chaim to arrive at such a late hour without calling first.

When the two were seated, Emanuel came quickly to the point. "What brings you here at such an hour, Chaim?"

"Rebbe, it was important that I see you as soon as Shabbos ended. I know you usually go quickly home to relax after we say farewell to Shabbat with Havdalah, so perhaps you have not heard the news. Yitzhak Rabin has been assassinated. Rabin is dead."

"Who would do such a thing?" Emanuel wanted to know. They looked across the coffee table at each other, their eyes locked.

"Rebbe, he is not one of ours," Rabbi Silverman added in a hushed tone.

"Thank God for that," Emanuel muttered. "But then who?"

"Non-Hasidic, ultra-nationalist, considered Orthodox extremist, learned Torah at Bar Ilan's yeshiva, maybe influenced by a Talmud teacher there."

Emanuel said, "Is this going to affect life at Kfar Rachel village? Is it going to change things for all our Beit Borisov learning centers and synagogues? Will it alter the support payments from the government to our yeshiva students and their families in Eretz Yisrael? Aren't these the main worries?"

Rabbi Silverman answered quickly, "Honestly, I don't believe anything will change in regard to our interests in Eretz Yisrael. Already Peres is acting prime minister. Their ship of state sails on. But Rebbe, I am here precisely because the powers-that-be in Eretz Yisrael have a plan for the continuation of leadership under such a circumstance, and you don't."

"Rebbe, for years you and I together have constructed a worldwide Hasidic presence. Borisov can be found in virtually every corner of the globe, and you, its Rebbe, have become a foremost leader of world Jewry. All those achievements provided my greatest joy in life.

"I must confess, Rebbe, to fifteen years of frustration with you in only one regard. I have begged, I have cajoled, I have counseled, I have pleaded and done all in my power to get you to create a full-fledged viable plan of succession. Who will be the new Borisover Rebbe? Or describe the movement's chain of command without our Rebbe. I am your faithful servant, but like Eliezer going to get a wife for Isaac, I cannot go and get another Rebbe, nor can I create a ruling council without your permission, your imprimatur.

"Your beloved wife Rachel is gone ten years now. She helped make your leadership outstanding. We have put her name on the map of Eretz Yisrael. We know that her mind and yours were entirely dedicated to spreading the message of Borisover *Hasidus*. We miss your beloved Rachel, but we have known that you lack an heir for decades now, and you do nothing to remedy that fact. Rachel's womb produced no successor, and we know of not a single relative of the original founding family who can undertake the task, nor have you given us a directive about succession. This issue generates huge tension among our Hasidim and our followers, who have grown legion during the 50-plus years under your guidance.

"Rebbe, we need to talk, and this stunning and horrible murder of Rabin should force us to focus on tomorrow. Yitzhak Rabin thought he had more time to lead Eretz Yisrael, and now, all at once, his time is up. Rebbe, you are young at heart, but your hundredth year is not that far away. You cannot avoid this decision any longer, and I'll not leave this room until you tell me how next to proceed to assure a smooth transition for the Borisovers."

Emanuel fiddled with a small decorative piece on the coffee table, his hand shaking slightly with an uncontrollable tremor. When he replaced the ceramic, he looked up at Chaim Silverman. He spoke softly, a new lightness in his voice. "Chaim, it is time for truth-telling. There may be an heir who can eventually preside over the Borisovers, but he is not yet ready. Indeed, he is completely unaware of the possibility that lies within him. He lives in Eretz Yisrael."

Rabbi Silverman sat wordlessly, his entire visage indicating, "Tell me more."

The Rebbe continued. "He's a lad, a *bar mitzvah bochur*. It's this year, his bar mitzvah."

"Rebbe, we must speak to his parents immediately, let them know that he is related to you. Surely they'll sense the great honor that history bestows upon them and agree to let their son move into our circle of Hasidim in Eretz Yisrael. We'll make a bar mitzvah for him such as the world has never seen."

"Chaim, that will not happen. His parents remain staunchly Zionist, essentially secular or nonobservant from our point of view, and they plan a bar mitzvah at the new Reform congregation in Tel Aviv, Beit Daniel. His parents have no interest in our ways. They reject them, and they teach him to reject them, as well."

"Rebbe, is this some distant cousin unknown to us, a nephew of yours stemming from your origins in the former USSR, or what?"

"No, Chaim, not that kind of relative. I am going to tell you a story in strictest confidence because I can trust you to guard the secret. You must not reveal it to anyone, unless that person needs to know in order to continue your work after your departure from this world. Are we agreed?"

"We are agreed."

"Chaim, this bar mitzvah boy is my great-grandson."

"What are you saying, Rebbe, that you fathered a child and there are further generations?"

"Exactly. A woman whom I knew in Berlin and with whom I was, let us say, close, had a child by me."

"Rebbe, I don't understand. You and Rachel – ever devoted, so much love and mutuality. How could this have happened?"

"Chaim, can you spare me a few minutes? I'll give you the full background."

Rabbi Silverman nodded yes and bent forward to hear the Rebbe's aged voice.

"In 1924 I was attending yeshiva in Minsk. Young, self-indulgent, and dissatisfied with my choice of the rabbinate, I walked away from the Minsker Yeshiva during a cigarette break, wandered about the town, and along the way stuffed my hands in my coat pockets. I found an old postcard from a friend visiting Jerusalem, a picture of the Wailing Wall, the *Kotel*, and instead of admiring the worshippers at its foot, I wondered about the huge stones and how such ashlars could possibly have been set in place without modern devices. That fascination led me to think about becoming an engineer. On my stroll I stopped at the new Byelorussian State University, but with chagrin I learned that as yet they had no courses in engineering. An official in the registrar's office recommended I take advantage of the Treaty of Riga, which would let me head for Poland to study. Maybe from there I could even get a visa to study in the technical center of the world, Berlin."

Emanuel paused to call his valet and ask that refreshments be brought into the salon. He then continued, "I trimmed my beard in Viennese style to make myself more acceptable to the officials, paid off a government agent with a few rubles to get the transfer papers, promised my poor parents I'd do my best to help them, and with the tuition meant for the yeshiva I bought a ticket to Warsaw. Let's call that tuition the Minsker's gift to Borisov.

"Warsaw was a great city, with almost 400,000 Jews and many more non-Jews. I found a kosher *pension* for residence, and lacking the resources to sustain myself, I decided to pay a visit to the then-Borisover Rebbe. He had moved away from the Bolsheviks and the USSR a few years earlier when they seized his properties and limited his religious prerogatives. I knew he maintained a prosperous Hasidic following in Warsaw, and my parents always reminded me that he was my second cousin once removed. That made him a sensible first stop.

"I donned my best Hasidic wear, including my fur *shtreiml* hat as if it were Shabbos, and knocked on his door. He welcomed me and called for his daughter Rachel to fetch some schnapps and victuals.

"Then entered a woman of twenty years, beautiful of appearance, her auburn hair tumbling in curls over well-covered shoulders and arms, her dress attractively shaped by her figure. When Rachel's gaze met mine, Chaim, I cannot forget how her brown eyes widened. I think she caught the discrepancy between my modern beard and my Hasidic attire, but certainly there were sparks already felt between us. The blush that crossed her face divulged her interest in me, as did the glance she stole as she headed for the kitchen.

"She returned with the liquor and food and then repaired to her room. After decrying the fact that Rachel was turning down all offers of matrimony from capable rabbinic scholars that the Rebbe and his late wife arranged; after pooh-poohing my career goals in engineering and my nascent hope to study at the Technische Universität in Berlin, the Borisover welcomed me to attend his yeshiva. In fact, he was so confident of Borisov's superiority that he promised to sponsor my university education if his yeshiva failed to excite my spirit. My empty stomach and I had nothing to lose, so I accepted his offer. As I raised the shot glass in grateful salute to him, I noticed that Rachel had placed a tiny note beneath it. I deftly scooped it up and tapped it into my pocket before thanking the Rebbe for his hospitality."

CHAPTER THREE

Anxious to move the story along, Rabbi Silverman said, "Let's come back to this other woman. Where does she fit in?"

Emanuel looked upward and sighed, as if Rachel might be listening to words he did not wish her to hear. "With that little piece of paper under the shot glass Rachel arranged our first date. We met at Kabaret Mirage, where the famous Yakub Kagan and his band played their upbeat compositions – fox trots, tangos. You've heard of him, Chaim – Yakub Kagan? No? Too bad – quite the musical stylist, that man.

"When we met, we both laughed at our change of fashion. I wore a business suit, tie, and black fedora." Rebbe Emanuel then smiled broadly. "And Rachel amply filled the bodice of a crimson silk dress with floral accents and a hem that touched just below her knees. Those are moments locked in my memory. Of course, her father the Rebbe would have condemned her immodesty, but he knew nothing of it because Rachel was supposedly visiting a friend. Secretly she carried in her traveling case her secular clothing for later wear.

"We glowed in each other's presence, and that night we drank wine, we danced, we chatted with ease, as if we had known each other a lifetime. Soon enough, our fingers interlaced, and we walked the entire distance to her friend's house hand in hand. At the door we embraced, and I spoke Hebrew softly in her ear, 'You have stolen my heart, my sister, my bride; you have stolen my heart with one glance of your eyes.' (Song of Songs 4:9)

"She kissed me tenderly and matched my sentiments, again in Hebrew, 'Come away, my beloved, and be like a young stag on the spice-laden mountains' (Song of Songs 8:14). All our lives, for the outside world we lived as two Hasidim, but inside our souls, just lovers. All our lives."

Chaim Silverman began to grow impatient with his Rebbe's maunderings, but with good *derech eretz*, proper courtesy, he tried not to show it. "Now tell me about the other woman." he said.

"It will only be a moment before I clarify that encounter." Emanuel was clearly unburdening his conscience while describing his personal history.

"When I started my studies at the Borisover yeshiva, my attitude was tepid. Slowly I had to admit it: the yeshiva teachers were wise and imparted both spiritual understanding and practical discernment. I decided to use what I learned to set in order the paths of my life.[6] Despite the excellence of Borisov, I could not get technical study in Berlin out of my head. Meanwhile, the Borisover Rebbe seemed to recognize my intellectual strengths in Talmud and to favor my pragmatic approach. He acted as if I were a spiritual hope for his followers, but he never flat-out told me he wanted me to marry Rachel.

"One warm evening – it was in 1926 – Rachel and I sat on a park bench far from the Borisover's neighborhood and planned the future. Chaim, it was like the midrash of Rabbi Akiba and his Rachel written in contemporary terms.[7] Rachel insisted, 'Go to Berlin, go and study. If you are to become an engineer, it should be there. Study with the best.'

"I asked her, 'If I become an engineer, would you join me in Berlin? Would you dare to leave your family and the sect?' She ran her hand down her garment in a flourish, inviting me to look at her closely. No long dress, no long sleeves. That night she could have been any cultured Polish girl. She said, 'If I am with you, I'll be happy. If you're happy with your work, I'll be all the more joyful.'

"We framed her suggestion as Plan One. The back-up plan was simple. If Berlin failed to materialize a future, I would return to Warsaw, dress in my Hasidic finest, and ask the Rebbe's forgiveness and permission to marry Rachel. I would then become his successor and bring an engineer's practicality and insight to mold an even greater

Hasidic dynasty. It would be no hardship to us provided we had each other. If we had to dance in the privacy of our own salon, so be it. And Chaim, ultimately, that's what we did, the dance of life, together."

Emanuel sat in silence for a moment, chewing on his lip. Then he said, "But I was afraid to leave the yeshiva. Learning Torah was all I knew. I wanted engineering, and yet I feared to turn the page, not only because I was uncertain of my abilities, but because I did not want to lose Rachel. She sensed how self-deprecatingly modest and timorous I was at that moment, so she said to me, 'If we engaged ourselves to marry, would you go away to study at the Technische Universität Berlin?'

"The words burst joyfully from my lips, 'On that condition, yes!'

"We were secretly engaged, and Rachel continually exhorted me to go. At last, I packed up and left for Berlin to study a full year.

"Rachel became quiet and withdrawn in my absence. The Rebbe demanded to know why, and she admitted that we two were in love, that she had encouraged me to study engineering in Berlin, and that she missed me deeply. My father-in-law hated failure, and he considered my departure for the Technical University a defeat for himself and his yeshiva. Failure made him irate. He blamed Rachel for cloaking our relationship from his view. He vented his ire upon her, driving her from his house, vowing to forswear from her any benefit of his estate. Although he knew she had the knowledge and ability to sustain herself in some small way, nonetheless he thought that being a woman without visible means of familial support might awaken Rachel to her tenuous situation and bring her to heel, resulting in an arranged marriage.

"Rachel left home in non-Hasidic garb, a shock to her father. She found an apartment to share with three young women, all of whom had left the religious life for the culture and amusements of secular Warsaw. She worked in an office at a salary sufficient for her portion of the rent, a modest diet, occasional clothing purchases, a few books, regular attendance at Yiddish theater matinees, and plenty of stationery and postage stamps with which to write me. She even saved a zloty or two. Clever, urbane, astute, and independent – that was Rachel.

"In the meantime, in Berlin I found a room in the home of an older woman who kept kosher. I started tutoring bar mitzvah boys to earn a livelihood, some of whose parents taught at the Technical University and arranged for me to audit courses. After a year's time, I took the entrance exam, then returned home to Warsaw with slumped shoulders. I failed the exam.

"During my few days leave from Berlin, Rachel and I took in a Yiddish play, and as I exited the men's room, I heard an old usher, apparently an acquaintance, say to Rachel, 'How long will you live the life of a widow?' She said that she'd be happy if I went back to Germany for another year of study. I had been fretting over whether to pack it all in and move to our back-up plan, but I took her words as encouragement and permission to try again.

"Now I'll answer your question.

"I returned to Berlin as penniless as ever, but honestly, Chaim, I was a young man, with a young man's needs. After a while I could take the loneliness no longer. I grew restive, desirous of female company. With nothing but a little pocket change, what could I do? Still, I felt confident about my future and thought to put myself in a neighborhood where people lived at the level I eventually hoped to attain. Maybe just a cup of coffee in Schoeneberg, a place of many Jews, a place of good entertainment venues, a place of affluence. Maybe that would lift my spirits.

"In Schoeneberg the Grand Café had opened in a section of the huge, ultra-modern Haus Nurnberg. You could not know it, Chaim, but it was very trendy. For the price of a cup of coffee I could enjoy an evening out, and who knew what might happen? I clothed myself in gentleman's black, topped by a black fedora.[8] I kept my beard neatly trimmed in those days, too. I looked the Berliner as I made my way to Haus Nurnberg and entered the immense coffee shop.

"The Grand Café was crowded, smoky, and noisy – such a clatter of coffee cups, with forks clanging like muffled bells against the dishware, and a drone of conversation echoing through the room. I felt excitement and urgency in the ambience, but the café was full. A few women sat alone at small round tables, their mouths overly-drawn in red lipstick, their black mesh stockings plainly visible – *nafkas*. Only one lovely woman sat alone at a table for two. Neatly dressed in skirt, blouse, and jacket, to me her youthful face looked Jewish and contemporary all at once.

"When I asked her if the seat was occupied, she eyed me up and down and responded coolly, even coldly, 'No,' but with a genteel 'May I?' and my sunny visage, she beckoned me to join her.

"We introduced ourselves with that strong German handshake – you know, once-up-lightly, once-down-hard. Her name was Hannalora Steinitz, and after we identified each other as Jews she told me that she worked as an organizer for HaShomer HaTsa'ir and planned to immigrate to Palestine soon. A left-wing Zionist, I thought, possibly unconstrained in certain attitudes.

"I questioned why she wanted to leave dynamic Berlin, a *faux pas* that made our interaction take a tense dive, but I changed the subject to jazz, and she picked up the threads of my conversation immediately. Together we wove a coverlet of interests sufficiently warm and broad enough to wrap us both in the illusion of unity, at least for the night. And so, hand in hand, we proceeded to her small apartment where we made love with a passion uncurbed by any restraint of conscience."

Rabbi Silverman winced at the words and looked away, his face both sour and stern. The old man's mind was failing to put limits on his tongue.

CHAPTER FOUR

Rebbe Emanuel carried on with his Berlin history.

"Understand, Chaim, I wrote to Rachel every day, but I saw Hannalora almost every night. After a month or two, I sensed my heart begin to shift its allegiance, and I urged Hannalora to remain in Germany a while longer so we could share a future in Europe. But no, she would not be deterred from her declared goal. She urged me to join her in Palestine after winning my engineering degree, a degree useful to building a Jewish state.

"Then I received a daring letter from Rachel. She yearned to see me and had saved enough to afford a brief visit to Berlin. I couldn't reject her, but I had to be careful. I told Hannalora that I was returning to Warsaw to consult with some professors about schooling in Poland 'just in case,' and I devised a plan to keep Rachel out of Hannalora's sight. We never spent time in the Barn District, Scheunenviertel, home to many East European Jews, poor immigrants hoping to receive visas to depart for America. In that district the Volksbühne at Rosa-Luxemburg-Platz, a worker's theatre, offered tickets at affordable prices. Its plays would provide evenings of entertainment and keep Rachel literally in the dark, away from a chance encounter with Hannalora.

"I had to admit that at first sight of Rachel pangs of shame for my betrayal afflicted me. Her beauty and grace charmed me once again. Though clothed in modern fashion, her clearly Jewish ways set me at ease. Staying in the Barn District made it simple to obtain kosher food, speak Yiddish, and feel as if neither of us had left Warsaw. At night, Rachel gave herself to me openly, freely, and with the innocent passion of romance that seemed pure, unlike my rapture with Hannalora."

Again Rabbi Silverman cringed. Could the aged Rebbe not control his tongue? Would that he finish soon. It was getting excruciatingly difficult to listen, and the hour was late.

Emanuel said, "At the end of Rachel's visit, we renewed our promise to each other: marriage and Berlin if I could study in the German capital; penitence to Papa, marriage, and Torah study in Warsaw if the Technische Universität rejected me. On parting, we kissed deeply at the *Hauptbahnhof*. I waited until her train disappeared from view and immediately called Hannalora from a pay phone. She answered crisply. I thought it was simply her Germanic way.

"We set up a meeting at the Grand Café. I have relived that night so often that it as if it were unfolding before my eyes at this very instant. At the café Hannalora said accusingly, 'I know you were not in Warsaw. I saw you at the Volksbühne with another woman. Explain yourself!'

"I fidgeted in my seat, played with my coffee spoon, and finally I said, 'There's a lot to explain, Hannalora. I have a heart-rending problem. I'm in love with two beautiful, giving, capable and caring women: you, who have become very dear to me, and the woman you saw at the theatre, to whom I'm engaged. Now you know the truth, but I'm baffled as to what to do next.'

"Hannalora pursed her lips. Her raw voice betrayed the irritation, the vexation she felt. She threw down the gauntlet, glaring at me with fiery eyes that flashed her anger. She said, 'How dare you! How dare you lead me on while you were engaged to be wed the whole time. Let me eliminate your problem and make your choice a simple one. My clearance to go to Palestine has arrived. I must leave in one week, and with anti-Semitic Brown Shirts threatening voters at elections here, and a Jewish land to build there, you can be sure I will leave Germany . . . and leave it without you.'"

Emanuel's voice choked as though he were about to weep. "Chaim, I can see Hannalora before me now. She stared at me fiercely from her seat. Tears streamed down her cheeks. Quickly she arose, steadying herself with one hand on the round table top and the other at her breast. I could feel the sharp edge of her anger escaping through clenched teeth: 'Emanuel, you son of a bitch,' she said. 'You stay here and continue to wait for your messiah to save you. I am going to Palestine, and what do you think will be my first job in our old-new land? It will be to nurse your baby!' Then she ran from the café."

Despite his disdain for such private revelations, Rabbi Chaim Silverman found himself enthralled by the unfolding tale of love. He waited for its denouement as if bewitched, waited for Emanuel to regain his composure and speak.

After a few moments' pause Emanuel continued, "Throwing a few coins on the table, I hastened after Hannalora. When I caught up with her, I cornered her against the wall of Haus Nurnberg, my arms over her shoulders. 'What? Hannalora? You're pregnant?' I demanded. Yes, and she had no doubt who was the father. She was maybe ten weeks into term.

"I kept my hands pressed against the outer wall of Haus Nurnberg, blocking Hannalora from an easy exit. I spoke words more noble than my heart desired, asking her to stay in Berlin. I told her, 'I'll do the right thing. We'll marry, I'll find work. We'll be a family. Let me be a part of the life of this child, *our* child. Stay. I'm a European, not a pioneer.'

"But she spat back, 'You could have done all that in Palestine. But not now. Now I want nothing to do with you.'

"I let one arm fall away and looked earthward in resignation. I knew myself. I knew that other factors besides romance could motivate me. I was neither a Zionist nor an adventurer. I wanted to climb the ladder of success in German industry. Failing that, I'd reweave the fraying strands of a Hasidic dynasty into an eternal garment, something great, something regenerative for Jews, something for myself, as well. But I could keep our secret. I begged her to let me be a part of the life of the child, and somehow, some way a part of her life, if not now, then later, when I could afford it.

"Hannalora wiped away her tears and focused on me as if through a gun sight. 'I . . . *we* are not just a line in your budget, a page in your little black agenda book.' she said. 'You chose to play a sharp, double-edged love game. With my edge of it, I am cutting ties. I choose to live without you. I leave for Palestine in short order. Don't ever follow me there. Don't interrupt my life there. Don't make an attempt to contact this child, from infancy through adulthood – nor this child's offspring. Promise you won't, or when you're well-ensconced in a marriage, I'll reveal this child's existence and bring you down, I swear it. Now you: swear an oath before God. Swear it!'

"I began to rock, *shuckling* as if to daven the words, as if reading from a tractate of Talmud, 'I deny myself the enjoyment of any possible child you may have, as of a thing sanctified.'

"Then Hannalora poked her index finger into my chest. With her other hand she touched her stomach and growled, 'To this baby, you will not exist.' She reached in her purse and pulled out what seemed no more than a folded scrap of paper, saying, 'Take this token to re-member me by, and to remember your choice and your oath.' She shoved the scrap into my hand, turned on her heels and rushed toward the *U-bahn* station. I stood as if rooted to the sidewalk, sifting my emotions for meaning, feeling the oddest mixture of deep relief and unfathomable loss. I looked at the wrinkled card in my hand. It certi-fied Hannalora's membership in Hashomer HaTsa'ir, and it bore her photograph."

Judah said to Tamar, who was pretending to be a prostitute, "Come, let me sleep with you."
"What will you give me to sleep with you?" she asked.
"I'll send you a young goat from my flock."
"Alright, but give me something as a pledge until you send it."

"What pledge should I give you?"

"Your signet . . . and the staff in your hand." He gave them to her and slept with her, and she became pregnant by him. (Genesis 38:18)

Tamar's words, divinely inspired, pointed to the future. "Your signet [chotamcha]" predicts royal offspring, because Jeremiah called a descendant of Judah and Tamar, King Jeconiah, "a signet, [chotam], on my right hand" (Jer. 22:24). "The staff,"— refers to the anointed ruler ultimately to issue from the union of Judah and Tamar, the Messiah, of whom it is written: "The Eternal will stretch forth from Zion your mighty staff." (Ps. 110:2)[9]

CHAPTER FIVE

Rebbe Emanuel shifted uncomfortably on the divan where he sat. He weighed his words, then he determined to bear his soul's less noble feelings along with his more honorable acts.

"Chaim, in confidence, I tell you that for days after Hannalora revealed her news, sleep evaded me, not because she was with child, but because I feared she might change her mind, knock on my door, and drag me to the *Rathaus* for a quick civil ceremony, Jewish wedding to follow. But Hannalora did not return, and as each day passed, I breathed easier, plunged myself deeper into the study of engineering, earned a little livelihood from the bar mitzvah boys, and avoided women and Berlin's night spots as I drew closer to the entrance examination date. With the testing concluded, I packed my bags and haunted the office bulletin board where they posted exam results. In a few days I had my answer. The Technische Universität rejected my application. I returned to Warsaw, praying to participate fully in Borisov once again.

"You should know that although Hannalora caused me to forswear myself from any contact whatsoever with her, her child, or any offspring, that oath never stopped me from tracking her life and the life of her family. Discreetly our contacts in Eretz Yisrael connected me to a lawyer in Haifa, where she lived, and through all these years I have anonymously sent child support for every generation descending from my involvement with that woman, and they all have prospered. I opened doors of opportunity for them without their awareness, and I saw to it that the life's work of each generation was regularly reported to me.

"I want you to track this very Zionist family of mine in Eretz Yisrael. If this current bar mitzvah boy or another of the family's males shows signs of deepening interest in Yiddishkeit, then amplify his prospects to become a halachically observant Jew using the dollars we have available to guide his path through open gates of learning and practice. If the interest becomes commitment to a life based on Jewish law and Hasidic interpretations of it, then you or your appointed agent will speak to that individual to discuss the Borisover connection and that person's critical import for our future."

"Rebbe, people will speak about the origins of the child in an illegitimate relationship."

"Yes, Chaim, people will speak, but every rabbi knows that halachically Hannalora's offspring are not illegitimate, not mamzers, because they stem from a relationship that had the possibility of sanctification by Jewish marriage. When necessary, that point will have to be clarified.

"Now, Chaim, prepare a document putting the temporary mantle of leadership of the Borisover Hasidim upon yourself in the event of my death or my medically proven incapacity to guide our followers. Under that mandate you shall be our *Epitropos*, our curator. The document shall also indicate that your curatorship can be passed by you to another individual of your choice under the same conditions of leadership, and so on, until a proper Borisover Rebbe, a spiritually and Jewishly qualified descendant of the family of the original Borisover, is prepared to assume the role of Rebbe and carry our *Hasidus* into a new generation. In the meantime, you and your successors shall continue support of my male offspring in Eretz Yisrael."

Rabbi Chaim Silverman sucked in a long breath, gave a *krechts*, the sigh of an afflicted soul, and sat at sofa's edge, leaning closer to Rebbe Emanuel. "I do not look forward to the day we must apply the mandate. To manage the Borisovers as if I were the Rebbe but without being so – it's a lot to ask. Should the time come for me to be curator of our movement, may God give me the strength to do it with the insight and spiritual intent that you have always taught me, and may I have the humility of Moses to endure pressure with equanimity. I have listened and acted upon everything you ever required of me, Rebbe, and it always benefited the Borisovers. When it is my turn to lead, I shall act and listen – listen to your voice, your commands, your Torah echoing in my mind as I guide us.

"Tomorrow I'll have one of our attorneys draw up the legal papers involved in creating this curatorship, and I hope to return tomorrow afternoon to have you sign them. Also, if you will, please open to me the secret files which tell of this possible heir in Eretz Yisrael so that I, too, may begin to follow his progress."

Rabbi Silverman arose to shake the Rebbe's hand to seal their agreement, but while seated, Emanuel drew the proffered hand toward himself and kissed it. "I thank God for you, Chaim. Silence is not always golden. Sometimes it weighs upon the shoulders like a leaden weight, and tonight you have lifted that kind of burden from my back and placed it upon your own. I pray it is not too heavy for you to bear. *Shavua tov*. I wish you a good week, and I'll see you tomorrow."

CHAPTER SIX

12 Heshvan 5756 – Sunday afternoon, 5 November 1995
Brooklyn, New York

Rabbi Chaim Silverman returned to Rebbe Emanuel's manse in the mid-afternoon, at his side a tall, somber-faced lawyer named Kenneth Handelman. Handelman carried in his briefcase the official papers that would create an *Epitropos*, or curator such as the Rebbe had outlined.

Once again the loud and persistent doorbell could be heard. The valet received them and escorted the two into the Rebbe's salon. Emanuel soon joined them. They sat facing the Rebbe across a low table, upon which the valet quickly placed a tray with coffee, tea, and their condiments, as well as a plate of cinnamon rugalach with hardy napkins alongside for hand wiping.

"The rugalach are according to Rachel's recipe," the Rebbe explained. "Enjoy."

Rabbi Silverman said, "Rebbe, this won't take long. Here's the legal document to create the curatorship over the Borisover Hasidim in the event of your death or medical incapacity."

Handelman the lawyer gathered the day's documents from his briefcase, placing them before the Rebbe, who, in turn, put them in his lap and read the text with a Talmudic eye.

After a few minutes Emanuel said, "Mr. Handelman, you have done an excellent job. And Chaim, thank you for taking care of this so swiftly. The text is clear, concise, and accomplishes exactly what I want. Where do I sign?"

The lawyer pointed to a number of X's on the original document and its copies. Emanuel Davidson affixed his signature to them.

"That should do it, then." Kenneth Handelman said, consolidating the papers into his briefcase and arising to leave.

"Please excuse me for not standing, but I do thank you for coming," the Rebbe responded, then added, "Chaim, I hope you can stay a few extra minutes."

After the lawyer's departure, Rabbi Silverman said, "Rebbe, I did not expect to stay long. Can we meet at another time?"

"Another time, Chaim? At my age, I may not have another time. I awoke this morning feeling incomplete. Please indulge an old man and give me a bit more of your time. Enjoy your coffee and Rachel's rugalach, Chaim. I want to tell you about my wedding to Rachel."

Rabbi Silverman gestured consent.

Rebbe Emanuel Davidson reflected on his return to Warsaw from Berlin. "When I came back from two years of study, no friend accompanied me, and certainly not one student[10], but I can tell you those bar mitzvah boys never had a better tutor. I brought with me to Warsaw only one scratched and stained suitcase, and mostly it was packed with suspicion. I'm a quick learner, but the Technische Universität rejected my application for admission twice despite concerted efforts on my part. All the way back to Warsaw I was filled with disquietude over the possibility that anti-Semitism, not incompetence, had done me in. Nevertheless, I begrudgingly accepted the end of my dream to become an engineer. But Chaim, my studies in Berlin taught me to ask how things function and to engineer the up-building of Borisov. That has held us in good stead, has it not?"

Rabbi Silverman nodded his full agreement.

"Before leaving Berlin, I sent a telegram to Rachel announcing my arrival. When I reached Warsaw, I followed our back-up plan 100%. I went straight 'way to Rachel's address to see her. The roommates handed me a letter from Rachel explaining that she had quickly gone to make peace with her father and pave the way for our plan. I dragged my battered suitcase to a kosher *pension*, where I took lodging. Once again, I dressed myself in Hasidic finery with a fur *shtreiml* as if it were Shabbos and went to knock on the door of my second cousin once removed, the Borisover Rebbe.

"He opened the door and said '*Sholom aleichem*,' but with such an aloof coldness to his greeting that my courage wilted as quickly as a flower in the first frost. Though discouraged, I went through the drill, saying, '*Aleichem sholom*, Rebbe. I am your cousin, related through my parents in Minsk, the Davidsons.' I confessed to him the error of my ways and renounced my plans for secular studies. I shared my soul's yearning to return to Talmud and Kabbalah, adding that his yeshiva was where my spirit flew highest. Frankly, I begged him to readmit me.

"I saw the corners of the Rebbe's lips turn slightly upward in what seemed a tentative welcome. He said, 'Come in from your long journey, rest here, and I'll fetch you some schnapps and refreshment.'

"The Rebbe escorted me to a seat on a couch in the salon, all the while calling out, 'Rachel, Rachel!'

"My eyes waited for Rachel to appear like the tongue awaits the first taste and touch of Shabbat wine. I told the Borisover that I was glad Rachel had returned home. The Borisover said that he, too, rejoiced, and he would make sure that Rachel was well cared for in the present. He admired her willingness to initiate the return by coming to admit her longing for the Hasidic way of life. She lamented her choice to leave and wanted to return in repentant *teshuvah*. Do you know what the Borisover said to her?"

Rabbi Silverman replied obligingly, though embarrassed that he might hear more personal revelations, "No, Rebbe, I do not."

"It is a line worth remembering, Chaim. He said, 'She opened my heart. I had only to open the door.' I have never forgotten the importance of that sentiment. We have opened many doors for people who came to us open-heartedly, have we not, Rabbi Silverman?"

Emanuel's second-in-command perked up. "Indeed, Rebbe. That's a lot of what Borisov is all about."

With a brisk wave of his hand Emanuel pressed on. "Rachel heeded her father's call, and upon entering the room her lustrous brown eyes widened to see me. She met my gaze and ran into my arms. Then we separated, perhaps only a couple of centimeters apart, but we could feel the magnetism of our love attracting us. When her father asked her to bring schnapps and refreshment, in a trice she re-entered carrying a tray with a flagon of whiskey, a carafe of water, some slices of cake, and several shot glasses.

"She said, 'Here, Papa, is what you requested, but there is something else we want to put on the table. Papa, Emanuel and I, we want to wed. We have love, we share convictions about life. We know we can be a devoted couple, and we believe your Hasidim will come to honor Emanuel as they have honored you.' Hastily I added, 'They will also honor Rachel as they used to honor your late wife.'"

"The Rebbe wiped the hard look from his face and wrapped his arms around Rachel tenderly, embraced me and shook my hand with joy. He said, 'We have reason to celebrate. Your two half-souls will soon become one in marriage.[11] We and all the Borisover Hasidim will celebrate your huppah. Rachel, how I wish your mother were alive to share this moment. Additionally, we rejoice in Emanuel's immediate return to the Borisover Yeshiva!'

"I recommitted to Torah study, and we held our *tenaim* engagement ceremony at the Rebbe's Warsaw home. An aunt of Rachel's, standing in for her late mother, broke a plate after admonishing us that it not only remembers the fall of the Temple, but it warns us that a broken engagement is an irrecoverable loss. She had no need of worry.

"I advanced rapidly in my yeshiva studies, so it came to pass that I was ordained a rabbi on the 16th of Adar, 5690. Rachel and I were wed a few days later, on the 20th of Adar, mid-March of 1930, amidst abundant wishes for good fortune and exuberant feelings of joy in the presence of throngs of Hasidim who crowded the hall to wish us mazel tov.

"Many appended a second wish to their congratulations. They prayed that a son be born speedily to us, not only because it would assure the future of the Borisovers, but because according to our tradition, the Borisover Rebbe descends from King David and therefore has the potential of becoming the messiah. As a relative of the Rebbe, I had that potential, and it's a major reason I want you to track my family in Eretz Yisrael. If one becomes the Borisover Rebbe, he could possibly be the mashiach. Do you understand now its importance more fully, Chaim?"

"Fully, Rebbe. We have always emphasized that miraculous possibility in our movement."

Emanuel's mind wandered a bit afield. "Reminiscing about my wedding day: do you recognize the name Alexander Zhitomirsky? Probably not. He composed music for Yiddishe weddings. I doubt you'll hear again the likes of Zhitomirsky's 'Der Eybershter Iz Der Mekhuten' (God Is the Father-in-Law) or the play on a Shavuot song, 'God is the groom, the Torah is the bride, Moses our teacher is the matchmaker. A pure bride, dear and beautiful, honest and refined, she surpasses all others.' It was the right song for my Rachel.

"We were married in the midst of the Depression, a fact the Borisover kept in mind. He could have afforded more luxury, but the times called for utmost restraint: food aplenty, yes, but opulence and sumptuousness, no. It's something to consider for the future, Chaim."

Rabbi Silverman sat bolt upright at the mention of his name. "Yes," he said, "You're correct, Rebbe."

"Well, Rabbi Silverman, here's the modest punch line of my tale of happy marriage. After our *Sheva Berachot* week of dinners to recite the seven wedding blessings, Rachel and I honeymooned in Berlin. The Depression dulled the city into a shadow of its old self, but still there were a few theaters, night clubs, and dance halls to visit. The

Rebbe would have disapproved, but we enjoyed every minute of those secular entertainments."

Rebbe Emanuel reached toward his amanuensis and tugged at his sleeve to gain his fullest attention. "So, Chaim, listen: someday, when you're *Epitropos* of the Borisovers, don't forget that even the most religious Jew can love the world of current culture, and make sure that Borisov stays up to the minute on that score, able to use it, able to participate in it, able to reach Jews through it. Failure to understand and involve the culture of the day will cost us our following. Do you hear me?"

Rabbi Chaim Silverman silently nodded "yes" a few times before he intoned, "Loud and clear, Rebbe. Loud and clear."

BOOK II

שמות

Exodus / "Names"

CHAPTER SEVEN

This is the name of the woman who went up to the land of Israel with a child in her womb: Hannalora Steinitz. A Zionist to the core, she abandoned the land of her birth to enter British Mandatory Palestine at the end of summer, 1928, 5688 on the Jewish calendar. She did not immediately wander in the Land, but settled where many German Jews already resided, in Haifa, whose hills and sea views rival and even shame those of Athens or Barcelona. Already equipped with excellent Hebrew skills and punctilious German, she shortly found work as a secretary to a German émigré lawyer.

Three years before Hannalora's arrival, in September, 1925, the British made a stern rule regarding the Western (Wailing) Wall, the *Kotel HaMa'aravi*. In those days as now, Muslims viewed the *Kotel* as part of the Al-Aqsa Mosque area, the third holiest site of Islam. They called it *al-Buraq* and believed that any changes to the area by Jews constituted an attempt to usurp Moslem religious rights by creating a synagogue. When Jews brought chairs and benches to the *Kotel*, the British banned them, even for the elderly and infirm.

On Yom Kippur of September, 1928, only weeks after Hannalora arrived in Palestine, Jews praying at the *Kotel* once again set out chairs and even added a separation between the men and women, a mechitzah. Previously such separations existed only from time to time. The British commissioner noted the changes as new and mentioned them to the *Waqf*, the Muslim community religious court in charge of the Wall. Along with agitated Muslim protests, the sheikhs demanded immediate removal of these items by the Jews. The Jewish prayer leader begged leave to withdraw them when the prayers of the holy day concluded, with which the British concurred, but after Yom Kippur, the Jews cleared nothing away. Ten armed officials forcefully re-moved the articles, and violence broke out, later adjudged as excessive force on the part of the police, who in mandatory Palestine were sub-stantially of Arab ethnicity.

Tension built month by month from that time forward, culminating in the Hebron and other massacres of August, 1929, when 133 Jews died in murderous attacks and 116 Arabs were slain in reprisals and by police seeking to stop the attackers. It was a month never to be forgot-ten by either side, Jew or Arab.

Hannalora Steinitz, who worried for the future of German Jewry, learned of the carnage in mandatory Palestine at third hand. Still she had no misgivings about her move. Her son Nachum had been born in Adar I, 5689, the month of February, 1929, and while the massacres took place in Hebron, Safed, and elsewhere, Hannalora quietly and attentively nursed her six-month-old child in Haifa. At peace with the baby in her arms, Europe felt ever farther away because, true to his promise, Emanuel never contacted Hannalora again.

Genealogy

These are the generations of Emanuel and Rachel Davidson. Emanuel begot Nachum with Hannalora Steinitz. Emanuel's wife Ra-chel had not an inkling of that child's existence. She and Emanuel prayed soon to generate an offspring to inherit the Rebbe's court, but Rachel was barren.

These are the generations of Hannalora Steinitz. Hannalora dwelt in Haifa and gave birth to Nachum, a good but not brilliant student who found every door opening for him when he needed to go forward with his education or his work. At age 19, Nachum fought in the Israeli War of Independence, 1948. He remained in service to *Tsahal*, and Nachum dwelt in Herzliya, just north of Tel Aviv. At the age of 22, Na-chum married Shoshana Tarivi, whom he met defending a kibbutz. He sired two sons, Yoram and Aviam. Nachum also fought in the Sinai Campaign, 1956, served in the intelligence service during the Six Day War, 1967, and again in intelligence during the Yom Kippur War, 1973. Rather than resign because of the military failures due to his office's mishandling of the last war, he accepted the obscurity of a sinecure that arose suddenly. After thirty years of service, he retired on his pension and briefly took supplemental work. He died in 1981, and his wife, thirteen years later.

After military service and near the end of his university degree studies at Technion, Yoram, son of Nachum and Shoshana, dwelt in Ramat Gan and married Leah Har-even. His brother Aviam was killed in the Lebanon campaign of 1982. Yoram and Leah gave birth to two girls and a boy, Talia (b. 1976), Noga (b. 1978), and Nachum Aviam (b. 1982). Yoram, too, seemed a fortunate man, for whatever he touched prospered, and his family fared well.

As for the next generation, Nachum Aviam did military service during the early part of the Second Intifada (2000-2005). He studied mathematics and aviation engineering at Technion and won an MBA on scholarship from Harvard Business School, then took a high management position at Israel Aerospace Industries, working in Lod at company headquarters, Ben Gurion Airport. Nachum Aviam dwelt in Ramat Gan and married Dina Ya'alon (2007), who would eventually bear two children, Hanna Liora (b. 2009) and David (b. 2012). An independent thinker, Nachum Aviam joined Beit Daniel Reform Jewish Congregation in Tel Aviv and studied Talmud with a *chevruta* group there. Outside of work, Nachum Aviam focused on family.

These are the generations of Hannalora according to their habitations in the land of their possession, the State of Israel. She is Hannalora Steinitz, *savta rabta di meshicha*, great-grandmother of the messiah.

CHAPTER EIGHT

Talmud Chullin 139b asks, "Where can we find Esther in the Torah? In Deuteronomy 31:18, haster astir panai, *'I [God] will surely hide my face . . .'"*

Rabbi Levi ben David v'Yehudit commented on Astir *[I shall hide]. The word approximates 'Esther' by its sound and spelling, as if the Torah took the exact spelling of Esther's name and inserted a letter of God's name,* yod, *in order to say, though you cannot find My Holy Name in Esther's scroll, I will hide Myself in Esther through her deeds.*

Rabbi Levi also noted a subtle meaning in Esther 2:10, "Esther did not declare her people or her country; for Mordecai ordered her not to." Esther could only enter the King's palace acting as if she were a Persian, and that is why Mordecai, oft-portrayed as an observant Jew, admonished Esther to hide her Jewishness, to act in the secular fashion of her time and place. Still and all, the 'yod' of Astir *in the Torah indicates God's presence with Esther. Hence, she became a messenger of the Eternal, hidden by the secular manners and clothing of her day. God does not always choose the traditionally observant to save the Jewish people.*

4 Tevet 5772 – Thursday night, 29 December 2011
Ramat Gan, Israel

I srael's foreign security operation is called the Mossad. Israel's internal security unit is called Shin Bet. Each office has its own director. Though Shin Bet had seen sixteen years and four directors go by since the assassination of Yitzhak Rabin, the joint Shin Bet

47

and Mossad Messiah plan, approved confidentially by one prime minister after another, carried forward.

Shin Bet's newest Director sat at the kitchen table with Nachum Aviam Steinitz and his wife Dina Ya'alon. The Director's knit kipa, installed immovably upon his shiny bald head by some mysterious means, declared to the world his Modern Orthodox convictions. Though he doffed his overcoat at the door, still he wore a thick knit sweater against what promised to be a cold night for Israel, 5°C.

After pouring coffee for all, Dina sat down and assured them, "Our little daughter is asleep. I don't expect any interruptions."

Nachum said, "We're both wondering what this is about, and we're a bit fearful, too. When the Director of Shin Bet comes to your home, it's worrisome. I'm vetted for my position at Israel Aerospace Industries and have been working there for a while, so why this meeting?"

The Director took a sip of his coffee, put the cup on the table, and shook his head. "There's no problem with your security clearance at work, none at all, and that's not what this meeting is about. First I have some secrecy papers to sign." The Director reached down to the briefcase sitting at his feet and withdrew from its outside pocket a file containing a sheaf of forms and other material. He handed the forms to Nachum and Dina to review.

"Let me make it easy for you both. Tonight, Nachum, I can reveal to you information about your family origins, and I can offer both of you unique positions with the Shin Bet, positions that will not presently alter Nachum's work at IAI, nor will you be put in danger. Dina, you've become a stay-at-home mom, but when you return to your work in marketing and public relations, your employment by Shin Bet will not alter your ability to be effective or to earn a salary in your field. You will both have high security positions for the benefit of the State of Israel, but the State may never call upon you to take a leave of absence to fulfill your roles for the good of the country. In short, we offer you a regular retainer fee which rises gradually with inflation, and if ever we call upon you to fulfill your tasks for Shin Bet and country, your pay increase will be dramatic.

"In order for me to fulfill this offer, I need to know that you both swear to guard the secrecy of the information you'll receive from me. And yes, Dina, we have already looked deeply into your background and believe that you pass all security safeguards, just as your husband does.

"Simply knowing the information about your family origins need not change your lives one iota, and you can decline my offer of a position with us tonight. In fact, you can leave our employ at any time. The retainers will cease when our relationship ends. However, the element of secrecy remains in effect, and if we find that either or both of you have broken the rule of silence on the matters entailed, you will be prosecuted to the full extent of our law, resulting in both fines and unhappily long jail sentences. Am I clear?"

"Honestly, I'm shocked by this whole thing," Dina sputtered. "It's like we're suddenly Arnold Schwarzenegger and Jamie Lee Curtis in that movie, *True Lies*, a secret agent couple. I'm not at all inclined to sign anything. I like our life the way it is."

"Fair enough," the Director said, "but the family background information may be of interest to you both, and though you would still have to agree to keep that quiet, it does not require you to sign on with Shin Bet."

Nachum shuffled through the papers as he listened. "Dina," he said eagerly, "look at this." He pointed to the proposed annual retainer. "500,000 NIS *tax free* annually. That's like 1,000,000 shekels! Do you know what that could mean to us, to the family we're making together, to you as a mother? How about a house in Herzliya Pituach? How about the best schools for our children, including American universities?"

"Let me see that." Dina snatched up the paper in question.

While Dina examined the contract, Nachum pursued the subject, "And we can turn you down tonight or cut the relationship next week or at any time?"

"Absolutely. Just maintain silence, or your offspring will become a jail orphan."

Nachum turned to Dina and spoke in hushed tones, "Dina, we have nothing to lose. Let's listen to the proposition. It must be important to Israel's welfare. Look who's here to speak to us." He tilted his head toward the Director.

Dina cautiously nodded her assent. "OK, Nachum, let's listen. But we go into this proposition united, or we don't go in at all. Each of us owns a veto."

Nachum agreed, gave Dina the contracts for her to peruse, and both found they read exactly as the Director outlined them. They signed at the red X's on several sheets of paper – Dina Ya'alon and Nachum Aviam Steinitz – promising silence, even to family members.

The Director of Shin Bet smiled and started his monologue.

"We have noted that you, Nachum Aviam, have a serious interest in Jewish texts, Jewish law, rabbinic interpretation, an interest in all matters of the Jewish intellect and spirit. Am I correct?"

Nachum grinned. "Correct. Some of my colleagues jokingly tell me that my MBA stands for Master of Biblical Analysis. One guy calls me the Master of Babylonian Aramaic. I probably talk too much about Torah and Talmud."

"Torah is on your lips since your bar mitzvah in 1995. Our agent at Beit Daniel attended services that day and left astounded at your grasp of the material. You thought for a time of becoming a Reform rabbi and studying in Jerusalem at Hebrew Union College, as well. All this redounds to our possible benefit," the Director continued.

"I decided instead to make a living, and I am respected in my field," Nachum responded.

The Director agreed. "Well-respected, but look, the goal we have in mind is an elusive one, depending on multiple factors including history itself. We may need to activate our plan, which is why you would be on retainer. But then again, we may never wish to put it in motion. Let me explain why the two of you are at the center of the process.

"You know, Nachum, that your great-grandmother was Hannalora Steinitz. That is obvious, because your little daughter's name is Hanna Liora, undoubtedly in memory of Hannalora."

The Steinitz couple agreed.

"What is the story you have learned about how your grandfather Nachum, *alav hashalom*, came to be born?"

Nachum Aviam did not even blink. He knew the story by heart as part of his family's oft-repeated lore, a tale both damning and exalting all at once. He felt no need to embellish it. "My great-grandmother came to Haifa from Germany in the late 1920's, pregnant with my grandfather at the time. The father of the baby, her lover, also knew she planned to go to Palestine. He, however, refused to make aliyah. My great-grandmother became so infuriated with his intransigence, lack of compassion, and egotism that she demanded he swear never to see her again nor inquire as to the child's welfare. She wanted nothing more to do with him and cut him off flat, period, never again mentioning his name. Then she made aliyah, surviving in Haifa as a working mother. She raised my grandfather Nachum, *alav hashalom*, with no one's help. The German Jewish colony in Haifa became awestruck by her audacity and her adroitness at making the best of her situation."

"Yes, all that is true, in part."

"In part? What are you saying?" the two asked.

"Yes, in part. The Mossad, our foreign security service, monitors overseas wire transfers to Israel from their source. Mossad detected a suspicious continuity of wire transfers from Brooklyn to Haifa and advised Shin Bet to follow the money using our network in Israel. We did so, discovering the final destination of the cash to a certain law firm's trust account. Further investigation into the firm's records showed that the transfers began much earlier, from Poland in the 1930's. The law firm held a portion as a fee, and the remainder they

deposited to the benefit of Hannalora Steinitz, and in later generations, to other family members. Sometimes the lawyers targeted
money to sources that would clear a path for the family member: for
example, a scholarship to a university or, less often, a well-aimed
bribe."

Dina grabbed Nachum by the wrist. They looked at each other with
eyebrows raised in surprise. Both thought of Nachum's MBA and his
full scholarship to Harvard. It even contained a monthly living allowance. Did it come from the same secret source of which they were now
learning?

The Director went on, "Our investigators perceived clearly that
these payments were intended for child support and as monetary sup-
plements necessary to, shall we say, grease the wheels of progress for
descendants of Hannalora Steinitz. We hesitated to reveal the source
or pursue the beneficiaries of the payments for taxes owed. Why? Because the payments involved a very public Jewish figure who could put
his followers on the street in protest here and whose charitable work
in Israel might be shut down by the American Internal Revenue Service if they knew how he used tax-deductible donations. We also
refrained from attacking the law firm that paid the baksheesh. We
simply didn't want to expose this very public American Jew to igno-
miny, at least not without a good reason.

"We did, however, take it upon ourselves to trace and identify the
source, and initially we thought it was simply an NGO in Brooklyn
supporting destitute Israelis, but on closer examination we found that
the source of the funds came at the personal behest of the Borisover
Rebbe. Borisovers still distribute all other funds for Israel through a
charitable organization designated 'American Friends of Kfar Rachel.'
Then those dollars transfer to an Israeli charity, 'Kfar Rachel Eretz
Yisrael.' Only the special funds related to the Steinitz family traveled
from 'American Friends' through the lawyer's pipeline on the excuse
that 'American Friends' needed to retain an Israeli lawyer to handle

any cases that might involve it with its Israeli partner, 'Kfar Rachel Eretz Yisrael.'

"We investigated the historic timeline of these two people, Emanuel Davidson, the Borisover Rebbe, and Hannalora Steinitz. He audited classes as a student at the Technische Universität Berlin when she was working for HaShomer HaTsa'ir as an organizer in that very city. Late on a dark and frigid night in Brooklyn's Borough Park neighborhood, Mossad orchestrated an operation whose results yielded us a view of contents locked in the files of the Rebbe's office. Immediately the Mossad found your great-grandmother's HaShomer HaTsa'ir ID card, along with two record books. One contained an itemized list of the wire transfers taken from 'American Friends of Kfar Rachel.' Ostensibly the Rebbe designated any money beyond the lawyer's retainer fees to support a Borisover family working at the Cave of Elijah in Haifa."

The Director looked in his file, and from it placed a copy of the ID card on the table for Nachum and Dina to see.

"We have no doubt that your great-grandfather was Emanuel Davidson, the Borisover Rebbe. He passed away about fifteen years ago, supposedly without an heir. But this little card tells us he did have heirs, and you are his male descendant in this generation."

Dina and Nachum turned to each other, eyebrows raised in surprise. In a low voice Nachum quoted, "*Haker-na l'mi ha-chotemet*, I am pregnant by the man to whom these belong; surely you must recognize the signet." (Gen. 38:25)

Dina said, "What do you mean, Nachum?"

"It's from the story of Judah and Tamar. Hannalora made it into the story of Tamar and Judah. She turned it upside down. Tamar marries one of Judah's three sons. Her husband dies. She marries the second son, Onan, to produce an heir in honor of the lost husband. He spills his seed rather than have intercourse with her, onanism. This angers God, who executes Onan. Judah refuses to give Tamar the third son, thinking she's bad luck, so Tamar disguises herself as a prostitute beside the road, and when Judah encounters her, he wants to buy sex.

She demands a sheep in payment. He doesn't have one right there, but gives her some valuable tokens to redeem later for a sheep, and she becomes pregnant by him. He later learns that Tamar prostituted herself. He wants to have her killed, but she presents the tokens to Judah, and he realizes that not only is he the cause of her pregnancy, but she forced him to fulfill what was then a custom, to provide an offspring in memory of the childless husband who died.

"But in Hannalora's version, the woman gives the token to her male lover. That means he played the prostitute in their mutual drama. It's a token of what? Of her contempt for him? The midrash has a more spiritual message, saying that Judah gave Tamar tokens of his power to point to a messianic time. Did Hannalora do the same? We can only surmise that she gave this scrap of paper to him like a calling card, a symbol that they had met, that she was in his life, that he was in hers, and that she retained the power to make trouble for him if he did not keep his word, if he did not stay far away from her. But why would he keep it?"

The Director conjectured, "Maybe he truly loved her and couldn't let go of that final symbol. Maybe their dalliance in Berlin gave him a memorable taste of freedom. Or maybe he kept it as a reminder that he owed her big-time, a goad to make himself into a better man than Hannalora believed he was. We'll never know. But you must admit it is potent proof of their connection."

"So I'm a descendant of the late Borisover Rebbe, Emanuel Davidson. So what?"

"So," said the Director, prolonging the moment, ". . . you could be the next Borisover Rebbe, if you wanted, if you qualified."

"I thought they were the group with the dead Rebbe who could never be replaced."

"Not so, Nachum. The mandate of Emanuel Davidson is clear. To replace him as Rebbe, he gave Rabbi Chaim Silverman management powers, including the power to search for a relative with sufficient commitment to what he called Yiddishkeit, and if Silverman could not find anyone, the Rebbe tasked him to pass the curatorship down to the next generation of Borisovers through another *epitropos* after him. Silverman also passed away, but before he died, he named Rabbi Avraham Stadlan as his successor-curator. We think Silverman enjoyed the influence and the challenge of his executive position among the Borisovers, which he carried out successfully. It was to his benefit not to find a new Rebbe. Mossad thinks Stadlan may also hesitate to fill the Rebbe's position, but he knows you exist, and he's watching. If your Jewish commitments are simpatico with the Borisovers, we agree with the Mossad that he will choose to turn to you.

"Before I outline our plan, you may recall that in my tale of the Mossad's skullduggery I mentioned that they found two record books. One listed all the wire transfers to Haifa and elsewhere for the benefit of the Steinitz family. But there was another record book of a different type."

The Director picked up from the table a stapled sheaf of papers.

"These pages," he said, proffering them to Nachum, "come from a lockable notebook that Mossad easily cracked open some time ago, photographed, and resealed. That book is a unique history text, a journal written by Emanuel Davidson, his personal recollections of events from the time he married Rachel in Warsaw until their earliest days in America. After that, the journal stops, perhaps because he was too busy, or perhaps because the Borisovers themselves recorded virtually his every move once he established himself in Brooklyn.

"I should emphasize that all the originals, the ID card and the two record books, remained in the safe of the Borisover Rebbe. Mossad photographed everything and sent a copy on to Israel. I can't vouch for the existence of the material any longer. Rabbis Silverman and Stadlan had access to it and might have decided to destroy some or all of it."

Nachum took the pages in hand and lifted the blank cover sheet. He and Dina were surprised to see a Modern Hebrew text, seemingly from a laser printer.

"He wrote in Hebrew?" Nachum asked.

The Director laughed. "No. Emanuel wrote in Yiddish, but I assumed you do not know Yiddish and had it translated for you."

Nachum offered his thanks, and Dina inquired, "What period does this cover?"

The Director screwed up his face as though deep in thought. "If I remember correctly, it's certainly not a daily journal. Rebbe Emanuel wrote extensively about their mutual quest to conceive a child, about their Borisover work in Warsaw to overcome the bitter times of the Depression, and about their exodus from Europe to America. In America he records some of his father-in-law's discourses and how the Borisovers came to establish Kfar Rachel in Israel. It makes for good reading, most of it, especially the story of their miraculous escape from Poland. It covers 1930 to 1939."

Nachum also had a question. "Before we meet again, would you mind if Dina and I digested this historical document? We might find some familial insights here, some light to illuminate my own disposition and attitudes in life. I'm sure the journal will take a little time to review. Is it possible to adjourn until next week?"

The Director lifted his briefcase from the floor and laid it on the table, inserting the file folder. "I understand fully. It's not a problem to meet again," he said. "Just remember your oath of silence. A week from today, then, same time and place?"

Nachum and Dina assented and bid the Director a good evening.

CHAPTER NINE

The next morning Nachum excused his family from his parents' weekly Shabbat dinner. By staying home, they hoped to find time to read Rebbe Emanuel's journal and ponder it together. That night, Erev Shabbat, the Steinitz family, including the presence of little Hanna Liora, lit Shabbat candles together in the tranquility of their dining room. After Kiddush, *HaMotsi*, dinner, and an abbreviated *Birkat HaMazon* blessing after meals, they played briefly with Hanna Liora, then put her down to sleep.

Nachum had made a copy of the journal for Dina so that both could examine it simultaneously and readily discuss its contents. They relaxed in their favorite chairs and began to read. The journal opened with a strange Torah text.

During the wheat harvest, Reuben found some mandrake plants. He brought them to his mother Leah, who had not given birth for some time. The childless Rachel said to Leah, "Please give me some of your son's mandrakes. They're reputed to increase fertility." But Leah said, "Isn't it enough that you are the favorite wife of my husband Jacob? Will you take my son's mandrakes, too?" Rachel said, "Alright, I'll let Jacob sleep with you tonight in return for your son's mandrakes."

When Jacob came in from the fields that evening, Leah went to meet him and said, "Tonight you're sleeping with me, because I traded my son's mandrakes for the right to do so." After sleeping that night with Jacob, God answered Leah's longing. She became pregnant and bore Jacob a fifth son, and later, a sixth son and a daughter. Then God remembered Rachel and enabled her to conceive. (Genesis 30:14-17, 22)

Less than an hour later, both felt eager to converse.

"A cup of mint tea, Sweetie?" Dina asked her husband.

"That would be great."

Dina poured hot water from the Shabbat urn into two mugs, dropped a tea bag in each, and brought them with a saucer for the used brew bags. The two sat across from each other in the living room, and both seemed fired up from their encounter with Emanuel Davidson's journal.

Nachum began immediately. "I like the way Emanuel brings Jewish texts into their struggle to conceive – the story of the mandrakes that Reuben gave to Leah, for instance, and how our Biblical mother Rachel at last became pregnant. What do you think Emanuel wanted to indicate by starting out his journal entry with that Torah text?"

Dina said, "Leah didn't need magical mandrakes to get pregnant, and Rachel really didn't either – just a positive answer from God to their prayers to conceive. I think he was belittling the superstitions."

"I think you're right, and Torah might agree. How about all the ways they tried to conceive?"[12]

Dina scoffed. "The whole episode seemed designed to help Emanuel fill a future job description as Rebbe. First they correlated berachah, blessing, with *breicha*, pool. To obtain blessing, they created a pool of goodness for others, hoping it would overflow to them. They gave tzedakah to orphanages, women's clinics, and mikvehs. Good deeds, yes, but not physically helpful. Then they tried that mystical claptrap, undoing the band that holds the Sukkot lulav palm frond with the myrtle and willow, like that's really going to unravel suspected 'knots that block a woman's conception.'"

Nachum said, "How about linking the etrog Sukkot citron to Eve and the pain of childbirth. Rachel has to bite off the stem of an etrog as if to say, unlike Eve, I wouldn't have eaten the forbidden fruit, so grant me a child.[13] At least he gave her a token of his love, that brooch featuring a red ruby,[14] a red stone to encourage fertility."

Dina frowned. "I don't get that one."

"Rubies symbolize the tribe of Reuben, who brought mandrakes to Leah. The plant, shaped like a small human, supposedly advances fertility.[15] Another hot Talmudic idea came along, garlic.[16] Since they both smelled of the stuff, it probably didn't interrupt their intimacy. Then they ate tons of fish because that phrase in Genesis, 'let them grow into a multitude,' (Gen. 48:16) contains the letters of 'fish' in Hebrew. Meantime, Emanuel keeps telling Rachel, 'What have we got to lose?' Nothing but time they could have spent in bed or exploring medical alternatives."

Dina sighed cheerlessly. "I feel sorry for them. They wanted a child so badly, and when they finally learned that Rachel had uterine fibroids, there was nothing safe that could be done: no ultrasound surgery like today.

"I especially feel for Rachel. When Emanuel suggested she change her name to escape the evil eye, she must have called it quits. Couldn't Rachel see from the outset that her husband was pandering to ignorant Hasidim by forcing his wife to act on useless superstitions? He was out to enhance his image and to curry their future favor, while she was obliged to abase herself by implementing those lies. What people won't do for love!"

Nachum demurred. "Love? Or was it mutual ambition? Also, they lived in a different age. Warsaw contained both cultured Jews and bumpkins from the shtetl. Many uneducated shtetl dwellers were Hasidim. How would snobbishness have served Emanuel and Rachel in their quest for leadership?"

"The two of them knew better," Dina snapped. "In this instance, they lacked intellectual integrity. Genetically, Nachum, there's a little bit of Emanuel in you. Whatever this Shin Bet plan may be, we mustn't let mountains of money pervert our individual character, the nature of our relationship, or our devotion to the truth."

"For sure. You're the mensch-maker in the family. I count on you that way."

Signaling his admiration, Nachum kissed his wife tenderly, and then a second time, more eagerly, more intently.

Dina pushed away her husband ever so lightly. "Before we call it a night, did you read the squib that came after the visit to the doctor?"

"Yes . . . what about it?"

"Pretty racy stuff for Emanuel the rabbi to put on paper, don't you think?"

Nachum thought for a moment, then said, "The doctor did indicate that Rachel might still have a child. I'm sure they spent plenty of time abed. After the enjoyments Emanuel described in such arousing detail, he wrote how they talked seriously about Borisov and its role in the community. That was the context in which she shared her ideas with him. For Emanuel to note Rachel's creativity and social concern was a generous gift to history, I thought. With this notebook, he insured Rachel's full credit for conceiving the first Borisover plans to combat the Depression. He followed the rule, *b'shem omro*, that we give credit to the one who first stated a concept. Enough discussion. Let's go to bed. We can read more tomorrow."

She pulled him closer and spoke sotto voce, "You said you liked the texts he used. Here's one just for you: 'How beautiful you are, my lover – handsome indeed!'" (Song of Songs 1:16)

Nachum whispered a second quote in her ear, "My darling, you are beautiful, and your eyes are like doves." (Song of Songs 1:15)

Together their words portended a blissful conclusion to a Shabbat eve of mutual discovery.

CHAPTER TEN

Nachum returned from Beit Daniel Synagogue at lunch hour. While Hanna Liora took her afternoon nap, the Steinitz couple pursued more of Emanuel Davidson's occasional journal, which began with remarks about public anti-Semitism's depredations against the Polish Jewish community, followed by a few dated entries.

19 Elul, 5696 (Saturday night, 5 September 1936)

In the worsening economy, our followers turn to the Rebbe for help, but he lacks an effective response. Last night, Erev Shabbat, during an extensive and for the times, luxurious meal, Rachel challenged her father directly: "Papa, when will you act to save your Hasidim from starvation?"

He claimed we have barely enough for ourselves to properly honor the Sabbath and to give the Borisover shul a full groaning board including challah, herring, kugel, and veggies after services on Saturday morning. What more could he do?

Rachel reacted strongly. She accused him of holding back, that since we ourselves never lacked for food or raiment, had he skimmed donations to set aside a private fund for these bad times? The family's money must come from someplace.

The Borisover rejected the whole conversation —not proper for Shabbat, not a talk any daughter should have with her father. We must thank God for our bounty because the times are dissipating our resources rapidly.

I thought Rachel came down on her father too hard, hammered him, in fact. I switched to soothing words, but the same complaint. I recalled a lesson he taught from the Midrash on Psalm 118, "In the world to come, they will ask you, 'What was your work?' If you reply, 'I used to feed the hungry,' then they will say, 'This is the gate of the Eternal. Those who feed the hungry may enter.' If the answer is, 'I satisfied the thirst of others,' they will say, 'This is the gate of the Eternal. Those who slake others' thirst may enter.' And so it will be for those who clothe the naked, raise orphans, give tzedakah, and do deeds of love and kindness. Then King David said, 'I did all of those things. Open for me all the gates.' For this reason David's Psalm 118 declares, 'Open for me the gates [plural] of righteousness. I will enter them and thank God.'"'[17]

I gently reminded him that he taught those incandescent words with tears in his eyes, as if the thought of such consummate generosity moved his very soul. Then I told him, "You are my Rov*, my Teacher, but you are also my* Shver*, and I am fascinated by the fact that in Yiddish the word 'shver' can mean both 'father-in-law' and 'difficult'. I have never found you to be difficult, and indeed you have become more than my father-in-law, but like my very own father to me."*

Rachel squeezed my thigh under the table to indicate that I had her father's attention. Then I proposed Rachel's idea, that we could achieve the goal of the Midrash on Psalms by having the audacity to apply what remains in the Rebbe's coffers for the good of his Hasidim: create more study halls and mitzvah groups; give our unemployed Hasidim a place to go in the daytime where they can feel like a mensch. Study or fulfilling labor – these are the keys to self-worth. We proposed to branch our schools into neighborhoods where Hasidim reside, give them projects to accomplish together: caring for the elderly, watching little children, helping the teachers of our youth, cleaning apartments, polishing the counters of stores so battered by the anti-Jewish retail boycott, removing anti-Semitic graffiti – anything to make them feel closer to the Holy One, more useful to society and to their fellow Jews.

Then I carried him to the mountain he would have to climb. I ex-plained that with his help and the contributions of others, we wanted to pay his Hasidim for their time, whether for study or for labor. If he did this, the Borisovers would earn a reputation in Warsaw for prac-tical piety, and it would redound to his benefit and the benefit of the Borisover movement.

Finally, I humbled myself. I begged my Shver to spend any re-maining Borisover treasure to open the gates of righteousness in a dark hour and provide light by which his Hasidim could see God's place in the world.

For a full minute the Rebbe turned aside as if to seek his answer on the wall. He said nothing. His blank facial expression revealed nothing. Then he turned his gaze to both Rachel and to me. Never have I seen such sadness in his eyes. Was it defeat, resignation, re-pentance?

He told us he would underwrite the venture, but its management touched areas beyond his ken. He surprised the two of us, empower-ing us to take the necessary steps or to find experts who could organize the action plan. He demanded we begin immediately after Shabbat's conclusion.

Rachel let go of my thigh, arose from her seat and went to kiss her father. In turn, I smiled at the Rebbe, nodded warmly, and offered, "Thank God."

19 Elul, 5696 (Sunday, 6 September 1936)
Sunday at our kitchen table. We parsed our strategy. I submitted that we could not refuse any Borisover Hasidim the right to study, to work, or to eat.

Rachel said, if others come for aid, we should not turn them away.

I disagreed. Our program is for Borisovers only. But Rachel right-ly indicated that our Hasidim would have first knowledge of the opportunities, and if others knock on our doors, they might even be-come followers of the Rebbe. We shouldn't turn them away. Then she cited a Talmudic case, how the author of the Mishnah, Judah the Prince, wrongly wanted to withhold tzedakah from someone he thought was not a rabbi.[18] With that proof, I had to relent.

26 Elul, 5696 (Sunday, 13 September 1936)

I put my Talmudic knowledge to work for our Borisover system of relief. We copied the method of the Mishnah from 1800 years ago.[19] We established a kuppah, a charity box in our central office to which anyone could contribute. We account for every penny. Payday for those working and studying is Friday morning, yielding them enough money to buy two meals a day for their families for an entire week. For tradition's Third Meal on Shabbat, they'll have to attend Borisov.

We also arranged a tamchui, a food shelf. In place of the Mishnaic beth din court of three to decide who is deserving, the relief office looks for bona fides that prove affiliation with Borisover Hasidism. We invite the unaffiliated to attend Shabbat services or a study hall, or engage in a mitzvah project. We quickly accept for benefits those who do even one of these acts. For trustworthy fund-raising, we send pairs of well-connected but unemployed businessmen to collect money for the kuppah and gifts for the tamchui. Unemployed accountants put sharp, practiced eyes on the whole system to keep us honest.

25 Heshvan 5697 (Tuesday, 10 November 1936)

Today one perspicacious accountant cornered me. He wanted to know why a small amount of our kuppah money goes to Palestine every month. I covered my Haifa connection by explaining that one Hasid with a large family who left Warsaw needs support. He goes daily to Elijah's Cave in Haifa to pray for peace. Elijah's Cave is simultaneously sacred to three faiths, Judaism, Christianity, and Islam, and we all share the space. This Hasid is our agent to pray for peace in Palestine, peace here and in all Europe, where so much hatred and *division now reign. Surely this Warsaw family deserves a grain of support.*

The amount being of little note, the auditor overlooked it. Thank God.

Nachum put down the text and went to the kitchen, made two cups of tea from the Shabbat urn, and carried them with some snacks into the dining area. Dina joined him there.

"Reactions to the journal?" Dina asked.

"I feel like I'm reading the Torah."

"Why do you say that, Nachum?"

"Because on the one hand Emanuel Davidson acts in concert with his wife Rachel to reach for holiness, to repair a very broken Jewish world, and on the other hand, he embezzles sustenance for his son in Palestine. He's a humanitarian and a rogue all at once, like our ancient forebears."

"Like so many human beings," Dina retorted. "Rachel's coming out a hero in this little drama. Or else they were double-teaming Papa with a good cop/bad cop routine. Rachel played the bad cop, tough on her father. Emanuel took the role of the good cop, giving him a chance – not to confess, but to redeem himself before them."

Nachum responded, "I think Rachel's less like the Torah's Rachel and more like the biblical Rebecca, the manager. Rebecca dreamed up the means to steal Isaac's blessing from Esau and give it to Jacob, the son she felt deserved it. She designed the future of the Jewish people. Rachel designs the future for the Borisover Hasidim with her open-door generosity. But a hero, Dina? No, and here's why: she almost destroyed the chances of success with her father by the way she chastened him. He perceived it as impudence."

"Impudence? She just called it as she saw it."

"Maybe so, but if you put the manager Rachel together with Emanuel's sweet-talking the Rebbe, what do you have? Management and sales. Every functional corporation needs both, trust me, Dina."

"Corporation? Borisov a corporation?" Dina said.

"Corporation, NGO, religious organization – any group of humans working together towards a goal needs management and sales. You're the marketing expert in the family. I've got the MBA. It's part of what makes us a team.

"Let's stop for now and take another look at the text tonight."

CHAPTER ELEVEN

As Shabbat vanished into the Israeli night, Nachum and Dina enjoyed a hurried dinner together with Hanna Liora in her high chair. She seemed to sense that her parents' minds were elsewhere and slowed their pace by squawking and spilling. Dina lifted her daughter from the high chair, bounced her lightly into her lap, and fed her from there. Hanna Liora collaborated, greedily taking her spoonfuls of dinner. Soon enough she seemed ready to sleep, and the couple resumed their reading of Emanuel's notes.

Purim, 14 Adar II, 5698 (Thursday, 17 March 1938)
I haven't opened this little notebook for so long — too busy with the kuppah *and* tamchui. *So much misery and so many Hamans in this world to persecute our people. The everyday hatred that we feel toward us submerges the joy of Purim. Haman? Read: Hitler, and certain Poles, too. It's all too real, and we have no Esther and Mordecai to save us.*

Public awareness of the Borisover Hasidim advances, enhanced by the ever-growing charitable work of the kuppah *and* tamchui. *We're bringing on professionals to help, though Rachel and I keep Borisov at the core.*

I hear the Rebbe reciting Psalm 118 every day. He thinks he'll meet his reputed ancestor, King David, at all the gates of heaven. Or maybe the Borisover relief work makes him think of himself as the messiah. Who knows? If the Depression continues much longer, he'll be penniless.

16 Heshvan 5699 (Thursday, 10 November 1938)

Kristallnacht last night, today in Germany and Danzig, syna-gogues destroyed, Jews suffered personal violence. Moses Hess diagnosed the disease almost 100 years ago: Germans have an in-born antagonism to the Jews.[20]

8 Elul 5699 (23 August 1939)

Must note the date: Today in Moscow, Nazi foreign minister Joa-chim von Ribbentrop and Soviet foreign minister Viacheslav Molotov signed the non-aggression pact between Germany and the Soviet Un-ion. What will this mean for us in Poland, wedged between those two powers?

17 Elul 5699 (1 September 1939)

Now we have the answer as to what the non-aggression pact means: Nazi Germany has invaded Poland. Hour by hour the de-struction grows.

Shabbat, 25 Elul 5699 (9 September 1939)

The bombs falling on Warsaw awakened me. I crawled up from the basement to our bedroom, hoping the whiny hinges on the oaken cellar door and the creaky basement steps would not awaken the Rebbe's family. It's Shabbat, but I'm impelled to write before I forget the full story of last night, and with the siege underway, I may not be here tomorrow.

Because of the bombing we dined in the cellar for Shabbat. Rachel prepared a dinner to exceed all expectations, given the combat over-head. With candles already aglow, the Borisover placidly poured an overflowing cup of wine whose surplus spilled over the sides of the silver vessel into the saucer upon which it sat. He sanctified Shabbat, his Kiddush cup held steadily in the manner taught by the mystics of yore to represent God's support of the world. While the house trem-bled from a nearby bomb, he slowly and serenely drank a long pull of the wine, and we followed suit. Then we cried out, l'chaim, to life!, partaking once again of the cup, for we did not want the first draught of wine, intended to sanctify, to be mistaken for a frivolity, a toast like l'chaim. After washing hands, the Rebbe uncovered and held two loaves of golden brown and braided challah which seemed, in the circumstance of war, as miraculous to us as the double portion of manna that they represented and that the Israelites gathered before Sabbath in their desert wanderings. He recited Hamotsi, *thanks for bread, tore the bread, dipped it in salt, consumed a morsel, and broke off pieces for us. He then began a table conversation that avoided mention of the Nazi invasion of Poland and of the German devastation of Warsaw.*

Over chicken soup I asked how many lives our Hasidim lost and how many suffered injuries. He said, "It has been a hot, dry summer, but what good fortune to bask in such beautiful sunshine. In the midrash, Rav Levi said, 'It should be sufficient for people that God causes sunlight to shine upon them.'"[21]

Rachel exploded. She said she knew that midrash and how it ends: "Let those who love God be like the sun when it comes out in full strength" (Judges 5:31). She acknowledged the fact of Shabbat and the calming speech it required, but this Shabbat was different. We run the risk of Nazi troops invading our city, the risk of death from their bombs, and we have a mission to fulfill. It is we who must be like the sun in full strength, doing mitzvah upon mitzvah.

The Rebbe interrupted and silenced her. Admitting the arduous nature of the day, he said, "We have our dead, our wounded, our refugees, and tomorrow morning, if the bombing continues, we'll set aside Shabbat in order to save lives. You and Emanuel have made our kuppah *program the talk of Jewish Warsaw, and you have added the rescue of life and limb to its record of mitzvah. But it's Shabbos. You bravely prepared for us a substantial meal that could be our last such repast. Our souls need rest, and I've never entered Shabbos with such dire talk as you have just heard from me. It was a long, trying* week. Surely something good happened to you within it. Tell me first about that, and later this evening we can speak of saving lives."

Rachel exhaled and quickly stated, "Something good? The able-bodied among our virtually unpaid laborers spontaneously formed squadrons that pored through the rubble to rescue the living and bring forth the dead. They co-operated with other such teams in the city."

I added, "Warm weather brought an early and extensive harvest, filling the tamchui for the needy. Air raids will create more hungry people, but our Hasidim generously open their hands to help. Good news."

Throughout dinner the Rebbe directed talk away from war toward spiritual topics, discoursing on the Torah portion of the week, Nitsavim. His monologue attempted to settle our family on an island in time, the Sabbath. At meal's end, the Rebbe suddenly paused. A weight seemed to tug at his visage. Grimly he looked around our makeshift Shabbat table, locking on each of us for a moment.

At last he said, "We have other survival worries. Every Hasidic rebbe worth his salt found followers, his Hasidim, and every group of Hasidim constituted its own movement with its own unique teaching and philosophy, what we call its Hasidus. Even while we busy ourselves with the welfare of our Hasidim, we must also consider how to insure the survival of our Borisover Hasidus.

"To you, my dear daughter and to you my dear son-in-law – no, let me rather say my only son, I confess: when the Soviets and the Germans signed their non-aggression treaty two weeks ago, I made a decision – not a simple one to execute, but a decision with consequences for all three of us.

"In Eastern Europe we develop a sixth sense gained from our history. With it I could smell war in the offing. Though our coreligionists hoped that Germany was different, civilized, educated, and this would somehow tame Adolf Hitler, I knew the Nazis intended to destroy the Jews. Hitler's writings and regime confirm it.

"Borisover Hasidus *must survive. Our movement must survive. We must leave once again and immediately, this time for America."*

Rachel grabbed my hand and looked aghast at her father the Rebbe. She protested that the vast majority of our Hasidim are here. How could we abandon so many needy people? And how make our way to America without visas?

The Rebbe shifted forward, his hand rapping the table before his hard-nosed response. "The Germans will seize what little wealth we have left in this country. Our mitzvah corps will grow unsustainable. Our funds for the kuppah will evaporate.

"Last month I contacted Borisover leadership in Brooklyn, New York, where we have a small, staunchly supportive group, individuals who immigrated there over the years. I urged them to employ every means to access the American authorities in Washington, D.C., as well as their New York members of the American Congress to promote our swift evacuation from Warsaw. Our New York Hasidim have some money to help our cause. On this side of the water, and I tell you this in strictest confidence, I have sequestered funds over a period of many years, and we, too, have sufficient to make our departure attractive to certain officials."

Rachel frowned and shook her head. "What do you mean you have sequestered funds?"

For years, the Rebbe explained, he built an emergency fund in Switzerland with a portion of the donations from our Hasidim and others. He asked, "Don't you agree that they want their Rebbe to be safe, the teachings of their Hasidus to continue no matter what befalls them here? We are not merely rescuing people with this money. We are rescuing a way of life, a particular Jewish way of believing, thinking, and practicing. It had to be done, and it must be used as foreseen."

Rachel wanted to know who approved the fund, and the Rebbe trashed the question by asserting that the Borisover Hasidim are neither a democracy nor a not-for-profit agency ruled by a committee.

Borisov is a theocracy which the Rebbe leads. Ultimately, all decisions are his to make with God's help. Then he clearly stated, "Someday it may well be your husband who will rule, and I do mean rule, over our thousands of followers. Who approved this fund? It was I who took the decision to create it and to harbor it in Lugano."

Rachel harrumphed that at last she understood why the family vacationed annually on Lake Lugano.

Then she infuriated her father by reminding him that the Israelites molded the treasure taken from the Egyptians into the Golden Calf, but used their own hidden gold to build the wilderness sanctuary, the Mishkan.[22] *However, the Torah text says, "Make for me a sanctuary that I may dwell within them" (Exodus 25:8). Every Jew has a divine sanctuary within his or her soul. Every Jew is a place where holiness resides. Rachel begged her father to use the Borisover gold to save as many individual Jewish "sanctuaries," as possible.*

The Rebbe pounced on her argument, saying, "Surely you can't believe that saving the Borisover Rebbe and his family using donated money is tantamount to worshipping the Golden Calf? Surely you agree that the hidden cache in Switzerland can build our Mishkan, *our place of worship and study, in another land. It is the future of our* Hasidus.

"If we live through the German siege of Warsaw, God willing, we'll find a way out of here with the help of those who are still neutral in this war, and chief among them are the Americans, where we may have influence."

Here I interrupted, hoping to subdue tempers with a different and new Torah interpretation. A strange conundrum exists in Nitsavim *(Deuteronomy 29:27). Why does the word* vayashLichem *have an oversized lamed? No one knows, but let me suggest a reason. Lamed is a useful letter for abbreviations in Hebrew. Lamed can abbreviate the word* l'havdil, *to separate. If so, the Torah says,* v'yesh l'havdilchem, *and the text would mean, "It's necessary to separate you to another land." I suggested that for the Borisover Rebbe, the war had created such a time.*

The Rebbe found the comment gratifying and cut off controversy when he launched into the blessing after meals.

For safety, we all slept in the cellar: the Rebbe on a mattress under the dining table, Rachel and I beneath the staircase. Rachel whispered to me that she considered the money hidden in Lugano as a kind of theft. People gave it for the welfare of the group, and the Rebbe will apply it for personal need.

I urged her to compare the Rebbe to a national leader, a symbol who had to be saved, as they did with some of the Polish leadership, spiriting them from the country. In the best of all possible worlds, perhaps Rachel is right, but today's Poland may be the worst of all possible worlds, and her father's plan shows foresight. Yet I admitted that we are all personally implicated in the matter, so how can our judgment be fair? What bigger conflict of interest than the fact of our own lives at stake?

Because tomorrow may never come, I must remember that whatever happens in this war, I still have a future and a hope. Part of me lives in Palestine, and I must try to fulfill my responsibilities there. The Midrash on Ecclesiastes/Kohelet has me pegged, alright. Recounting the vanities of every stage of life, of my moment in time it says, "When he has children, he grows brazen like a dog to supply their food and wants." [23] *Just how brazen remains to be seen.*

Dina and Nachum sat across from each other quietly awaiting the discussion to open. Nachum broke the silence.

"Who's in the right, Rachel or the Rebbe?"

Dina bit her lip and responded, "*Elu v'elu divrei Elohim Chayim.* Both of these are the words of the Living God.[24] I can understand the Rebbe's choice to abandon Warsaw, particularly in hindsight, and I can understand Rachel's objections. I especially honor Rachel for her chutzpah. She never hesitates to let her voice be heard for social justice. Could it be that her father's earlier abandonment of Rachel developed within her the grit and self-confidence to stand up for the causes she most respected?"

Nachum agreed. "She's the altruistic hero of the story. But the Rebbe reveals his cleverness. With the Nazis capturing Warsaw, he decides that it's every man for himself. He could rely on that old Talmudic tale of two men in the desert, only one possessing water.[25] If he shares the water, both die. If he keeps the water, he alone lives. Rabbi Akiba decides the owner of the water has priority and lives. Why? 'Your brother shall live *with you*' (Leviticus 25:36). We have a responsibility to ourselves to survive. The Rebbe owns the water, so to speak, that fund in Switzerland."

Dina shook her head. "A fund whose existence Rachel rightly called a theft from Borisov's donors."

"Hold on, Dina. Let's assume he set it aside for an emergency. Was it really theft, or was it self-insurance for the future of the Borisover Hasidim?"

"Nachum, it's all so gray, no clear black and white, right or wrong. War suspends the normal course of morality, I guess. As for Emanuel, he admits to conniving for cash to support your grandfather as a child."

"For sure, but . . ."

"But what, Nachum? He ripped Borisov off to support Hannalora's family, and he did it for generations."

"Dina, this is going to sound crazy, particularly since we don't know what Shin Bet and Mossad have in mind for us, but what if his actions were more than a personal desire to send child support? What if he took the long view and thought to himself, someday I'll be the Borisover Rebbe, and one day I'll die. I have one child. That child may have other offspring. Maybe one of those offspring will know enough Yiddishkeit to take my place. Therefore, the support money I send ultimately redounds to the benefit and future of the Borisovers."

"Wow! There's a stretch if ever I heard one. We all want to think well of our ancestors, but what you just said sounds to me like a whitewash, like you've elevated Emanuel's motives beyond the facts at hand. No offense meant, Nachum. But I think we should talk more about the journal tomorrow."

"Not tomorrow. I have to go early to the office for a meeting. I'll be whipped by evening. Monday?"

Dina nodded consent, and their session adjourned.

CHAPTER TWELVE

Again Nachum and Dina relaxed at the kitchen table with Emanuel's private notes in hand.

4 Tishri 5700 (Sunday, 17 September, 1939)

The Soviet Union invaded Poland, grabbing the portion of the country that must have been consigned to it by the non-aggression pact. Jews will run from Hitler into the arms of Stalin – from my Russian experience, not a blessing.

14 Tishri 5700 (Wednesday, 27 September 1939)

Today, the eve of our festival of thanksgiving, Sukkot, Warsaw fell to the Nazis. After Black Monday and its intensive bombing by the Germans, thanksgiving for what? Twenty thousand dead? Probably more. Poland's capital in ruins: Warsaw looks like a vast city of sukkah lean-tos after a storm – roofs stripped away, fragile walls crumbling, contents strewn across the landscape. God help us.

18 Tishri 5700 (Sunday, 1 October 1939)

The Rebbe spent the day frantically attempting contact with the new German bureaucracy that flowed into the city after the surrender. He returned weary, drawn, and discouraged. No exit visas from any embassy, either. As a Jew, he has no more status with the Germans than any simple Yiddisher street sweeper. Me? I thank God because we're fortunate still to be alive.

25 Tishri 5700 (Sunday, 8 October 1939)

One week changed our world. Today I write from the safety of an Italian ocean liner. Rachel is strolling the deck with her father, allowing me to log this record during ostensible nap time.

Last Tuesday, 3 October, 5 AM, violent pounding on the door of the Rebbe's home awakened us. At the entryway we encountered two Wehrmacht officers, a chaplain major and a captain, who flashed swastika-stamped orders from the German Foreign Office to escort us out of Warsaw under the aegis of General Gerhard Steinmüller. They gave us fifteen minutes to dress and pack.

The chaplain tried to calm us, but the cross emblazoned on his uniform added to the nerve-wracking tension and terror. Where were we going? Why? Would our transit be safe? With no choice but to comply, we felt jittery, emotions over the edge. Outside the house, the captain plucked the keys from the Rebbe's hand and relieved us of our identity papers, which he tucked into a leather envelope. He directed us to an automobile at the ready.

The noise of our car fractured the deadly silence of streets strewn with loose brick and scarred with bomb craters. The homeless huddled in doorways and crouched for warmth before corner ashcans where they burned the remains of their houses. We zigzagged through the rubble and arrived at Warsaw's central railroad station. An officer met us, received the leather envelope, and said he would accompany us. We sat in the station, quietly praying from our pocket siddurim or reading psalms. The Rebbe and I began to lay tefillin just after dawn, but the officer loudly and crudely halted us.

About 9 AM we left for Poznan, where we bought water, fruit, and kosher candy in quantity and departed for Berlin close to 3:30 PM. Ten hours later, after endless stops, the train pulled into Friedrichstrasse Bahnhof. There we transferred by army vehicle to Anhalter Bahnhof, gateway to the south. Our official guard changed to a certain Lieutenant Baecker, who took possession of the crucial envelope.

On Hoshanah Rabbah, 21 Tishri, Wednesday, 4 October, 6:30 AM we entrained for Zurich after sleeping fitfully on benches. Baecker let us daven in our compartment, but without the willow from the lulav to drive away the last of the previous year's sins and absent a congregation, the holiday did not inspire. Near Freiburg, Baecker suddenly disappeared. He returned in a rumpled civilian suit that would not draw attention from the Swiss. At Weil am Rhein, prim Swiss customs officials scrutinized our papers and approved our transit. Baecker directed us off the train at Basel.

It was already dinner hour. The lieutenant offered to buy us a meal, but we ate of our kosher food and davened quietly in the station. Our Swiss Railways train left promptly for Milan via Lugano. After midnight the Rebbe stepped to the door of our compartment, slid it open, and asked the officer for a moment of his time. Lieutenant Baecker jerked his head to the right as if to say, "Come out."

The Rebbe closed the door behind him and initiated an inaudible conversation which he later detailed for me. The Rebbe stated that he knew our destination. Clearly the lieutenant was accompanying us to Italy because the few refugees the Swiss deigned to accept were political, and we did not qualify. Mussolini's racial laws of 1938 proved Il Duce wanted no more Jews in his country, so Milan wasn't our final destination. We must be en route to a port like Genoa.

Then the Rebbe said, "Lieutenant Baecker, I'll make you an offer." That surprised the German. Through the glass window of our compartment I saw the soldier's eyebrows shoot up. The Rebbe explained that this day was a sacred Jewish holiday, Shemini Atseret. He asked if the schedule allowed us to detrain in Lugano for rest and a chance to attend synagogue to honor the memory of his late parents with Kaddish at Yizkor remembrance services. He assured him that trains aplenty to Milan departed from Lugano. The Rebbe pledged to Baecker not merely deluxe accommodations, but a reward, and asked him to name his price.

"I promise that when we leave your company, you'll receive a worthy payment in Swiss francs. This war is only beginning. When it's over, how much will your reichsmarks be worth? You may need hard Swiss currency. How much do you want? Name your price to give us a night's rest and the opportunity to pray to God."

With 900 reichsmarks, 1200 Swiss francs, Baecker could buy a Volkswagen, if he could find one. Our guard must have thought, go for the moon, and he asked for 10,000 francs. He probably wanted his own Swiss bank account for family use after the war. The Rebbe agreed to pay the 10,000 francs on condition we not depart Lugano until mid-afternoon, and Baecker would have to arrange the railroad connections.

When we reached Lugano, we left the train and awakened the station's single somnolent cabbie, who took us to Hotel International. Elegant and historic, it's on the lake, a favorite haunt of the Rebbe for our family vacations.

Our bedraggled entourage walked from the taxi to the portico of the imposing hotel. The Rebbe asked Baecker to give us our passports, or he would not be able to fulfill the lieutenant's fondest hopes. Baecker complied, and we entered.

Seeing us at the door, the registration clerk cried out, "Signor Rabbino, benvenuto!"

The Rebbe recognized him. "Roberto! So good to see you."

As the Borisover reached the reception desk, Roberto asked in a near-whisper, "Do you have food you want stored in the cooler, as usual?"

The Rebbe replied in a low voice, "Not tonight, Roberto, but maybe you could wait until tomorrow afternoon to submit the record of our papers?"

"Sì sì," he winked with an air of confidentiality. "It will be the same day as you checked in. No problem." Roberto took our passports for the record and returned them to us. At 3:45 AM we entered our lavish quarters and slept until our wake-up call.

Shemini Atseret, 22 Tishri 5700 (Thursday, 5 October 1939)

I let Rachel sleep late. Bathed and dressed, I met the Rebbe in the hotel lobby to walk to synagogue. The Borisover's presence created a stir, with many congregants leaving their seats to hear firsthand stories of the war and inform themselves of the status of Polish Jewry. Later, a sudden buzz of voices in the upstairs women's section announced Rachel's presence in Lugano's single Jewish Tempio. That day the Rebbe was honored with a Torah blessing; I was honored to offer blessings at the meal.

We were ravenous for something kosher and solid, but we pretended not to be famished and ate refinedly. The president of the congregation quietly offered a couple of shopping bags of food for our journey, which I gratefully accepted. He sent them by messenger to the hotel. Good to have because kosher food in Ticino Canton comes at a premium.

The Rebbe instructed Rachel to await us at the hotel. We walked to BSI Bank, steps away on Via Magatti. A secretary greeted "Signor Rabbino" warmly, knew enough not to extend her hand to him, and rang up a bank executive, Signor Luccicato. With open arms he gave the Rebbe a two-cheek kiss, strongly shook my hand, and escorted us to his substantial office paneled in dark wood, with parquet flooring covered by an impressive, intricate Persian rug.

The Rebbe explained that because of the unstable times he wanted to add my signature to his account. Also, he wanted to withdraw 50,000 francs in cash, and later he would be wiring money from Lugano to other sites. Any problem with wiring money during the war?

The bank executive assured the Rebbe that all his requests could be faithfully fulfilled. He returned with the cash, five envelopes of 500-franc notes, 10,000 in each, which he handed immediately to the Rebbe, who put them in an inside pocket of his long black coat. We signed the necessary documents, thanked Signor Luccicato, and departed.

As we wordlessly walked the lakeside path under colorful fall foliage and in sight of alpine terrain, the Borisover seemed rapt in thought. Then he put his hand on my shoulder. He offered me a shiur, *a lesson on the permission to break Jewish law in order to save life, employing as an example this very Shemini Atseret.*

He said, "Look what we'll have done – from riding in a taxi to banking and handling money, transacting a business deal, paying for hotel rooms, and more. Why? To save our lives, because if we do not follow the plan of this Baecker, we are dead. One government or another will remand us into the grip of the Nazis, and I am convinced Hitler will kill us. Usually questions of pikuach nefesh, *of saving lives, are about saving the life of another. We must trouble ourselves with these questions in speaking of ourselves. I suppose it's as simple as 'You shall live by the commandments and not die because of them.'"* (Lev. 18:5)

I felt as though the Rebbe read my mind. I, too, was pondering whether we could justify all these transgressions against holiday tradition.

By 1:45 PM we rejoined Rachel and Lieutenant Baecker, who sat impatiently in the lobby with our luggage and the bags of synagogue food spread around them. Baecker had transferred our tickets to other trains without problem, but with a 2:30 PM train to catch, the Rebbe quickly paid the hotel bills, and as we hastened up the hill by taxi to the nearby station, Baecker reclaimed our documents, which in turn passed inspection at the Chiasso border stop, and by 4:45 PM we chugged toward Genoa, leaving Milan's huge and heavy Babylonian style Stazione Centrale. *During the trip, Baecker stepped away for several minutes and re-emerged in uniform once again. In fascist Italy, the German military garb would not present a problem and might even alleviate a few. Italy was not at war, yet no one questioned Mussolini's closeness with Hitler, who considered Il Duce his best friend.*

We arrived in Genoa just before 8 PM and went directly to the Grand Hotel Savoia, across the piazza from the railroad terminal. Baecker approached the desk clerk with a fistful of documents and a voucher drawn from his leather envelope. While he arranged our rooms, we scrutinized the lobby, seeing a number of families in brisk conversation. We heard Yiddish – more Jews bolting from Europe. They looked at Baecker's Wehrmacht uniform with fear, disgust, and disdain. Certainly, their heightened tension overwhelmed the usually staid social atmosphere imposed by the lobby's overstuffed elegance and mahogany veneer. When they saw Baecker approach the Rebbe, they murmured among themselves, then went mute as we passed by, following a bellboy who pushed a cart loaded with our bags.

23 Tishri 5700 (Simchat Torah), (Friday, 6 October 1939, 7:45 AM)

We met Lieutenant Baecker in the hotel lobby. The last morsels of the synagogue food had sated us with a nourishing breakfast, though the bread had grown crusty. Baecker led us to a waiting taxi where he instructed the Rebbe to sit between the driver and himself. Baecker said simply, "To the Rex.*"*

During the brief ride, the German extended the passports, visas, and information sheets concerning the voyage. The Rebbe took the material in his left hand, and at the same moment, using his right hand, he drew from his coat a single unsealed envelope of 10,000 Swiss francs and subtly glided it into the lieutenant's possession. Baecker tipped its opening toward the window and with two fingers inspected the envelope to verify the currency within. His nod indicated acceptance.

When the taxi stopped at the edge of the ship terminal area, Baecker emerged from the vehicle and waved the rabbi out, holding his hand palm-forward to halt our exit. He took the Rebbe by the elbow, turned toward the docks and forced him to walk a number of steps further. With the Rebbe's back to me, I could not see or hear the soldier, but we all watched as the Borisover reached in his left-hand pocket for another envelope, gave it to Baecker, and accepted what Baecker tendered him. The two returned to the taxi, Baecker grinning, the Rebbe scowling.

We alighted from the vehicle while the taxi driver assembled our luggage on the sidewalk. Baecker pointed toward the ship in port. "You are travelling on the S.S. Rex of the Italian Line, one of the finest ocean liners afloat, and count yourselves fortunate. This is her last voyage to America for the duration of the war. She leaves port at 11:30 AM. All tickets and documents you need for travel and admission to the United States at the Port of New York are in your possession. You may not leave the ship at its Naples port of call. Berlin has full relations with the neutral American government, so today I'll request our foreign office to apprise the Americans of your arrival six and a half days from now. You are free to use the ship's communications system to contact anyone in the United States or elsewhere once the vessel reaches the open Atlantic. As they say here, 'Buon viaggio.'"

With that, Baecker turned heel, entered the taxi, and sped away.

Rachel and I walked alongside the Rebbe toward the gangway. We asked him what the lieutenant took from him at the last moment. He relinquished another 10,000 Swiss francs. Without that payment, Baecker would have withheld our tickets. The Rebbe said he played tough with the lieutenant: A soldier has orders to follow. He and his family could suffer if he failed to complete them. Baecker snarled that the disappearance of a few more Polish Jews, even famous ones, would ruffle neither the Fuehrer's nor Roosevelt's feathers. He planned to report that we slipped away from the hotel before dawn to hide in Italy. Checkmate.

The Rebbe was glad he didn't put the bills in a single envelope, or we'd be penniless right now, though even that could be overcome once we arrived in America. The cash was already divided into five parts, one part in each of his coat pockets, one in each shoe, and the *last in his suitcase. He told us he couldn't wait to get to our state-rooms so he could take the money out of his shoes and walk like a normal human being.*

I couldn't help but laugh. I asked if he drained much from the Lugano account. The Rebbe shook his head, telling me the withdrawal cost less than 1% of his Swiss savings. He believed we stood in good position to begin a life in America and carry our Hasidus to the New World.

I did the math in my head. 50,000 is 1% of 5,000,000. But the Rebbe said "less than 1%." The man possessed a fortune, over a million US dollars, and my name now sits securely on that Swiss account. Comforting news.

Our staterooms, remarkably, are first class and with balcony. The ship is heated, air conditioned, and boasts a kosher kitchen, indicating that Jews aplenty have escaped Europe aboard the Rex. There's more than a minyan of us on board.

When the ship left port on Friday morning, Rachel drew close and kissed me. She tried to smile while tears formed in her eyes. "We're free," she said, "but our people are sold into slavery." I held her close and responded, "I'll believe we're truly free when we survive the sea lanes and make it to America. Maybe from there we can be of greater help."

Our shipboard Shabbat mixed the sweetness of our liberty and safety with the stingingly bitter sadness of surrendering our friends and relatives to the animus of our adversaries.

"Where are you in the text, Nachum?"

"They're aboard ship."

"Wait a minute. I'm almost there." Dina guided an index finger swiftly across the lines, a speed-reading trick she had learned.

"OK," she said. "Reactions?"

"There are two stories here, the one we know from the printed page, and the one we don't know, the one that took place behind the scenes and moved the family across, what?, 2000 kilometers? It's that last story I'd like to read."

"Maybe the answer is yet to come in the notebook," Dina speculated, "but even if we examine what's on the surface, it's plain that your great-grandfather watched every financial move of the Borisovers carefully to advantage himself, to scout secretive means to send child support to Hannalora. He consciously avoided raising red flags, but he put his hand in the till."

"The notebook itself raises red flags," Nachum pointed out. "Mossad photographed it surreptitiously. We are reading a journal kept under lock and key. I have to wonder whether Emanuel didn't destroy it before his death. You can be sure that I would have, were I in his place."

Dina added, "Or he could have torn out the incriminating parts. Only a few indications of malfeasance pop off the pages so far."

Nachum frowned. "Obviously Borisov was not a squeaky-clean operation. There were too many loopholes in the management of it, too much power in one man's hands. I wonder if it's still the case."

"Let's leave that question to the tax authorities. We'll never know the answer, just like we'll never know who was bumped from two cabins on the *Rex* to make sudden room for the Borisover family. What happened to them?"

Nachum shrugged and shook his head in bewilderment. "Why don't we take a few more minutes and read ahead? Are you game? Maybe there are answers."

"I've got to get some sleep. Hanna Liora's been getting up early. And what about you? Don't you have to be at the office tomorrow?"

"I do, but I'm impelled to finish this section. I'll fill you in over breakfast." The two kissed. Nachum settled into the chair while Dina headed for their bedroom.

CHAPTER THIRTEEN

I n the morning, Dina awakened her drowsy husband, who had followed Emanuel's journal late into the night.

"So?" she said. "Wake up and fill me in."

In a bit, Dina sat at the table while Hanna Liora played with blocks at her feet. Nachum outlined the contents of Emanuel's notes as he ate.

"First he cites a Talmudic tale of a wayfarer who asked a lad which was the correct way to his destination.[26] The boy told him of two routes: one he called the short long way, and the other was the long short road. The short long way quickly led to the city wall, yes, but at its end, no entry was available. The long short road led over a more tortuous pathway directly to the city gate. Emanuel says that with their long journey concluded, the American Borisovers opened their gates and their hearts to the Rebbe and his family in short order. Nice use of the Talmud, though I think they traveled the short short way, given the times they lived through.

"The Hasidim in Brooklyn prepared everything to establish the family quickly and easily in Borough Park: a house for the Rebbe, an apartment for Emanuel and Rachel, furniture, linens, kitchen and dining needs — every detail. From Ellis Island they went to the Statue of Liberty for a photo-op with the press. Then they swept the family through clothing stores to restock and get fitted for new apparel.

"While Emanuel waited with one of the local leaders for Rachel to try on some dresses, Emanuel asked how the Brooklyn Borisovers managed to spirit the family out of embattled Warsaw.

"The fellow said that the Rebbe's social work outreach, the *kuppah* and *tamchui*, received some notice in the American Jewish press.

Borisover leaders assembled a dossier of the Warsaw efforts with English and other translated press clippings, adding large pictures of the Rebbe and family. They contacted impressive names in Jewish communal life to obtain endorsements, even well-known Reform and Conservative rabbis. They twisted the arms of key New York politicians, portraying the Rebbe not only as Eastern Europe's most recognizable rabbi, but as a religious dignitary equivalent to the Anglican Church's Archbishop of Canterbury, or even the Pope in Rome!"

Dina laughed out loud.

Nachum went on, "They promised strong contributions to certain New York congressmen and senators should their efforts move the State Department to demand that the German ambassador arrange the immediate transfer of the Rebbe and his family to the United States. They connected to American families whose grandparents followed Borisover Hasidism in Europe to cajole them to urge officials to endorse the Rebbe's immigration.

"The big breakthrough came at the outset of October, 1939, when a former justice of the United States Supreme Court, a federal cabinet member, and a long-time New York City member of Congress – all Jews – twisted the State Department's arm. All three used the same argument, saying that surely the publicity for the entry of three prominent Warsaw Jewish religious lights might embellish the murky reputation muddying State's name for its rejection of entry to 936 desperate Jews only four months previously, when President Roosevelt decided not to 'send the homeless, tempest-tost' of the *S.S. St. Louis* past the Statue of Liberty and extinguished Lady Liberty's 'lamp beside the golden door' to the ship's refugee passengers, who disappeared into the maw of the impending Shoah.

"Their pressure could not have had better timing. The Brooklyn Borisov leader himself didn't know what transpired, but he's guessing that the State Department summoned the German ambassador, who in turn contacted Foreign Minister von Ribbentrop in Berlin to endorse the family's release as a means to cover negative publicity damning the Nazis for war crimes in Poland. Or maybe State contacted von Ribbentrop. The American Borisov leader pictured von Ribbentrop consulting with Nazi propaganda mastermind Goebbels, who approved the plan, or maybe von Ribbentrop simply wired Nazi overlords in Warsaw to move the family out.

"But Dina, I did my own research last night, sitting at the computer and surfing the net. At that crucial moment for Emanuel and Rachel, I believe General Gerhard Steinmüller, mentioned by Emanuel, was the highest ranking German officer in Warsaw. He's the general who witnessed Nazi troops burning rural synagogues packed with screaming Jews. He wanted to confront Hitler with these and other war crimes but stood down when he learned that the vicious atrocities came at the instance of the Führer himself. He clandestinely relayed that information to MI6 intelligence service in Britain, which wanted to make the U.S. an ally in the war effort. The British then disclosed the horrifying information to the departments of State and of War. That might have helped the Rebbe's cause, too, and notice that the transfer was carried out by the Wehrmacht.

"Steinmüller was in Warsaw in an official administrative capacity. I think he received a call from the Foreign Office ordering the Borisover Rebbe and his family out of Warsaw, and given what he'd seen in Poland, he was ready to use staff and materiel to extract the Rebbe and his family. Hard work by Brooklyn's Borisovers combined with their fortuitous timing and flat-out mazel to accomplish a miracle."

Dina nodded in agreement. "It's a plausible reconstruction of events. And what a compliment to the Brooklyn Borisovers. In the midst of a blazing war, they refused to give up."

"Yeah, well . . . both the German and American governments wanted to whitewash their actions before the American public, and the Borisover family provided an opportunity that neither could refuse."

"Look, Nachum, the governments were pretty stupid about marketing their actions. That's my field, hey, and I can tell you that neither side gained anything from the rescue. Most people never heard of this particular Rebbe. The ones who recognized the name probably threw their sheitels and yarmulkes overboard when they landed in the States, happy to be rid of his autocracy. The publicity came forth, and I'll bet, even with positive reviews of the Rebbe's social work in Warsaw, most Jews and all non-Jews said, 'Who?' The name Borisov meant nothing in those days. The whole Borisover movement only became well known after Emanuel took over. The winner in the deal was the family and ultimately, Borisov, because they got Emanuel and Rachel's leadership.

"Enough for now, Nachum, you've got to go to work. Let's finish the last of the notebook tonight. The Director is coming the day after tomorrow."

Book III

ויקרא

Leviticus / "And he called"

CHAPTER FOURTEEN

Ohr HaChaim comments on Leviticus 1:1 – And he called to Moses:
Why doesn't the text mention the name of the one who called, and
also, why is the subject of the sentence mentioned later? It should
come at the outset. In any case, it's understood that God is the one
who is speaking, as if it said, "God called." [27]

Rabbi Levi ben David v'Yehudit commented on the Ohr HaChaim:
Out of piety and grammatical knowledge, Ohr HaChaim, Rashi, and
others assume that God called to Moses. However, since Ohr HaCha-
im asks why the text fails to mention the name of the one who called
to Moses, he not only admits to the text's obscurity, but he admits to
doubts whether God did, indeed, call to Moses.

The biblical text that follows delineates sacrifices to be brought
when individuals, the community, or even a ruler might sin, on pur-
pose or accidentally. If not a divine call, its source is at least the
Jewish superego requiring fulfillment of God's charge to Abraham, to
become a people that does what is just and what is right. [28]

The Steinitz couple finished their perusal of Emanuel's journal in the evening. Not much remained – a record of two of the Reb-be's speeches at his first Shabbat dinners with Borisover leadership and a policy change that Emanuel initiated. They sat across from each other, a low table between them.

Dina screwed up her face and pointed at Nachum's slippered feet on the coffee table. "Off," she said.

"They're only slippers."

"They're only slippers that walk all over the floor. Who knows what's on them. Off." She flipped her fist with a thumb outstretched.

Nachum complied with a groan and leaned toward his wife. He asked, "Anything stand out for you in those two speeches of the Rebbe?"

"For sure," she responded. "He addressed almost two dozen people at dinner, and he tried to share the emotions of living through and fleeing from war, but he didn't belabor those points. He made them feel like family with warmth, thankfulness, and some humility. The discourse came from the heart, but he organized his table talk well."

Nachum chimed in, "And he turned immediately to his goals for their community. I like his interpretation employing the three groups in the Torah that had responsibility for the wilderness tabernacle and its movement from place to place. The Merarites managed the framework items. The Gershonites had charge of fabrics. The Kohathites oversaw the most sacred objects, like the Ark of the Covenant where the Ten Commandments were kept. The Rebbe designs their future by declaring that the Borisover Hasidim must take the role of all three.

"He hopes to save lives in Eastern Europe, but correctly predicts that Hitler will destroy the framework of European Jewish life and calls upon Borisov to rebuild it in the New World according to a Borisover blueprint, to become guardians of the framework like the Merarites."

Dina said, "From the women's angle, I like how he turned to local needs and endorsed the work in Warsaw by both Emanuel *and* Rachel as examples of tzedakah and community organization that could be followed in Borough Park. He empowered the whole couple, not just Emanuel, to help reweave and strengthen the economic and social fabric of the Borisover group in Brooklyn. He volunteered his children to accomplish the task of the Gershonites, and I'm sure they were pleased."

Nachum's eyes glowed as he described the third challenge. "To conclude, the Rebbe offers a general sense of his role as a leader, and it's all about Borisover *Hasidus*, exactly what he dwelt on a few Shabbat eves before in Warsaw – saving the movement and its philosophy.

He understood that during the war and after, most efforts in Jewish life would center on fighting the enemies of the Jewish people. He wisely advocated strengthening Borisov instead.

"From my MBA's perch, it's like a company that finds itself in the midst of a terrible recession. They can cut back to fight the economic times, or they can spend more on advertising, research, and development to emerge the major player when better times return. That's the way the Borisovers became like the Kohathites, literally taking charge of the most holy objects, and in our time, having an impact on the physical world of synagogues and schools, as well as the realm of Jewish ideas and ideals as they expanded their movement. The Rebbe made his coterie of leaders feel as though they could conquer the Jewish world."

"They've done pretty well at it, Nachum. The goal was the Rebbe's, but it took his children to carry it off. Anything to note in the second Shabbat table talk?"

Nachum scratched his head as if trying to provoke a thought. "The Rebbe became more specific about the details of his plan because in a week's time he was able to acquaint himself with the main players in Brooklyn, one by one, knowing their strengths and inviting their participation in his plans. That showed good management.

"Also, Emanuel noted that the keynote quotation from *Pirkei Avot*, 'The day is short, the work is great, . . . and the Master is urgent,'[29] left out any reference to lazy workers or great rewards, complimenting them for their diligence and warning them that they may never see the reward of all their labor, but still, the work must be done. The group probably understood the references. Then the Rebbe moves to the Torah portion, *Vayera*, which is the kind of after-dinner discourse the Borisovers expect."

Dina picked up the theme. "He brands the *Akedah*, the binding of Isaac, as one of Abraham's tests, then brings current affairs into the picture and makes their moment in 1939 a test not of one person, but of millions. He wants to raise money to save lives in Europe by sending out emissaries, *shlichim*, if possible, and he hopes personally to improve the Borisover's education system in America. OK. Good ideas, nothing fantastic, though, because the Rebbe knows that in wartime the money they raise can't penetrate through the enemy's lines, and the only refuge is in the east, the USSR. He hates the Soviets.

"From my publicist's point of view, the Rebbe succeeds in his closing remark. He lets his Hasidim know that he's both a realist and a leader who can bring them to a stirring future. He does it in a way to inspire the Torah-hungry group and display the Rebbe's depth of knowledge. Using that midrash about Joseph and his brothers from Tanhuma[30] he tells them of his full awareness that among Jewish people the Borisovers are virtually unknown, an unrecognized group of Hasidim in America. As he put it, 'They don't know us, but Borisov recognizes our Jewish people, and we know their spiritual neediness. Let us welcome them in our midst to taste of our *Hasidus* – our philosophy, our love of Torah. This we cannot do until we have thoroughly prepared ourselves, and that preparation begins now. Help me build the Borisovers into a force for Torah and mitzvah in America.' That's pretty inspiring stuff for Hasidim, Nachum. I give him credit."

"It's a good speech, but Dina, shouldn't we give some of the praise to Emanuel? Forgive the metaphor, but he engineers the fundraising by convincing the Rebbe that despite the Borisover's non-Zionist philosophy, the Rebbe must recognize that a vital escape route for European Jews would be legal and illegal immigration to the British Mandate of Palestine. He asks what the Borisover is doing to help his Hasidim feel at home in Eretz Yisrael, and he advocates working with the Jewish Agency for Palestine to create a Borisover village in an area of Eretz Yisrael suitable for settlement and within reach of Jerusalem. He says . . . let me read it, 'We have to keep alive our *Hasidus* and keep alive our Jews, both.'

"The Rebbe is disgustingly reticent about Zionism, almost antiZionist, I'd have to say. But Emanuel convinces him that Zionism has robust fundraising legs in America and that Borisov should run with it and capitalize on it. It sounds deceptive, but they did create Kfar Rachel eventually."

Dina interrupted her husband. "Hold on. Are you aware that the words 'State of Israel' never escaped Emanuel's lips, nor his father-in-law's? Borisov concedes only that you and I live in Eretz Yisrael, the Land of Israel, not the State. I'd also like to know how much money the Jewish Agency supplied to establish Kfar Rachel. I can't believe the Borisovers did it alone.

"Fact is, the money the Rebbe raised in America for saving lives actually went to build schools and shuls after World War II. Emanuel was correct when he wrote . . . what page is it on? Here: 'I told the Rebbe he would be withdrawing some of the valuable goodwill that American Jews invest in Zionism. Why not put this goodwill to work for the best purposes of Borisov?'

"Furthermore, you must realize that Emanuel also chose to send some of the Kfar Rachel money to your family, Nachum. See, I've done some homework, too."

Nachum frowned. "Given my family history, who am I to sit in judgment on these matters, right? That's it, then. The record ends even before Emanuel became the Rebbe. I'm not sure how that event happened."

Dina had checked the net. "The Rebbe died on Long Island in a horrible winter traffic accident while returning from a cemetery service for a major supporter. The Rebbe's last testament nominated Emanuel as his successor; the Borisover Council quickly endorsed it. Emanuel's road to the Rebbe-ship had been well-paved ahead of time."

"It's strange, Dina. I feel personally joined to the records in the journal, yet totally disconnected from them. The notes are part of my history, but in so many ways not a part of my life. They help me understand how I might be inclined to love Torah study, but much of the ethic and action is alien to me. If Thursday evening's meeting with the

Director deals with Borisov, I'm going to rely on your help and insight to overcome my confusion."

Dina stood, leaned across the table, and kissed her husband with a caress. "Count on me," she said.

CHAPTER FIFTEEN

11 Tevet 5772 – Thursday evening, 5 January 2012
Ramat Gan, Israel

O nce again the Director of Shin Bet sat in the Steinitz home. He took a sip of coffee and asked what they thought of Emanuel's journal. The Steinitz couple shared bits and pieces of their conversation, dancing around the core question, their opinion of the drama's players.

The Director discerned their reticence and asked, "Let's get down to brass tacks. After looking through Emanuel's narrative, what do you think of the Borisovers?"

Nachum answered, "We know today's Borisovers from their many, let's say, installations here and around the world. Reading the journal put us on the ground floor of Borisov's creativity, and we respect what they achieved, though we might not agree with all their philosophy."

The Director paused momentarily, looked at the Steinitz couple, and said, "In short order I'll describe for you our plan. We began to brew this plan well before Rabin's murder, when we became suspicious about the source of the wire transfers. The presence of a legal document signed by Emanuel Davidson affirming the search for a genetically related successor all but confirmed that your family was the eligible link they sought, or shall we say 'awaited,' since the successor had to qualify religiously. That's when we started to look at your family cohort as possibly useful to the State of Israel in a risky counterthrust against the Haredim, with other political possibilities added to it.

"The inordinate rise in population and influence of Haredi and Hasidic Jews acutely troubles Israeli security services, all of them, because the situation could put the State of Israel in jeopardy. The Haredi generally don't serve in *Tsahal*. Secular Jews do not have a high birthrate. Therefore, as the Haredi grow larger, the available number of draftees is growing smaller. They are part of the Jewish people protected by *Tsahal* and our police, yet many follow leaders who refuse recognition of the Jewish State. They are usually supported by the State as yeshiva students, and the bill for this is rising exponentially. Today Israel has about 80,000 state-supported *kollel* Talmud students over the age of 20. Multiply that by 3 to get the number in a generation or so. Does Israel really need 250,000 Talmud lawyers? They are badly educated for a modern workforce, sometimes not educated in secular pursuits at all.

"The Haredi have separate school systems which do not develop good Israeli citizenship. Example? Shas, the Sephardic ultra-Orthodox party, gets 500 million government shekels a year for their separate school system which teaches loyalty to a theocratic leader. The Haredim have exceptionally large families, averaging close to seven children. In the main, they cannot properly support them. The load on welfare payments and social services increases month by month. Because of family size, they've gone from 1 or 2% of the Jewish population in 1948 to 12%, 750,000, in 2011.

"They tend to vote *en bloc* according to their rabbi's command, a practical method of obtaining more from the government, but this habit entirely and anti-democratically discounts the will of thinking individuals. They overturn secular Israeli law in their neighborhoods, requiring people who enter to dress in certain ways, women to walk on separate sidewalks and sit in the back of buses, and so on. I can give you other reasons, but maybe the greatest reason for concern is the simple fact that the Haredim are creating a deep split in our society. Inevitably we refer to them as 'they,' as if 'they' were not a part of 'us,' and in turn, we whom the Haredim call nonobservant," the Director ironically tapped his knit kipa, symbol of his *Dati Leumi* "National Religious" Modern Orthodox ways, "even we have become 'other' to them.

"You're both secular or only somewhat traditional Jews. Surely you must see these facts as a cause for concern. Please, if I'm wrong, and you favor the growth of the Black Hats, tell me, and we can cut the conversation right now."

"Do you want more reasons to fear their rise?" Nachum asked. "Can this little land readily sustain many more people? We're clever about desalinating water to survive, but still, I wonder how much pressure the land can bear. Plus, I work hard and pay heavy taxes, while scarcely 50% of Haredim work at all. Fair it's not."

Dina said dismissively, "But they're far from a majority right now."

"You're right," the Director said, "still, demography predicts the conclusion of the tale: a Haredi majority around 2060. Do you want to leave it for your daughter to deal with, or do you want to do something about it today?"

Nachum scoffed. "There's nothing we can do about it."

"Oh yes there is. That's why I'm here, and that's where our plan comes in. But first, for our plan to function, we need to qualify you, Nachum, for acceptance by the Borisovers as a part of their life. To accomplish that, we need to qualify Dina as a co-operative wife in their movement." He turned directly toward Dina. "So, Dina, this involves you, as well. Before you both push the panic button, let me underscore some aspects of the late Borisover Rebbe Emanuel Davidson and his wife Rachel that you may now comprehend, that Borisover leadership also understands, but of which the public is hardly aware. I may repeat items of which you're cognizant, but to some extent I want to reframe your mental portrait of these two Borisover leaders.

"By all accounts, I wouldn't describe either Emanuel or Rachel as Haredi or truly Hasidic at the outset. Think about it: Rachel refused a number of matches and waited until romantic love struck her in the person of Emanuel Davidson. She well surpassed the usual Hasidic age of marriage. Using some subterfuges, she enjoyed going out on the town as a single woman in Warsaw. Friends reported that her clothing often exemplified secular fashion, not the usual Hasidic style. When she endorsed Emanuel's desire to leave the Borisover yeshiva and study in Berlin, her father threw her out of the house, and she became all the more secular and independent for a time.

"Emanuel came to Poland from the former Soviet Union. He knew how to be a Hasid, but he did not cut the figure of one unless he entered their quarters. Then he bedecked himself in full costume, and that's how he might have considered it, as costume, masquerade. He intended to become an engineer, kept his beard cut short, apparently doing so to advance his future. In Berlin, his Jewish involvement centered mainly on teaching bar mitzvah lessons to Reform Jewish kids."

Nachum and Dina looked surprised.

"Yes, the b'nai mitzvah were mostly at Rabbi Leo Baeck's congregation. Emanuel dressed in the secular style, and only his severely limited budget kept him from living as a bon vivant who spent his evenings at nightclubs. He did not commit to a fully Hasidic lifestyle until he returned from Berlin, having failed his entrance exams, failed in his desire to become an engineer. Only then did he give himself over completely to the Borisover dynasty. He married Rachel, and the results are well-known.

"You see, the Borisover Hasidim are accustomed to elevating for themselves a rebbe from what they might term a sketchy background. For them the question that remains to be answered is whether the candidate-Rebbe is a knowledgeable leader, and whether he and his wife have left their secular past behind them and given themselves entirely to their Hasidic project."

"What does that mean for us?" Nachum wanted to know.

"To start, you two need to make Emanuel and Rachel your model. If they can provide any example for you, you might find it by comparing the Borisover literature about them with histories of the Davidsons written by university scholars and secular biographers.

"To carry off our design, you both need to return to tradition by becoming *Chozrim biTeshuva* whose behavior is obviously kosher to the Borisovers. Nachum, you've got to grow a beard, maybe for openers something short like Emanuel's original Viennese style. You've got to go to the local Beit Borisov to daven on a regular basis, meet the folk, get to know them, see if you're simpatico, and if so, attend some larger meetings to make yourself known. You should join their Talmud study and quit the Beit Daniel Reform shul altogether. You don't have to change costume for Borisov, but you do have to add a black kipa worn at all times, and maybe later, their typical *shtreiml*, and you've got to start wearing a *tallit katan* under your shirt. In particular, let the fringes show. Those tzitzit make a statement. Have you got a portable siddur? What if someone wants a minyan at the office? You have to be available. Quietly *bench* your blessing after meals with the siddur. Above all, you need to guard your observance of kashrut and of Shabbat so that you conform to Borisover standards of behavior. It's not all that hard to do in Israel. I myself could qualify, if I wore their traditional outfit to synagogue on Shabbat and holidays."

The Director turned to face Dina fully. "For you, Dina, how does kashrut fit?"

"We already keep it, not out of religious conviction but because we both have friends who couldn't visit us without its presence in our home, and in Israel, it's easy to do. We'll have to buy a few more things: more timers, maybe a bigger hot water urn, and the like."

"OK. Now three – no, four more items for you, Dina, just to begin. You would have to make your presence felt at the mikveh after your time of month, and for now, you must at least cover your hair with a kerchief or some shmatteh in public, eventually perhaps a sheitel, because the Borisover women expect the Rebbe's wife to wear a wig. Check your wardrobe and the modesty qualifications for *tsni'ut* to make sure the clothes conform. Modest dress comes with the territory. If you buy in, I'll see you get an extra budget to shop for proper clothing. And the two of you must get a Jewish bed: you know, one that's composed of two single beds you can split apart. It's in the domain of your privacy, so whether you use it according to halacha is up to you."

"Is this what we need to do to earn the 500,000 shekels annually?" Nachum demanded.

The Director looked around the house and, satisfied to spot mezuzahs at every door, nodded yes. "It's a start. Additional actions may be necessitated, but for now, that should do it. After all, you're newbies at the return to halachic tradition, so leave space to grow."

Nachum took his wife's hand. "Well, Dina, what do you think? A lot of it is on your shoulders to decide. We're both feminists in our own way. Plenty of halachic demands fall on you and run counter to our outlook."

Dina responded, "Look, I'm willing to give all this a try if we have the possibility of saving our daughter from a Haredi majority in her lifetime while moving our standard of living up more than a few notches. It's not that hard to do these things, but I'd be play-acting."

"So was Rachel, the Rebbe's wife," the Director interjected, "at least for a time, but her social activist philosophy led Emanuel and the Borisovers to be the foremost advocates for Jewish humanitarian aid in Poland during the Depression and an inspiration to Borisov in Brooklyn. You never can tell what might happen."

"Anyway, Nachum," Dina continued, "if I can't stand it, you can be sure I'll exercise my veto. What about you? Are you in?"

Nachum said, "I'm in so far. But there's more to hear. You have some kind of plan that involves the two of us. What is it?"

"Remember that you're sworn to secrecy. The plan that I'm about to set before you is tentative, but we ask that you not be too skeptical. We ask instead that you consider the broad and worthwhile implications of it to our country. We ask that you imagine yourselves at the heart of it, because without envisioning yourselves in that central position, we might as well end our brief acquaintance, and the retainer will not go into effect. But if you can buy into the plan, you both could become instruments of immense and positive change for Israel's future, should the strategy be implemented. Just listen. Judge the project later in the privacy of your own discussions. I'll check back with you at a future time to learn whether you're still on board."

In a matter of minutes, the Director of Shin Bet outlined the plan and took pains to explain that if it ever went into effect, it would probably occur after a number of years, and during that intermediate time a great deal depended on the Steinitz family's ability to integrate into Borisover Hasidic life. If that did not take place, the project would fail, and if the project were canceled for whatever reason, their stipend would cease after one year.

"I hope you noted that fact in the contract," the Director said.

"I did," Nachum said, "but that's fair enough."

The Director continued, "Again, don't say yes or no to our plan yet. Talk it over between the two of you, and I'll contact you in about a month. If you make a decision before that time, you can let me know – from a pay phone, Nachum, not from here – to this number." He handed Nachum a card. "Just say the word 'yes' or 'no.' Our mutual work will either cease or begin at that point."

27 Tevet 5772 – Saturday night, 21 January, 2012

With three stars in the sky to end Shabbat, the Director of Shin Bet checked his message line using a cell phone app with an unscrambler. The sole message on the line arrived at 2:15 PM from a pay phone at the Ramat Gan Rimonim Hotel. It contained only one word, "Yes." The Director thought to himself, they're in, and they're making a statement about their secularism at the same time, calling on Shabbat, using a pay phone. He requisitioned a monthly payment of 41,667 NIS to a specially numbered account in the name of the Steinitz couple at Bank Leumi. Later he'd have them informed of how to withdraw cash from it and make transfers. Then he requisitioned VISA debit cards for 50,000 NIS with the names of the couple on them for use in the purchase of clothing and other requirements to fulfill the standards the

Director indicated at their meeting. The cards could be hand-delivered by an agent and explained verbally.

Using facial identification technology, the Director opened a secure computer unconnected to the internet. He brought up a certain file by clicking on it and swiping his thumb across a fingerprint reader at his desk. He read the opening page of the action plan for the project involving the Borisovers and ticked off those aspects successfully accomplished. He saved the work, automatically placing it on two equivalent drives, one in the machine, and the other hidden elsewhere in the room, connected by scrambled, low-range Bluetooth. As the computer shut down, he pushed his kipa securely onto his bald scalp before he arose, and as he did so, a verse from Isaiah came to him, "Declaring the end from the beginning, and from old times the things that are not yet done" (Is. 46:10). Then, speaking to himself, "We shall see. We shall see."

And all the acts of Nachum and Dina as they transitioned from secular to observant Jews, can they not be found inscribed in the lists of their purchases made by credit card during the months that followed, and could they not be seen in the mode of dress which Dina adopted or in the tzitzit that dangled over Nachum's belt? And could not the change also be noted in the pregnancy which began almost immediately after their decision to return to tradition as *Chozrim biTeshuva*? Was it not witnessed by Rav Shoshana Shekedia of Beit Daniel Reform Congregation when she visited their home in Ramat Gan to discover why her faithful members no longer attended? The rabbi observed the couple's changed appearance, viewed bookshelves filled with brand new gilt-edged classical rabbinic texts like Talmud, Shulchan Aruch, and Zohar, and noted two refrigerators and two ovens in the cramped kitchen, and she immediately perceived the cause of their absence.

CHAPTER SIXTEEN

Although Dina harbored a secret ache for simpler and more secular days, she made friends at Beit Borisov while sitting in the women's section and while studying texts on weekdays with a class for mothers that also provided day care.

Nachum quickly became bored with the constant repetition of the prayers. Some people used them like a mantra, but he was no meditator. He often spent the services doing mental reviews of his Torah study, which continued to grab his imagination. He concentrated on Talmud at the Borisover's evening *kollel*, plunging deeply into the analysis of ancient texts led by the *kollel* teacher, a true *lamdan*, learned in the texts, who taught the most difficult arguments with ease. In turn, his teacher found in Nachum a mind exceptionally attuned to the agile parsing of abstruse sections whose logic almost always evaded the others.

One early summer's day in the midst of Dina's pregnancy, the Talmud teacher pulled Nachum aside. "Listen to me, Nachum. You came well-prepared from previous study, and now I have nothing more to give you. It is not that I can't teach you more Talmud, but simply the fact that you can read the commentaries as well as I, and you certainly can take apart the argument straight from *Shas* (Talmud) as swiftly and as surely as I can. You need someone to challenge you. I want you to move your studies over to our yeshiva in Kfar Rachel with the Gaon. He teaches an evening *kollel* there, and they will provide dinner for you, as well, so you can come straight from work. Talk to your wife about it."

But there was nothing to discuss. Both Dina and Nachum understood that he had no choice. The evening *kollel* met three times a week, Sunday, Tuesday, and Thursday. The location of Kfar Rachel, situated at a slight detour off the road from Tel Aviv to Lod, did not present an obstacle, however the frequent extension of the class towards the midnight hour often made it difficult to arise for work the next day at Israel Aerospace Industries. Nachum began to keep a change of clothing and toiletries in the car so that he could sometimes sleep at Kfar Rachel.

Nachum's and Dina's son David entered the world on 3 Tevet 5773, 16 December 2012, the last day of Chanukah. Given the largesse available to them from Shin Bet, they both decided it would be wise to hire help for Dina so that Nachum could continue to learn at Kfar Rachel. Still, he proved himself a conscientious husband, father, and helpmate during his hours at home, particularly attentive to young Hanna Liora, who sometimes felt bereft of *Ima* because of her baby brother David's early crankiness and his demands on mama's time.

By 5775, that is, 2015, Nachum Aviam integrated himself into Borisover life. He davened regularly at Beit Borisov near his home. He befriended a number of Borisovers, and they in turn expressed admiration for his warmth of personality, as well as his comprehension of Torah law and use of midrash in his comments. He began to teach Talmud and responsa literature to a receptive and admiring group at his local shul on the odd days he didn't attend *kollel* in Kfar Rachel, where he progressed rapidly under the Gaon's guidance.

One evening at *kollel*, while studying in Talmud tractate *Yevamot*, the group came across the phrase, "Where we have both Beit Shammai and Beit Hillel cited, Beit Shammai's is not the Mishnah's ruling."[31]

Nachum said, "Gaon, can we consider the consequences of this decision?"

The Gaon responded, "The School of Hillel was more lenient than the School of Shammai. Beit Hillel compassionately weighed societal needs into their decisions. The Shammai group usually decided cases according to strict legal lines, and their outcomes could make life unbearable."

Nachum said, "Beit Hillel puts people first and pays attention to their social context. Responses like that exist within certain historical frameworks. When society changes, the old, socially driven outcome might not apply anymore. Let me give you an example.

"We might think that putting people first results in greater leniency, Beit Hillel's reputation. But consider the case of a wife whose husband died far away. The wife testified that she witnessed her husband dead. Shammai says she can receive the value of her ketubah marriage contract and remarry. Hillel the lenient one says she can remarry, but she cannot receive the value of her ketubah contract. For that, she needs two witnesses of the husband's death in court.[32] Since others like the brothers of the deceased stand to gain monetarily from the death, Hillel uses the payment of her ketubah as a way to ensure the woman's honesty and the equitable distribution of the estate. Meanwhile, the woman is penniless. But Shammai cites the ketubah's promise that if the woman remarries, she receives her ketubah payment, almost like insurance, almost like a second dowry. Beit Hillel then concedes the case to Beit Shammai based on the wording of the contract.

"Gaon, in this case strict interpretation gives the widow's welfare first priority. Beit Hillel seems bereft of social conscience for the widow because their decision would impoverish her. Beit Hillel does not see her need for rights and autonomy. Only strict interpretation gives the woman a second chance at life.[33]

"In our own time, a destitute woman came to the Chief Rabbi of Haifa, She'ar Yashuv Cohen, with a palimony case. Even though she contributed as an equal partner while living with a man outside of wedlock, her paramour remorselessly snatched her contribution and evicted her from their house with nothing but the clothes on her back. She asked Rabbi Cohen for a legal remedy to recoup her losses.

"Rabbi Cohen asked her to bring witnesses to testify that the two lived together like husband and wife. She brought witnesses, and the rabbi's court declared her married with a ketubah by virtue of *yedu'ei tsibur*, public knowledge that they lived like a married couple. He then told her to divorce him Jewishly with a *get* and obtain the value her ketubah promised.

"Thousands upon thousands of couples in Eretz Yisrael live together as husband and wife without benefit of clergy, yet we only apply *yedu'ei tsibur* when absolutely necessary for the social good. Nevertheless, in the strict interpretation of halacha, the rabbinate could force marriage upon all such couples to ensure certain rights of women. Because of changes in our civil law, Israel now has palimony, but nonetheless, the strict interpretation of halacha, the Shammai version, could help meet the legal challenge of couples who live together and then separate, a major alteration in our social norms.

"My point? At times, strict adherence to the law according to Shammai's interpretation can actually handle societal changes better than Hillel's, who may still be adjusting Jewish law to life in the second century C.E. In the meantime, Israel's democratic positive law solves problems that halacha can't because Beit Hillel always trumps Beit Shammai when cited together and because Jewish courts are held back by the dictum that 'a court cannot annul the opinion of a previous court unless it exceeds it both in wisdom and in number.'[34] How do you react to this?"

The Gaon tensed his jaw a few times before replying. It gnawed at him that Nachum's question revealed both his strengths and weaknesses simultaneously.

Strengths? He absorbed Jewish law with ease. Nachum brought commentaries, responsa, and new decisions to illuminate his discussions and debates. He had moved quickly to the head of the class. The Gaon found Nachum more than a student: he was approaching collegial status, all in a short period of time. Dare he even say it? An *ilui*, a Talmud prodigy.

Weaknesses? Nachum came from a liberal milieu, and at times he could not shed its effect on his world view. Nachum viewed the azure sea of Talmud from a high and removed vantage point when he should have been swimming in its waves and confronting every drop. Sometimes the Gaon thought Nachum picked up legal details like sweet delights to be savored, or like fine gemstones, treasures to be collected, every facet to be carefully polished, then shelved for later display, not part of a fuller spirituality that lived the present moment connected to the whole Jewish past.

The Gaon finally answered, "Hillel turned, if you will, strictly lenient when the group saw that the Shammaites were correct from the point of view of the contract before them. In the Haifa chief rabbi's case, I also agree that a strict interpretation brought justice for the woman and maintained her autonomy. But the rabbi overturned nothing from the past in that case, and I am certain that Rabbi She'ar Yashuv Cohen would not manufacture halacha out of thin air. He applied existing law.

"We who accept the origin of the Torah at Sinai, as soon as we admit that one word of that Torah is the product of the human mind and hand, the whole Torah is in doubt. Why? Because tomorrow someone will make the same claim about a different word, and soon enough the divine origin of all 79,847 words of the Torah will be suspect. This already occurs in the realm of the so-called scientific biblical 'higher criticism.'

"Likewise, with halacha, if you find that a single halachic moral conclusion in a particular case is immoral based on standards taken from outside halacha, you've just judged the halacha as deficient, and that finding becomes the leading edge for rejection of the morality of the whole enterprise because essentially you've declared that your standard from outside halacha is God's will. If that be God's will, then the theological center of halacha collapses and you've got *hefkerut* – a legal free-for-all, or some kind of positive law.35

"Positive law considers today's sum of knowledge as greater than yesterday's. In Jewish tradition, Sinai is the summit, and the farther we stand from Sinai, the less right we have to make changes. We must work by extending pre-existing halacha into the present, with its majority decisions and minority reports. We cannot manufacture halacha out of whole cloth, whether our own or someone else's, and so the Mishnah quotation about wisdom and number, the basis of why we honor decisions of earlier ages, still stands."

Nachum nodded his head slowly as if in agreement, but then he asked, "And what of Rabbenu Gershom Me'or HaGolah and his *takkanot* legal remedies for us Ashkenazic Jews from 1000 years ago? He and his synod endorsed huge changes, everything from personal matters like requiring the wife's permission for divorce or banning polygamy, a seeming response to the Christian reality around him, to a business matter like not reading other people's mail."

The Gaon said, "You're aware that these still apply today, but for what reason? Some say as law, and others say they apply as customs, with custom gaining force of law in Jewish history. These are worthy of discussion at another time, since we are closing in on midnight. *Laila tov*. A good night to all."

The Gaon closed his Talmud, slapping the covers together, revealing for all to see that he read the book upside down. His grandfather lacked the money to buy a Talmud of his own and always shared the various books at a table with three others. He read the book of the yeshiva student across from him, thus upside down. From grandfather to father to the Gaon himself, the tradition of the upside-down Talmud lived on. Maybe the upside-down Talmud would someday give the Gaon a unique point of view and add to his insight, but it did not seem so to Nachum that evening. In fact, the Gaon's book served as a symbol of Nachum's world, not the Gaon's. The Gaon's contentious discourse against an academic, humanistic approach to Jewish texts still stung his ears. He resolved to learn more and confront less. He knew how the system worked. Firmly convinced that confrontation had dismally failed to produce results for centuries, he privately rededicated himself to work within the system with the hope that he might initiate liberating, positive results.

CHAPTER SEVENTEEN

How good is the one who says, "I want to study so that the Talmud might bring me to action, to upright qualities of character, to knowledge of the Torah, and I do this for the sake of feeling unity with the Shechina (divine presence.)" This is termed "Torah Lishmah, Torah for its own sake."[36]

Rava demonstrated an incongruity in two verses. One psalm states, Great is your loving-kindness, reaching to the heavens (Ps. 57:11), while another says, Great is your loving-kindness, higher than the heavens (Ps. 108:5). Why the difference? Psalm 108 refers to those who do commandments for their own sake, lishmah. They reach high into heaven, toward divine realms. Psalm 57 refers to those who do commandments with an ulterior motive. Their deeds reach at least to heaven's lower realms. This agrees with Rav Judah, who said in Rav's name: Always occupy yourself with Torah and commandments, even if not for their own sake. Though you start with an ulterior motive, you'll eventually follow the Torah lishmah.[37]

Seven years later
8 Kislev 5780, Night of Thursday, 5 December 2019

During the mid-class break, the Gaon asked Nachum if he could spare him a moment. Nachum approached his Talmud master with trepidation.

"Nachum, I should have asked you earlier, but the Tel Aviv Museum of Art is exhibiting impressionist landscapes alongside landscapes of Reuven Rubin, and there's a recap of Shalom of Safed's work, as well. It closes this month. I'll want to spend several hours at the museum with these shows and take care of some shopping needs, too. The sun sets so early in winter that I worry whether I can get back to Kfar Rachel in time for Shabbat. Would you mind if I stayed with you and your family over Shabbat?"

"Gaon, it would be our honor, our pleasure. I'll call Dina right now to let her know. She'll be delighted to welcome you, I'm sure."

Nachum opened his cell phone, spoke to his wife in front of the Gaon, smiled and nodded yes to his teacher, told Dina he'd be home late again, and ended the call. Shabbat with the Gaon was set.

The arrival of Shabbat with the Gaon caused them to double check their every step toward the day. In the dining room, candlesticks and dinnerware, polished to an extraordinarily high gloss, sparkled under halogen lighting. The home smelled of baked challah dough. Everything for the meal and for Saturday's dining, too, awaited the coming of the Shabbat bride, save some dishes still cooking, nearly ready to place on their warmers before Shabbat began. The light bulbs in the refrigerators were disabled, timers set for the family's convenience, hot water readied in the large all-day urn. The installation of toilet paper dispensers containing individual sheets folded one into the other obviated the need to tear tissue.

The children were finely scrubbed and bedecked to look like model seven- and ten-year-olds. Nachum visited the dry cleaner before returning home on Friday afternoon. His Borisover "uniform" appeared crisp, clean, almost new. For Shabbat, Dina dressed elegantly, yet in clothing that both honored the Sabbath and posed her as the well-dressed homemaker. She chose a sheitel with extensive curls.

When Dina made the transition to a sheitel, she investigated sources everywhere, and finally she settled on the wig store of another *Chozeret biTeshuva*, a woman in suburban Toronto. Nachum backed her choice and suggested the family celebrate it with a vacation in Canada, where she could try out wigs around people who did not know her. The women in the gallery of Beit Borisov of Toronto complimented her on her sheitel and helped Dina feel at home in their world. She returned to Israel with greater confidence in her new life than ever before. Her smile and posture on this particular *Erev Shabbat* emanated self-assurance.

The Gaon arrived at Nachum and Dina's home in Ramat Gan at 3 PM, cutting close to the edge of Shabbat, since sunset came at 4:36 PM. They showed him to his bedroom, usually Nachum's study. He laid his luggage on the floor, obtained permission to use a shower, and attended to his pre-Shabbat ablutions. The Gaon dressed with care. Then, finding two small Shabbat candlesticks with candles and a matchbook stationed on an open ledge in the room, he took the mitzvah upon himself to light the candles and say the blessing, inwardly pleased that Nachum knew of this obligation of guests.

When the Gaon emerged from his room, he, too, appeared in full Borisover dress from shoes to *shtreiml*. It was time to walk to shul. Even before Shabbat arrived, the two men found themselves strolling at a slow Sabbath pace because Hanna Liora and David, the children, went along with them. Hanna Liora skipped and ran ahead independently to every corner, while second-grader David clutched his father's hand, walking directly, but with smaller steps.

After welcoming Shabbat at Beit Borisov, all four languidly returned to the Steinitz residence. They came to the table where they immediately sang "Shalom Aleichem." With sincere and admiring eyes directed at Dina, Nachum recited Proverbs 31, the Woman of Valor, to honor his wife. He summoned the two children to the head of the table and blessed each one, asking that God make Hanna Liora like Sarah, Rebecca, Rachel, and Leah, and make David like Ephraim and Menashe, and he bestowed on each the well-known priestly benediction. Four Shabbat candles, lit by Dina when the two men were at synagogue, put their glow upon the children's faces from the other end of the table. Two candles represented the minimum number for Shabbat, and two more for the light of the children in their lives.

All stood while Nachum poured the sweet wine of the Sabbath into a small *becher*, a silver cup the shape of a thimble. He allowed the wine to overflow onto the vessel's waiting saucer, hoping the Gaon would not mind the petite cup. Two opinions about the volume in a *revi'it*, the amount of wine prescribed by tradition, competed for favor. Because alcohol tended to give him a headache, Nachum chose the 86-cc *revi'it* rather than the 150-cc version. Shabbat with a headache was no Shabbat at all. Nachum proceeded to sanctify the day with the Kiddush prayer.

After "Shabbat shalom" all around the table, a traditional hand-washing took place. Silence reigned as Nachum removed two challahs from their upper and lower coverings. He held one on top of the other, the bottom challah a bit closer to him, recited the *motsi* blessing over the bread, lifting the bread somewhat higher at the mention of God. He placed the two loaves down, and from the lower loaf tore a piece for himself, which he consumed after dipping it in salt, a practice taken from the sacrificial cult of the ancient Temple, a reminder that every home's dining table is a small temple in itself, a *mikdash me'at*. Then he broke off pieces for all to enjoy.

Dina served an ambrosial meal including soup, fish, meat, vegetables, and dessert. They filled the air with discussion of the weekly Torah portion, *Vayetsei*, including consideration of Dina's namesake, born to Leah in that section of the Torah.

The conversation rotated around the meaning of the name Dina, judgment. Who was being judged in the tale, Shechem? Jacob? Simeon and Levi? All of them? And what was being judged – marriage outside the tribe, or . . .? Suddenly silence arose like a roadblock, as if all agreed that discussion of *Vayetsei*'s pre-marital relations, rape and rapists, violent tribalism, and more did not befit a Shabbat table conversation, nor were they topics for children's ears.

Quickly Nachum broke the silence by opening an escape valve. "And what about Jacob's famous ladder and his dream of angels going up and down on it, a text that cries out for interpretation?"

He outlined a comment by the first Borisover Rebbe. In Jacob's dream, the angels of God were going up and down on the ladder – first up, then down. Clearly, they began to scale the ladder from the ground up. So how could they be angels? Alright, let's just call them messengers of God, *mal'achei*, same Hebrew word for both.

In order to understand why the messengers started on earth, the first Borisover asked how God is revealed through dreams and visions. He explained that the receptor of God's message is the soul. God calls the soul or parts thereof upward during the dream as a messenger to be filled with divine communication and returned to earth to inhabit the dream and the heart of the individual. Perhaps the soul makes many such trips within the dream, like messengers going up and down the ladder.

When Jacob learned what God promised him, he awoke and conformed his will to the new vision within his soul. He made an oath pledging to believe in God, his first move toward becoming Yisrael, the God-wrestler, not Ya'akov, the cheater.

Nachum explained, "The first Rebbe taught that we, too, need to consult and scrutinize our own dreams, whether received when asleep or awake. He called it 'bending higher', for these visions that illuminate the soul cause our will to bend and conform to God's will, which in turn causes our will to reach toward higher inspiration. Every Borisover must learn to bend higher. The first Rebbe said that the best way to arouse such dreaming is through prayer, because prayers constitute the dreams of the whole Jewish people."

Nachum credited his explication of the first Rebbe's commentary to an obscure notebook written in Yiddish in 1817 by a Borisover who jotted down his master's many Torah interpretations.

"Hebrew University of Jerusalem somehow obtained it and saved it on microfiche. I decided it was time I learned enough Yiddish to translate it," Nachum said.

The Gaon, who listened with rapt attention, nearly broke into applause because the particular commentary and its source completely surprised him. They continued their conversation about the dream through dessert. Then, lacking a total of three adult men, they offered the blessings after the meal individually.

Dina gathered up the children to put them in bed. When she returned, the two men were singing Shabbat songs along with some Borisover *niggunim*. Knowing that the Gaon's Orthodoxy would not welcome her woman's voice, she said Shabbat shalom and retired to the bedroom.

After all the singing and table rapping concluded, the Gaon said, "Nachum, I must talk to you about something serious, but altogether happy. For seven years you have studied with me at the *kollel* in Kfar Rachel. All the time you studied, you maintained your steady work schedule at Israel Aerospace Industries. I hope they are as happy with your leadership in the office as I am with your influence among our students. You are far and away at the head of the class, at the same time prompting others to probe deeper and read more widely. Tonight provided a good example. How you found that commentary, how you found the time to learn Yiddish in order to dig it out, both are a miracle."

Nachum responded, "Sometimes a student must be like an archeologist, sifting the internet for rare finds. That's how I discovered the microfiche. Then I went up to Jerusalem and couldn't read it. After a couple months' study and armed with a good dictionary, I could manage the text.

"My attention to Borisov has not affected my work situation. My promotions at the office indicate their contentment with performance. As to my influence in the class, our *chevruta* group likes to co-operate for growth. It's nothing like corporate competition. We're out to discover Torah together."

The Gaon said, "You're allowed to be modest. And you're allowed to acknowledge your assets. Let me admit that I utilized a visit to the art museum as a simple subterfuge to permit me these moments in your home with you and your family. Indeed, you have a lovely family.

Would that God bless you with more children like Hanna Liora and David."

Nachum thought to himself, more children? Dina eliminated that possibility when she obtained a prescription for birth control pills from her gynecologist and coaxed the doctor with shekels to write a note that having more children would not be healthy for her – just in case anyone from among the Borisovers might inquire. Nachum agreed fully with the plan. From the point of view of ecology, economy, and yes, Dina's health, neither husband nor wife found acceptable the thought of living life as a Hasid or Haredi with seven or eight children. Besides, didn't the Torah teach that Jews have only the obligation to replace themselves with one male and one female child?[38] He and Dina had fulfilled their halachic duty.

The Gaon continued, "I spoke to the other rabbis who teach at the *kollel*. All say that you are prepared and ready for the best possible *smicha*. All agree that you should receive a Borisover ordination which enables you to both teach and judge, to decide matters of ritual law and monetary cases: *Yoreh? Yoreh! Yadin? Yadin!*"[39]

A tear came to Nachum's eye. He wiped it away as he tried to discern its source: a tear shed for the joyful honor of continuing Jewish tradition through his love of Torah and dedication to the Borisovers? Weeping for the shame of playing a dual role as Hasid and agent of Shin Bet, possibly committed to opposing masters? He said, "You trust me so completely that you would bestow this upon me without my asking? *Baruch HaShem,* I bless God for granting me this kindness."

"You are not being given a kindness, Nachum, but rather recognition of high achievement, deep understanding, and unfailing reliability. Early on, I had my doubts. Not about your ability, not about your comprehension, no, but about whether you could ever see the world through Torah eyes, whether you could live in the world of tradition and specifically Borisover Hasidic tradition without dragging your Western liberal baggage along with you.

"Some years ago, you challenged me in class, and I gave you a philosophical swat across the cheek. I admit it. I meant to force you to decide which path you wanted to walk. You absorbed that blow to your autonomous, individualistic, rationalist ego and threw yourself all the more into our midst and into your studies, swimming with intention and faith in the sea of Talmud. The simple joy you took in this *Erev Shabbat*, its prayers, its customs, its salutary effect on your family, its time spent turning the Torah portion over and over – all that and the clear evidence that you seek Torah inspiration independent of classwork tells me that you'll make a fine, no, a great and spiritually dedicated rabbi, one who can become a leader here and abroad. After your ordination, I plan to speak to Rabbi Avraham Stadlan in Brooklyn about your future. He may have something in mind for you, possibly in the States."

"With all due respect, Gaon, we cannot move from Eretz Yisrael. First of all, the Mishnah forbids moving from a better place to a lesser place, and Eretz Yisrael is considered a better place. We'll move within Eretz Yisrael, yes, and if we reach Yerushalayim, that is the best place, and from there we'd never move. We take that Torah seriously."[40]

"Well then, Nachum, let me look into something worthwhile for you either at the *kollel* or our yeshiva. By the way, how's your English?"

"My English is fine. It was better when I studied in Boston and used it daily at Harvard, but it's a key part of my communication at IAI."

"And what of your speaking skills? Could you hold a class's attention in a lecture?"

"There I could improve," Nachum admitted.

"We can talk about these things after Shabbat. It's customary for me to report to Brooklyn about all those we're ordaining in Eretz Yisrael, and that report contains ability ratings. Yours will be of the highest caliber because you are the finest student of halacha it has been my privilege to teach, Nachum Aviam."

In the morning, while the Gaon and Nachum davened at shul, Dina set the table for Kiddush and their second Shabbat meal. Upon their return, Dina laid nourishing salads and appetizers on the table and served cholent from the crockpot connected to a timer, which allowed it to slow-cook overnight and turn off at the usual hour of Nachum's return.

After lunch, both men delved into Torah privately for a time, napped, and then, due to the early sunset in winter, returned to Beit Borisov for a study group where the Gaon had promised to lecture at a *Seudah Shlishit*, the traditional third meal sponsored by the shul. All knew the Gaon needed to return home to Kfar Rachel, so they purposely abbreviated their *Melaveh Malka*, accompanying the Shabbat Queen out the door in less than an hour. By 7 PM Nachum and the Gaon departed. At Nachum's home, the Gaon changed his clothes, folded his tallit back into its regular weekday creases, packed his bags, thanked his hosts, gave the children a hug, loaded his car and drove away, leaving Dina and Nachum at curbside.

"Dina, we've got to talk," Nachum said urgently. They went inside and sat at the table.

"He's going to have me ordained a rabbi, Dina. Not just any rabbi: the movement's highest ordination, the level about which they're so selective. He didn't say when they'd give the *smicha*, but I imagine soon, in the next few months."

Dina offered her mazel tov, leaned over and kissed her husband. "*Kol hakavod!* Congratulations, you've earned it. How will it impact our future?"

"I can't be sure right now, but the Gaon indicated they would offer me a job. He said maybe in the States, but I refused it. We're happy here. Why relocate, considering the circumstances we're presently in? So maybe it'll be a teaching position at the yeshiva in Kfar Rachel."

Dina said, "The pay will be nothing compared to your job at IAI."

"Why don't we deal with that when the time comes? Maybe Borisov will take that into consideration. The Director will need to know about this when they make the offer. Maybe Shin Bet will increase our allowance. Let's see what happens."

"Honestly, Nachum, I don't know if I could stand living in Kfar Rachel. Tel Aviv suits my style, however devotedly frum I may have to act."

"Again, let's see what develops. In the meantime, we'll carry on as before and play a waiting game. Unfortunately, I've got some preparation to do for work tomorrow." Nachum gave Dina a light kiss on the cheek and headed for his study.

CHAPTER EIGHTEEN

5 Tevet 5780 – Thursday evening, 2 January 2020
Sonol Gas Station and Steakiah 443 Restaurant
Modi'in, Israel

Nachum received a voice mail on his cellular phone, a message with no traceable source, but though they had not spoken in years, the Director's voice resonated unmistakably in his ear. He let Dina know he wouldn't be home for dinner because of a late meeting and left the office at 5:20 PM, allowing himself extra time for the twenty-minute trip because of rush hour.

Nachum Aviam Steinitz laughed out loud as he pulled his car into the Sonol Gas Station on the alternate four lane highway from Tel Aviv to Jerusalem, the 443. The Director of Shin Bet was turning this meeting into something off the pages of 007. "See you at Sonol Modi'in on the 443 tonight at 6 PM," he said, but where was he?

Nachum waited in the car a while, saw a flashlight in his rearview mirror – someone checking his license plate – followed by a muffled tap-tap on his passenger side window. In the light of the parking lot behind Steakiah 443, the restaurant located at the Sonol Station, he could see the Director. Nachum unlocked his doors, and the director slid in beside him.

"Shalom, Rabbi Steinitz," the Director said, and extended a hand. Nachum took it and said, "Not rabbi yet. On Tu BiShevat."

"Mazel tov, Nachum. I'm here to give you some news, and I didn't want to involve an agent in the process. Mossad informs me that Rabbi Avraham Stadlan will be coming from Borisover headquarters to ordain you personally. As soon as Stadlan registered his reservation for the flight, we knew of it. If Stadlan's coming to give you your *smicha*, something is up. At the least, they plan to offer you work at their yeshiva in Brooklyn. Don't leave the country. We need you in Israel."

Nachum shook his head. "Not to worry. I already told the Gaon that we would reside only in Israel. It was to me a *klara gemorra*, as plain as day that moving away from Israel would not be good for Mossad and Shin Bet's plans, and frankly, not good for us, either. Here we are at home."

"*Me'ah achuz.* 100%. OK, let's look at other possibilities. Stadlan may offer you a position with the Borisovers in one of the schools in Kfar Rachel, or even their outreach institute in Yerushalayim. If he offers a teaching position, negotiate the salary up as high as you can. Pretend you've got the last bottle of kosher wine in town and it's five minutes to Shabbat. They need you. Then we'll make up the difference between IAI and that salary. Understand?"

"*Me'ah achuz.*"

"Now let's take it to the nth degree. Suppose he shunts you aside after ordination and says something like, 'My son, we've watched you all along. You're the great-grandson of the last Borisover Rebbe, and the time has come for you to take up his work and become our Rebbe yourself.' Nachum, we need you to say yes. Our entire plan revolves around your saying yes. If you say no, you'll have resigned from our special support network. The money you've got is yours, but there'll be no more. It's OK to say no. I keep my word, but we need you to say yes. Before you react, let me finish.

"Should you become the Rebbe, your special account at Bank Leumi will be moved offshore. We'll assume that all your personal and familial requirements will be supplied by the Borisover Hasidim. It will not be necessary for you to draw from that account, but we'll provide you the means to do so, just in case, and we'll add to it at double the current rate."

Nachum said, "Because you have offered me double today's stipend, I think it is safe to assume you're prepared to pay triple. Am I right?"

The Director hesitated, then nodded, "*Me'ah achuz.*"

Nachum responded, "If they offer, I will accept the mantle of the Borisover Rebbe, but then I will not accept any more money from Shin Bet, none. I shall be your unpaid agent, still with the right to abdicate the position. I have but one condition: in the event of my death, my wife Dina and family will receive the regular compensation you have offered, three times the current stipend, tax free. If she dies, the children should receive it until they have completed their normal army obligations and university or other education."

The Director agreed. "I'll have the paperwork completed, and an agent will visit you for a signature." They shook hands. The Director moved to go and hesitatingly turned back toward Nachum.

"Why are you doing this?" he asked, "I mean, why give up the money?"

"I want it clear that I take whatever tasks you lay upon me because I love this country. I am a Zionist of the old stripe, like my great-grandmother Hannalora. Yet if something should happen while fulfilling my mission, I want my family looked after."

"Fair enough." The Director squeezed Nachum's shoulder in approval and left.

Possessed by a cavernous appetite, Nachum walked from his car to Steakiah 443. The waiter brought the normal repast, a small plate of nearly every imaginable Middle Eastern appetizer. He delivered refills of the empty dishes in a moment, and when Nachum started waving off the seconds and thirds, the meal concluded with grilled beef on skewers – all very kosher, all delectable. Nachum then drove around the building to the Sonol station, filled the tank, and headed home.

Dina heard Nachum unlatching the door and met him with open arms.

"Big meeting?" she said, giving him a peck on the cheek. "Mmmm, you smell like a *steakiah* restaurant. Where'd you go to eat?"

"Steakiah 443."

"That dive on the highway to Jerusalem?"

"Yeah, that's the place. Nothing fancy, but lots of families, all kinds of folks, and what good food! I ate a ton." Nachum patted his stomach.

"How come there?"

"The Director called a meeting. Big news."

Dina said, "Take off your coat, sit down, and let's talk."

Once settled in, Nachum explained, "They know from Mossad that Rabbi Avraham Stadlan is coming for the ordination on Tu BiShevat. They think that's a sign of something big just around the corner. He went through the drill of what to do in the face of each possibility. He wants me to refuse to leave Israel, but I already have. They'll make up any difference in salary if I accept work as a teacher for the Borisovers. If Stadlan offers the mantle of the Rebbe, he wants me to clinch the opportunity."

"Would you do it?"

"Yes, Dina, I'd accept it. At that point, there's no use taking money from the agency. The Borisovers would provide whatever we needed. If Stadlan offers the rebbe-ship, I would decline further stipend from the agency, but I did arrange for triple pay for you and the kids were I to die in office. If, God forbid, you should pass away thereafter, the stipend would continue for the kids until they're full adults. He agreed."

"You don't want to build up a nest egg?" Dina asked.

"Nest egg? By the time the stipend would start, what with inflation, it would probably be a million shekels a year tax free for your lifetime, plus what we've already managed to save and invest. We have the nest egg, and now we've got superb life insurance. I think we're OK. Besides, I want to feel like I'm acting for the good of both Borisov and Israel, and not taking the Shin Bet money helps me to feel that way."

Dina leaned over the corner of the table and gave her husband a hug.

"Oy, you're such a Zionist! What am I going to do with you, Nachum Aviam? Look, the result of your ordination could be nothing more than a fancy *smicha* document, so we'll play the waiting game."

CHAPTER NINETEEN

Tu BiShevat, 15 Shevat 5780 – Tuesday morning, 10 February 2020

asidim overflowed the Borisover shul in Kfar Rachel. If the men in the foyer could have occupied the women's gallery, they would have. Instead they settled for seats in the social hall below, where the festival of *smicha* appeared on large television screens. It wasn't often that Rabbi Avraham Stadlan came to visit Eretz Yisrael. In fact, the late Rebbe Emanuel Davidson never set foot on the soil of Eretz Yisrael, so the infrequent visits of Stadlan from Brooklyn always felt like a gift.

After the murmuring, the *shuckling*, and the cantorial *chazanut* of the prayers; after the thumping of the benches during a few Borisover *niggunim*, the congregation was called to order. The Gaon and his beth din sat on the bimah of the synagogue, along with Rabbi Stadlan. In the first four rows sat the new *musmachim*, the about-to-become newly ordained rabbis. Students receiving *Yoreh Yoreh*, an ordination which entitled them to teach and to advise on matters of ritual law, occupied rows 2-4. The first row, with only four men, seated the rabbis receiving *Yoreh Yoreh Yadin Yadin*, the right not only to counsel on ritual matters, but also to serve as a judge on a Jewish court. The Borisover Hasidim preferred to graduate their top rabbis from the Brooklyn yeshiva, but some few could only study in Eretz Yisrael, and today they'd receive their strong ordination.

The ceremony did not begin with the singing of "Hatikvah," the Israeli national anthem. As far as the Borisovers were concerned, Kfar Rachel existed in the Land of Israel, but not in the State of Israel, which in their theology depended for its establishment upon the coming of the messiah. Instead, they sang a hymn, *Adon Olam*, well-known to virtually all Jews, but chanted in a singular Borisover melody. The *Rosh Yeshiva*, head of the school, spoke about the accomplishments of the class, especially praising Nachum for opening the door to greater understanding of the first Borisover Rebbe with his research in Jerusalem. Then he introduced Rabbi Avraham Stadlan.

Rabbi Stadlan offered essentially the same speech delivered to last year's class in Brooklyn. He spoke in English, which he handled with greater ease than Modern Hebrew, and besides, using Modern Hebrew would have created controversy among old line Yiddish-speaking Borisovers if they heard about it in New York. His words did not inspire greatly, but they complimented the new rabbis and pointed to a growing Borisover pervasiveness in Israel and abroad, which heartened all present.

He concluded by saying, "It is especially my honor to present a *smicha* and a blessing to each new rabbi present here today on Tu BiShevat, the New Year of the Trees. The Torah is a tree of life to those who hold fast to it (Proverbs 3:18), and those whom I am about to call are its finest produce. We honor them all for their accomplishment, and we trust that they will tend to the Torah, our tree of life, with great love and care, even planting new seeds that will flower into love of tradition."

Called to the bimah by name, the new rabbis ascended the stage one at a time. The first group received their proper level of ordination verbally: *Yoreh? Yoreh!*, followed by the Aaronide priestly benediction, "May God bless you and keep you," with Stadlan's hands laid upon the temples of the head. The beth din then presented the *smicha* documents with handshakes all around, and often parents and family cheering from the seats below and above. Each new rabbi returned to his original place, then all the new rabbis were bidden to stand, and the emcee invited the congregation to welcome the new *musmachim* with applause. Applause did indeed follow, overwhelmed by hands pounding benches, feet stomping the floor, and many a cheer. The first group sat down.

Rabbi Stadlan explained that the next four rabbis merited the high level of *Yoreh Yoreh Yadin Yadin* and someday they might actually be standing on this very bimah to ordain others. Called by name and given the same ceremonial welcome as the previous group, each remained at the corner of the bimah until Rabbi Stadlan arrived at the last name on his list. Before calling up that new rabbi, he invited the congregation to appreciate the achievement of the previous three. They did so with the same enthusiasm and more than the first group received. Then the three sat down.

Rabbi Stadlan *shuckled* a bit as he spoke. "When Jacob was returning to Eretz Yisrael from Haran, Esau appeared. Jacob fretted that Esau would attack and wipe out all his family. What did he do? He put the maidservants and their children at the front, facing Esau and his troops. He put Leah and her children after them, and finally he placed Rachel and Joseph at the back of the group. Rashi asks why Jacob put his family in such an order, and he answers, *Acharon acharon chaviv*, the very last is the most beloved.[41]

"Without taking a whit away from the achievement of the other rabbis here today, I must tell you in all frankness, and I think the students will agree, that Nachum Aviam Steinitz mastered Talmud, Codes, Responsa, and current halachic literature, while making a significant contribution to our understanding of Borisover Hasidism. In addition, his colleagues view him as their leader. So we have decided to call up our leading student last. With the Gaon, Nachum's teacher and rabbi, I will share the granting of his *smicha*."

A rarified silence reigned in the hall.

Nachum arose, ascended the bimah and bowed his head before the two rabbis standing in front of him. Before uttering a word, they opened the holy ark of the Torah. The entire congregation immediately stood to honor the sanctity of the Torah, even as they witnessed Nachum's ordination blessing from the Gaon. Rabbi Stadlan followed, conferring his benediction, which seemed longer than the Gaon's. Nachum received his *smicha* document and handshakes from the beth din. The ark was closed, and the crowd, acknowledging the exceptional spirit of the moment, broke into the Borisover *niggun*, beat on the benches and the floor, applauded, and danced in the aisles. Nachum smiled up to Dina, his face warm with love for her, but also reflecting his surprise.

At last the *Rosh Yeshiva* returned to the pulpit, calmed the crowd, and invited them to close the ceremony with *Yigdal*, a hymn extolling Maimonides' Thirteen Principles of Faith. Outside, Dina found her husband and blew him a kiss while he hugged and shook hands with the multitudes of male Hasidim as the two tried to reach each other walking toward the community center for the celebration. Surrounded by a gaggle of students and family members, each entered their proper side of the community hall.

When they reached a section of the room away from the buffet tables, they spoke through the grillwork of the division between men and women. Dina asked why Rabbi Stadlan's blessing seemed to take so long. Nachum leaned over and in sotto voce told his wife, "Rabbi Stadlan took a moment to tell me how privileged he felt to complete my ordination. Then he said he must see me at 2 PM in the *Rosh Yeshiva*'s office. How much longer can you stay at Kfar Rachel before the kids get home?"

"I'll take the car, and you take the bus to Tel Aviv, or call a taxi. We've got the money, you know."

Nachum grinned. "You're right. After all this time, I still can't get used to it. Let's eat something."

The office of the *Rosh Yeshiva* included a small meeting and dining table located in an alcove at its side. Nachum sat just across from Rabbi Stadlan, who occupied the head of the table. Rabbi Stadlan poured water for both. A bowl of mints stood mid-table between them.

"Nachum," Rabbi Stadlan began, taking a mint, noisily peeling off the cellophane wrapper and dropping it in the bowl, "you do not know me, but I, on the other hand, know you."

Nachum forced himself to give the rabbi a curious look. He knew the denouement, but he couldn't reveal it.

The rabbi said, "Not long before Rebbe Emanuel Davidson died, he charged my predecessor with the task of finding the next Borisover Rebbe. In turn, that *epitropos* mandated me for the same task. The qualifications are simple: a descendant of the Borisover Rebbe dedicated to Yiddishkeit, to Torah and to the Jewish people, and who could be, in particular, dedicated to the Borisover Hasidim.

"Nachum, I have carried the burden of this search for almost twenty-five years. Once I was a young man and now I'm an old man . . ., well, an older man, and I have seen the righteous *tsaddikim* of Borisov hunger for bread, not bread to nourish their stomachs, but bread to nourish their souls.[42]

"You, Rabbi Steinitz, are the man for whom I have been searching. You are dedicated to Torah, you're a Talmud *ilui* with much to teach us by your genius, and you understand that our type of Hasidism requires careful and inspiring spiritual interpretation. What's more, you are the great-grandson of Emanuel Davidson. You are fit and fully qualified to inherit the mantle of the Rebbe, and now is the time for you as an ordained rabbi to accept the challenge."

"Rabbi Stadlan, you have told me so much while I stand, so to speak, on one foot.[43] You are certain my heritage stems from Emanuel Davidson? What is your proof?"

Rabbi Stadlan reached to the floor and brought up a small brief case, unlocked it, and withdrew a file. He spread it wide before Nachum, revealing a small, stiff paper yellowed by time. "Here," he intoned, "is the HaShomer HaTsa'ir identity card of your great-grandmother, Hannalora Steinitz."

Nachum took it from Stadlan's hand as if cradling a holy object. He had seen the copy, but now he held the real thing, the card that described his great-grandmother's commitment to Zionism.

"According to the late Rebbe," Stadlan went on, "she gave that card to him as a token of their relationship in Berlin when, pregnant with your grandfather, she forced him to forswear any contact with her or her offspring in Eretz Yisrael because Emanuel refused to follow her to Palestine. Through the years the Rebbe paid a form of child support via Borisov, and that secret sustenance continued until your generation, when you finally seemed well-launched, and we simply stood back and watched your Jewish commitments bloom, very pleased that they were growing in our Borisover soil. You see, we have been tracking your family since 1930, almost a century, and you are the first member of the family with whom we feel confident to entrust the position of Rebbe."

Nachum shook his head vehemently no. "Rabbi Stadlan, even if I accept what you say about my ancestry, and even if keen to become the Borisover Rebbe, the group headquarters is in Brooklyn. I cannot and will not move to the United States, so I believe that ends the matter."

"Not so fast," Rabbi Stadlan countered. "As curator in the absence of a Rebbe, I am empowered to speak for the Borisovers. We are prepared to set up the Rebbe's headquarters here in Kfar Rachel or in Yerushalayim. You presently reside in Ramat Gan. We are not prepared to center our work in the Tel Aviv area, including B'nei B'rak, where we might be mistaken for just one more Hasidic or Haredi movement among many. So yes, you would have to move, but your choices are good ones and easily facilitated within Eretz Yisrael."

"Nevertheless, Rabbi Stadlan, you can understand that this comes as a shock to me, and certainly it is something that must be discussed with my wife. How quickly must I let you know?"

"Listen to me, Nachum. You're the man, not just for this hour, but for any hour you choose until you are too old to serve as the Borisover Rebbe. Your acceptance is not a now or never proposition.

"Right now you're in your thirty-eighth year of life. You have a huge grasp of halacha and of Borisover *Hasidus*. I beg you to seize the opportunity to lead while at the peak of your faculties. Saying yes is not up to me. It is up to you to decide, and once you do, everything will fall into place as you wish. You will become the Rebbe of a major branch of Hasidism in our time.

"Be honest with your wife. Tell Dina the drawbacks. Tell her that she'll have to go with you from time to time to New York City. Tell her that she, too, like Rachel, the wife of the late Rebbe for whom this village is named, can play a strong role in the development of our religious life if she wishes. She is a professional woman with much to give. If she wants to work, we could readily apply her marketing skills to the benefit of the Borisovers. She could be very helpful. Or she can be a wife and mother, as she chooses. I'm being straight with you.

"I urge you to make a swift and positive decision. It's a life changing decision, but not just for your family. It will bring life and renewal to the Borisovers. I need to hear from you. When?"

"Soon, Rabbi. I won't keep you dangling, but absorbing all this in an instant – it's just not possible. There's the shock of my ancestry and the shock of its implications and the shock of your offer. Give me a moment to breathe.

"Thank you, Rabbi Stadlan, first for this day of ordination. You uplifted my soul. Thank you for the trust you place in me and the important leadership in Torah that you are prepared to invest in my person. May God give me the strength and the insight to make the right decision."

Nachum and Rabbi Stadlan arose at the same time. They shook hands. Then Rabbi Stadlan grasped Nachum by the shoulders, pulled him towards himself, and whispered in his ear, "Say yes, my son. We need you."

CHAPTER TWENTY

After the death of Emanuel, the servant of the Eternal and Rebbe of the Borisovers, no Rebbe arose among those Hasidim for a generation. Then Nachum Aviam Steinitz, son of Yoram and Leah, accepted the mantle of their leadership, for he descended from Rebbe Emanuel and was versed in the laws of the Eternal.

The first installation of Nachum as the Borisover Rebbe took place in a massive celebration at the *Kotel HaMa'aravi* after evening prayers on the eve of Rosh Chodesh Nisan, 25 March 2020, as the nations of the world count time. Echoing across the great plaza could be heard words based on Joshua 1:5-6: as the Eternal One was with Emanuel, so may God be with you, never to fail you, nor forsake you. Be strong and courageous; for you shall cause this people to inherit the land, which God swore to their ancestors to give them.

The second ceremony of installation took place three days later in Borough Park, Brooklyn, on Saturday night, *Mots'ei Shabbat Vayikra*. There the Borisovers and followers overflowed from the shul into many streets. Nachum spoke to his Hasidim, saying to them a version of what he had promised at the *Kotel*, "as God was with Moses, so I will be with you; I will not fail you, nor forsake you. Let us be strong and courageous together!"

His Hasidim vigorously applauded and lustily cheered. Musicians struck up an exuberant melody. Men danced with men. Women danced with women, and the notes of the Borisover *niggun* were heard chanted on every male tongue until suddenly, one booming voice changed the *niggun*'s birri birri bams into Joshua's *Chazak ve-ematz*, Be strong and courageous. The men began to sing the words over and over as they danced, and the *niggun* remains that way for many Borisovers until this very day.

While Rebbe Nachum visited Brooklyn, he changed Rabbi Avraham Stadlan's status from *Epitropos*/Curator to American Manager of Borisover Hasidic Life. The rabbi came to the office of his newly appointed Rebbe with a statement and a question.

"Rebbe," he said, "there's something you should know."

"You seem agitated, Rabbi Stadlan. What is it?"

"The last few days generated a great deal of publicity about you. That's only natural. But I want you to know how we monitor and manage that publicity."

Now it was Nachum's turn to be agitated. "What are you trying to say?"

"You're an Israeli citizen. You served in the Israeli army. Educated at a prime American business school, you worked for a major Israeli defense contractor. Only in the last decade have you proved yourself an *ilui*, a genius in the study of Talmud and halacha. You have become the Rebbe of an important sect of Hasidim by virtue of your great-grandfather's affair with a secular Jewish woman in Berlin almost a century ago. All of this could make difficult publicity for us."

"Rabbi Stadlan, what's wrong with the truth?" Nachum probed.

"We need *sh'lom bayit* and to get peace in the house, everything must seem as normal as possible. Toward that end I made some decisions before the installations took place, and you should be aware of them."

"What have you done?"

"Let's take them one by one. That you're an Israeli citizen: we try to put that fact at the very end of any articles we have written, and we've sought to push it to the bottom on everyone else's publicity output. We want to emphasize the great and vital fact that a Rebbe leads Borisov once again. Between you and me, we Hasidim discount citizenship in favor of leadership. We think tribally, and consider Borisov a worldwide band within the Jewish tribe. As a group, we have been at most non-Zionist. We always speak of Eretz Yisrael."

Nachum could not help but frown and roll his eyes.

The rabbi continued, "That you served in the Israeli army: We have not mentioned the fact at all. Others have done so. When they have, our local people sometimes – not always – contact the press to ask that any further articles de-emphasize your army service simply because every Israeli confronts that obligation and many rabbis served Israel in its armed forces."

Nachum nodded.

"That you earned an MBA at a prime American business school: we have trumpeted your degree in the forefront of our publicity. Our last rebbe brought some engineering background as well as a traditional Jewish one. In this day and age, a business school like Harvard's offers practical lessons for rebbes and professionals alike, and Harvard stands out in people's minds. You're the rebbe who understands the business world.

"That you worked for a major Israeli defense contractor: this we have played down, similar to the matter of the army. We want to present a more spiritual face to the Jewish public.

"That you are a Talmud *ilui*: your ingenuity with Talmudic law and your understanding of halacha offer us heavyweight publicity opportunities, and we have taken advantage of every opening to tout those facts, your own modesty notwithstanding. We have placed your halachic legal novellae in the best journals, and when your work influenced a decision in a humane way, we tried to get a squib in print.

"The last and perhaps most difficult fact, the one regarding genealogy: let me be frank with you. Too many secular or uneducated Jews translate the word mamzer as bastard. Of course, a mamzer is the offspring of a union that can never be made legal, while a bastard in English or American law points to a child born of a union outside of wedlock. As you're aware, there's a huge difference. Your great-grandfather had every right to marry your great-grandmother if the two of them desired, and therefore the resultant child of the union was no mamzer. Under Anglo-Saxon law, a bastard, yes, but definitely not a mamzer.

"Before we announced your installation ceremonies, we placed articles about the large difference between mamzer and bastard in major Jewish newspapers and news services around the world, and since it's a controversial topic, we think we received strong readership. However, we found discussion and articles on the internet surfacing over that issue and over others that I mentioned, the ones we wanted to play down. Therefore we hired a firm whose main job is to suppress and push down topics that we did not want searched or investigated."

"Suppress? Push down? Do you mean censor?"

"No, Rebbe. How can you censor a Google search? No, we just make sure that a hundred other responses more satisfactory to our public relations come up first. The PR firm pushes the unwanted material back to page ten or eleven of the search. It's done all the time. Someone bad-mouths a retailer on line, for example, and it starts to ruin his reputation. He can hire an agent to submerge the negative review under a ton of positives. The negative remarks won't appear until several pages into the search. It's reputation management, essentially."

"And that's what you did for me?"

"Yes."

"It sounds like *genevat da'at*. Aren't you misleading people, 'stealing their mind'?"

"There are those who dislike us, Rebbe. Most of them are farther to the right religiously than we are. The liberals think it's wonderful that you're a captain in the Israeli army reserves. Their non-Orthodox so-called rabbis also serve as you did, in regular units, not as chaplains. The middle-of-the-roaders approve of your working for Israel Aerospace Industries. They're protective of Israel in attitude. It's the right wingers who want to knock you off your pedestal, and we need to cover our behinds to remain in their good graces."

Nachum conceded, "I understand."

"Rebbe, I have a serious question. What will be your first important act as our new leader?"

Nachum said, "*Kedoshim Tihiyu* (Lev. 19:2), you shall be holy – I have always considered this one of the great mandates of the Torah, particularly for our Hasidim."

"But Rashi considers this a command about proper sexual relations," Stadlan objected.

"You are right about Rashi, but others say that it is not a command at all, simply a prologue to what follows. I take it as an overarching command, a commandment to observe all the other injunctions of Leviticus 19, just as the tzitzit on the tallit ought to remind us of the other 612 commandments. I want to begin the era of Rebbe Nachum by devoting ourselves to the ethic of this chapter of Torah and its mitzvot."

"Why does that so concern you, Rebbe?"

Nachum picked up a file folder that lay before him on his desk. A good 15 cm thick, it contained newspaper clippings which protruded from its edges.

"Look at this, Rabbi Stadlan." Nachum turned the file around so the rabbi could see it. He plucked the top four clippings from the bunch and spread them out in front of his administrator. Tapping a sheet of newsprint, he said, "This one is particularly odious. Borisovers in the American south raised funds with a most creative plan. They walked into many family-owned businesses with a briefcase in hand, a briefcase filled with cash. They asked for a $100,000 contribution to their cause, and you know we sponsor many good causes besides our Beit Borisov shuls, many organizations that feed the poor or house the homeless or look after other needs of the unfortunate.

"They went to one businessperson after the other with their stash of $100 bills, and for every $100,000 check they received, they issued a tax receipt for that amount and handed over the briefcase, usually filled with $60,000 in old banknotes. First class money launderers and tax cheats, they are. One entrepreneur they solicited knew the Talmudic dictum *Dina diMalchuta Dina*[44], which makes the tax law of a country into Jewish law, so he blew the whistle on them to his state's revenue agency, and that's how this headline about $30,000,000 in fraudulent tax receipts appeared. It took place a few years ago, and no prosecution followed. Rumor has it that the revenuers were bribed to shut down the investigation. The feds, now looking into it, may not be so kind. 'You shall not steal or deal falsely or lie to each other' (Lev. 19:11). I take that command to include all human beings.

"Here's another one." Nachum pointed to the next clipping. "Take your clunker car to a certain garage, donate it to one of our charities, and receive a tax receipt for full retail value of the auto in average to good condition, regardless of true market value. The garage owner sells the car for whatever the market will bear, often at a value less than the receipt. From the proceeds of the sale he gives money to our tzedakah group, taking an agreed upon commission at a high percentage. We must also ask the question of whether we should be party to the sale of used cars not checked for safety. Some family is likely to buy that donated, unsafe vehicle. 'You shall not put a stumbling block before the blind' (Lev. 19:14) means you don't mislead people who can't adequately judge the goods. We should not aid and abet that transgression. As for the tax receipts: 'You shall do no unrighteousness in judgment or measures.' (Lev. 19:35)

"Check out the third clipping. One of our West Coast yeshivas gave large tax receipts for furniture supposedly donated to outfit the homes of its students. Used furniture decreases greatly in value from the original cost, but in this case our Hasidim decided to be extra generous to the givers. The state revenue agency notified the yeshiva of a date when they would visit to verify recent gifts at the warehouse. When the revenuers arrived, our people told them that an all-consuming fire occurred, and sadly nothing remained to see of the furnishings. The agency ascertained from the local fire department that no such fire ever took place. It cost the yeshiva their charitable status. They have closed. 'You shall not defraud your neighbor.' (Lev. 19:13)

"Here's a day school we operate where the teachers generally don't receive their paychecks on time. Month after month they consistently pay the teachers late, and still the staff await salary that's two months overdue. 'You shall not keep the wages of the hired person overnight.'" (Lev. 19:13)

Nachum reached in his pocket and withdrew a small paper. "Here's an investigation I did myself, very easy to do. I went to the Revenue Canada website and looked up one of our charitable organizations in that country. They've raised a lot of money. We should bring the Hasid in charge to Brooklyn as a fundraiser for us. According to their annual report, published by the government, most of what they raise stays in the bank. If we don't push them to spend it for their charitable purposes soon, the revenue agency will get on their case. We need to ask some serious questions there. 'You shall reason with your neighbor, and not allow sin on his account.' (Lev. 19:17)

"To me it's a *klara gemorra*, Rabbi Stadlan, really clear. The vast majority of our Borisovers conduct their organizations properly, but some of our Hasidim, in the name of doing good, transgress the Torah in major ways and give us a bad name in their localities. You ask my first order of business as the new Rebbe? I want to clean house. I want squeaky clean books. I want attention to tax laws. I want us to accomplish the ethical mitzvot of Leviticus 19 and better.

"I've already discussed the matter with an accounting firm of international capability that offered the Borisovers good professional and financial support over the decades. I'm sure the name Kamtsen Vantsman means something to you. I've asked that firm to monitor the books of every single Borisover charitable organization throughout the world. They have agreed, and you'll see – it will earn us the respect our movement deserves."

Rabbi Stadlan said, "Rebbe, I want you to know that I've dealt with each of these cases on a quiet local basis, and I'm convinced they do not represent general practice. However, if you want to discover if the house needs cleaning, you've picked the right firm with which to work: incorruptible, competent, international.

"I honor your efforts. We should splash the word across the Jewish press that we demand and assure full compliance with tax laws regardless of locale. It can only help our cause. If you don't mind more from *Vayikra* 19, 'The priest shall make atonement for him and his sin shall be forgiven.'" (Lev. 19:22)

After all these things, at the cost of many talents of silver and much gold, Nachum acquired land to build the House of Borisov on King George Street in Yerushalayim next to the Great Synagogue. Without offering either comment or interpretation, he gave for his reason the Book of Joshua (1:1-2): "The Eternal spoke to Joshua saying, Moses My servant is dead; now arise, cross over the Jordan, you, and all this people, to the land which I give to the people of Israel."

So Nachum and Dina and their children lived in Rehavia in the west of Yerushalayim and established the seat of Borisover Hasidic life in the city of David, that is King David, Nachum's ancestor according to the claim of the House of Borisov, and they patiently awaited the completion of their new global center.

BOOK IV

במדבר

Numbers / "In the wilderness"

CHAPTER TWENTY-ONE

Comment on Numbers 1:1-2: "Take a census [lift up the head] of all the congregation." Compare this to the official who says to the executioner, "Lift up this man's head." This hints at a double entendre, for if the Israelites are worthy, they will go upward to greatness, heads lifted high, as it is said, "Pharaoh will lift up your head and restore you to your office" (Gen. 40:13). And if the Israelites have no merit, they will all die, as it is said, "Pharaoh will lift up your head from off of you and hang you on a tree." (Gen. 40:19)[45]

1 Iyar 5781 – Tuesday, 13 April 2021
Jerusalem, Israel

Irving Kamtsen sat confidently in Rebbe Nachum's presence leafing through a thick volume containing the numbers that summarized hundreds of Borisover non-profit accounts. The tricolor report revealed pages at the front tinged in green. Farther back could be found a section tinged in yellow, and finally, pages in pink. A similar copy lay on the Rebbe's lap.

Kamtsen said, "Rebbe, we completed a worldwide survey of the last five years' finances of all the Borisover NGOs, all Beit Borisov shuls and schools, and the central office's books. I want you to feel good about the condition of the Borisover Hasidim today. Your central office bank account remains solid, with no deficit. Borisover Hasidim can well afford the construction of the new center here in Yerushalayim, and the further development of Kfar Rachel as a Hasidic focal point in Eretz Yisrael faces no financial hurdles."

Nachum signaled his approval and Kamtsen continued, "We have indicated problem areas. Turn, if you will, to the yellow section. So far as we can tell, all these not-for-profits operate at the edge of the law or the limits of proper fiscal behavior. Some do not sufficiently reinvest the funds they raise. Some may rely on questionable evaluators to determine the tax-receipt amounts for gifts in-kind. Some pay salaries edging toward excess. Some transfer funds to other non-profits, an action which certain tax authorities do not accept. Some report deficits caused by inexplicably vague reasons. Some just don't seem to understand the rules of accounting. In short, the agencies in yellow need to be warned of their deficiencies and to correct them before problems arise."

Nachum asked, "Do you think a warning letter to the rabbis in charge should best come from me or from your accounting firm?"

"I think," Kamtsen offered, "that we should sign the letter together, provided that you concur with its form. I'll send you a copy of what I would propose to say, and if you can endorse it, then by all means, do so."

"Very good, Irving. Now what about this last section?"

"Ah, the pink sheets. Obviously pink sheets are easier to read than red ones, but if I could choose a proper color, I'd rather a sinner's deep scarlet. As you can see, considering the size of Borisover operations around the world, the pink sheets form a fairly small problem group. These outfits have broken the law. You've seen reports on several of them in the press. The bulk of them are in North America, Australia, and Western Europe, since those nations hold not-for-profits by a tighter rein. Transparent disclosure has become more public to encourage compliance. Still, you might find a few surprises in the lot."

"Your recommendation for these?"

"Everyone is innocent until proven guilty. Our accountants believe with near faultless certainty that every administrator of these pink sheet operations violated civil legal and Jewish religious standards, but I would appoint a group of, say, three rabbis with knowledge of accounting and the law to hear their various cases. Maybe we misunderstood something. Maybe there are extenuating circumstances in various countries of the world. Who knows?

"After a fair hearing, if not found culpable of wrong-doing, dismiss the case. If found to be more like those listed in the yellow sheets, deliver them a corrective warning. If they remain worthy of the pink sheets, close the organization down forthwith, turn over what the Borisovers know about it to the competent authorities, and let the law take its course. On the surface it may seem cruel, but it will put the Borisovers' central office in the good graces of the different revenue agencies and send an unmistakable message about financial rectitude to all your local leadership. Each of these charitable organs is separately incorporated, meaning that Borisov Central, which, by the way, is cleaner than a kitchen on the morning before Pesach, will not be touched.

"Of course, you may want to create a new tzedakah unit to replace the old one that is being shut down. You'll give it a different name, provide a different leader, and carry on with your work."

Nachum paged through the pink sheets. "Here's a Beit Borisov in South America. How do we rename that?"

"Rebbe, I'm sure we can respond creatively to the issue. In some towns, you've built sufficient momentum to simply assume the reins of pre-existing community organizations that provide similar services. For example, the Borisovers might leverage themselves into control of the local synagogue, making Beit Borisov unnecessary. That might be one approach. You'll think of something."

Nachum arose and shook the accountant's hand. "Irving, we owe you greatly for this."

"No, Rebbe," Irving Kamtsen stated, "you don't. The bill, steeply discounted, mind you, was paid last week from Brooklyn. In my opinion, you've taken the Borisovers a massive step forward, and as a camp follower, let me suggest that once you conclude the handling of the yellow and pink sheets, use your accomplishment to make hay."

"Make hay?" Nachum asked.

"Publicity. The fact that you're monitoring the legal compliance of all your not-for-profits will help you raise more money and earn you respect in Eretz Yisrael and abroad. If I were you, I'd regularize this global analysis. Do it every five years. It'll pay dividends."

"I hear you, Irving. Let me talk to Rabbi Stadlan about setting that in motion. *Na'aseh v'nishma* – we'll do it, and afterwards I'm sure we'll better understand its significance. Thank you for work well done."

Two days later, Rebbe Nachum signed a joint letter with Irving Kamtsen announcing a rotating system of examination for the account books of all Borisover organizations, to begin the following year. Press releases extolled the transparency of the Borisovers under their new rebbe's aegis.

The next day, all Borisover organizations received an email of a hard-copy, posted letter co-signed by Kamtsen and Steinitz. Non-profits that passed muster were informed and complimented on their good practices. Those which were marginal received a yellow-tinged email similar to the posted letter warning of irregularities that needed correction. Kamtsen Vantsman gave six months to conform to proper accounting and tax practices.

Leaders of organizations which received a pink colored letter were granted three months to prepare a defense, after which they appeared before a Borisover beth din close to their home to answer diverse charges of mismanagement as listed in the complaint. They could also choose simply to plead guilty to the Rebbe's office, which acted immediately to repair any damage.

Nachum treated the 50% who pleaded guilty with forbearance, if not full clemency. He relieved them of their duties and dispatched them to different outposts to serve under rabbis whose organizations passed inspection flawlessly. Often that took the transgressor out of the country where he or she had broken the law, making prosecution less likely. Too often it meant that the local fiscal authority negated tax receipts, presenting the giver with a higher tax bill, but many givers, too, were involved in the cheat and deserved to face the consequences.

Rabbi Stadlan looked after the public relations aspect of the house-cleaning, using a nationally recognized American firm for press coverage and website development. Despite unfavorable publicity about a few bad apples in the lot, ultimately the transparency of the Borisovers won them recognition across the Jewish world, and donations swelled. The Borisover financial office, never before so awash in new gifts, grants, and bequests, used their abundance of cash to advertise to anyone who sought Jewish information or entertainment on well-frequented web sites. Donations to Borisov rose ever higher.

CHAPTER TWENTY-TWO

Yom Yerushalayim, 28 Iyar 5781 – Monday, 10 May 2021

Nachum Aviam Steinitz, the Borisover Rebbe, stood immediately next to the mayor of Jerusalem at the city's Yom Yerushalayim celebration, held in the square outside the Hurva Synagogue of the Jewish Quarter in the Old City. Most Borisovers could not believe their eyes: their Rebbe associating himself with an Israeli politician, drawing nigh a purely Israeli festival celebrating the unification of Jerusalem in 1967. And then they, along with all Israel, could not believe their ears, as the mayor announced, "I call now upon the Borisover Rebbe, *Seren* Nachum Aviam Steinitz, to speak on this great day."

Nachum stepped to the podium. "Thank you, Mayor, for that truthful introduction. Yes, I was a *seren*, a captain in the *Tsahal*, and I served my country honorably, but since I have taken on this new post as Rebbe, they have forgotten me! To be honest, in a few months I'll be exempt from duty in the army reserves, but I thank you for including my rank, for I am proud to have served and protected the State of Israel."

The State of Israel!? Borisovers never heard those words come from their Rebbe's lips before – ever and only Eretz Yisrael, the Land of Israel. A drastic change was taking place before their eyes and ears.

Nachum went on, "We Borisovers delight to announce that before next Yom Yerushalayim, the construction of our international center on King George Street in Yerushalayim will begin, and within two years from this very day, it will be, God willing, completed. Just as this Hurva Synagogue belongs in the heart of Jerusalem, so we Borisovers, who touch the mystical soul of the Jewish spirit, belong here, too.

"Why do we belong here today? The connection is through Kabbalah. Over 300 years ago, a mystical Ashkenazic rabbi named Yehuda HeHasid brought his 500 followers to this very spot, thinking that together they might induce the messianic time through their quiet religious lives in Yerushalayim. Yehuda HeHasid soon died, leaving the group leaderless. Nevertheless, they built a small synagogue, and then, to enlarge it, borrowed money that they could not repay. Their Arab lenders torched the shul and made it a *hurva*, a ruin, in 1721. That name has stuck for 300 years. Another group constructed a second synagogue here in 1864. The Arab Legion laid waste to it in our War of Independence, 1948. In 2010 our government dedicated this structure, based upon its predecessor. Still, we call all synagogues occupying this space the Hurva Synagogue, the ruined synagogue.

"Now the Jewish Quarter and all of Yerushalayim vibrate with Jewish life, yet today we celebrate the unity of Yerushalayim here at the Hurva, the ruin. Why? Is it to remind us that for the sake of Yerushalayim time and again our hearts have been made a ruin? How many times have our hearts broken as we prayed for the rebuilding of Jerusalem? At last we have our nation once again, our Israel, with Jerusalem its natural and rightful capital.

"Whenever we pray for the peace of *Medinat Yisrael*, the Jewish State of Israel, the whole country, the whole Jewish world calls it 'the first flowering of our redemption.' What does that mean? In creating and sustaining Israel, we have taken a step toward what those 500 Ashkenazi Jews under Yehuda HeHasid prayed and worked to achieve when they built the original Hurva Synagogue. We have taken a first step toward the messianic age.

"To my Borisover Hasidim I say, to all of Israel I say, thank God for the unity of Yerushalayim. Thank God for the existence of *Medinat Yisrael*, the first flowering of redemption. Let us tend this garden, nourish its efflorescence, work together hand in hand, step by step toward the time of complete redemption, a hope without time limit, a hope that draws life from the ideal of a sacred tomorrow. And it will be said of the Holy One of Israel, as Isaiah wrote, 'For the Eternal has comforted Zion, comforted all her ruined places.' (Is. 51:3)[46]

"Even if our hearts are ruined and broken a thousand times more, Yerushalayim, we will not forget you. We are united with you as a people, and you, O Jerusalem, are united – by us, for us, and with us, the first flowering of redemptions yet to come, the birth pangs of a new age aborning."

Rebbe Nachum sat down in his chair on the dais, but all around him rose from their chairs in tumultuous applause. Given the occasion, a chief moment on the secular Israeli calendar, slim numbers of ultra-Orthodox and Hasidim attended, but Borisovers worldwide listened on the internet to their Rebbe's speech in astonishment. In one stroke, their Rebbe reversed 150 years of anti- and non-Zionism, save for their successful outpost of Kfar Rachel in Eretz Yisrael. Today, for the first time on the tongue of the Borisover Rebbe, Kfar Rachel attained a physical address in the State of Israel. Nachum wondered how it all would be received. He did not have long to wait.

By noon, news flashed around the Jewish world of bold new leadership in an important Hasidic group. Borisover rebbes had never once spoken the words "State of Israel" until Nachum Steinitz's sudden about face shifted the group's position. "Captain Rebbe Recognizes Israel" one headline proclaimed. "Zionism Comes to Borisovers" cried another. "Talmud Genius Drags Borisovers into 21st Century" wrote *The New York Times*. A cynical editorialist at *Haaretz* must have seen the *Times* piece, because his headline read, "Borisovers Reach 1948." Some Hasidic and ultra-Orthodox leaders repudiated Nachum's move, but most stayed silent. They did not read secular newspapers, watch television, or listen to the Voice of Israel. The day at the Hurva Synagogue did not matter to them.

Nachum's office began to receive calls for interviews and speaking engagements across Israel. Callers from Europe and the Americas wanted to know when he planned to visit so they could schedule him, never mind the fee. His office took note of the offers but promised nothing. Rebbe Nachum had become hot, and life at Borisover Central in Israel simmered with the allure of new and heightened influence.

In early afternoon Dina received a phone call letting her know that a security service officer would meet that evening with the two of them to discuss their safety. She informed Nachum upon his return home and added, "Nachum, have you listened to the news?"

"No."

"Listen for the beep beep beep on the hour at Kol Yisrael radio and hear what they're saying."

Nachum heard the 3 PM newscast in which the national radio service replayed parts of Nachum's speech at the Hurva Synagogue. The announcer then switched to interviews with the average Israeli in the street, who never expected to hear the Borisover Rebbe endorse Israel's political existence prior to the arrival of the mashiach, and many hoped that Nachum would become the leading edge of a major shift in attitude among certain Haredi and Hasidic groups. Kol Yisrael noted that Nachum Aviam Steinitz came from a family that arrived with the Fifth Aliyah. He served in *Tsahal* with the rank of captain and before returning to tradition as a *Chozeir biTeshuva,* immersing himself in study and developing as a master of Talmud, he occupied a position as a key player at IAI. To most Israeli ears, the Voice of Israel made Nachum seem both a brilliant and an eminently normal Israeli.

CHAPTER TWENTY-THREE

No ordinary security agent rang the bell of the Steinitz home in Rehavia late that night of Yom Yerushalayim. Once again, the Director himself chose to call.

Social niceties concluded, the Director went to the heart of the matter.

"My dear Nachum and Dina, this visit has two purposes. One is security. From now on, no matter where you go, you'll be protected by a Shin Bet operative or our hired agent. Sometimes he or she may get in your way, but believe me: it is for your safety and well-being. Treat our guards well, because they're prepared to sacrifice their lives for you."

Nachum asked, "At this point in my affairs, do you really think we require such tight security?"

"*Me'ah achuz.*" The Director's copyrighted response to his every assertion. 100%.

Nachum conceded to the demand. Dina sighed in relief. "Our kids will be protected, too?" she asked.

"*Me'ah achuz.* And now the second part of my visit. Today's gathering at the Hurva confirmed to me your great potential as a leader. I didn't expect you'd be such a powerful orator, Nachum."

"My teacher at Kfar Rachel insisted I take speech lessons privately, which have helped me greatly, but when I feel profoundly moved to speak my own truths, it liberates my tongue and connects to my strongest emotions."

"In any case, well done today. We have no particular assignment for you, but we want you to grow more recognizable in the public eye, yet not so regularly seen and heard that they tire of you. Stay fresh. Stay in demand, but play hard to get. Don't sidle up to politicians. Let them come after you. It's a tall order, but you and Dina have good instincts about these things. Nachum, what does it say in *Bava Metzia*? 'If your wife is short, bend down and hear her whisper!'"[47]

"Director, I forget that you're a Talmud student yourself. Yes, that's what it says, *me'ah achuz*."

The Director laughed, arose, shook Nachum's hand, bowed slightly to Dina, thanked them for their time and asked to be excused by the back door.

Maimonides' seventh cause of inconsistencies and contradictions: It is sometimes necessary to introduce metaphysical material which may partly be disclosed, but must be partly concealed.[48]

Rosh Chodesh Sivan, 1 Sivan 5781 – Wednesday, 12 May 2021

Naturally the Borisovers provided their Rebbe a house in Kfar Rachel. Nachum sat in the dining room of that residence, the Gaon across the table from him. They stared at a meat and potatoes lunch. Nachum made a berachah over the bread, and the two began to eat and converse.

The Gaon said, "What you did a couple days ago, first, it astounded all of us."

"Why? I'm an Israeli, I carry an Israeli passport. It's a fact of my life, of your life, too, Gaon."

"Ah, but passports belong to the material world, the ordinary world we live in. Nations need to exist in that world, but our life is meant for a higher existence. Your new home, where you actually reside, is in this world's Yerushalayim. We want to bring about *Yerushalayim shel ma'alah*, that higher, ideal, heavenly Jerusalem for which we have dreamed and yearned. And still we wait. The waiting is holy, and the waiting room is where we Hasidim live."

"Gaon, 'When someone is looking for something to happen, and his expectation is not met, his heart is pained. When his expectation is met, he's like someone who was given life.'[49] Is it so terrible that we reveal to our Hasidim the possibility that a bloom of their great hope exists today? It gives them life. I did not say that redemption has come, although for many of us in Israel, just to be here on this land, just to have a Shabbat table full of food and to share it with family, that alone is redemption."

"Well, that leads to my second point, Nachum. In my opinion, you gave permission to our people to accept this world, this nation as the answer to their prayers." The Gaon took a minute to enjoy his stew, pointed his fork at his student and Rebbe, and confessed, "But I don't blame you. It's been a long time since our Hasidim have grown excited about an idea – more than an idea, an ideal. If you can carry them beyond this point, beyond the 'first flowering' to realize that full redemption of this world will take a greater effort – prayer, deeds of love and kindness, tzedakah, mitzvot – you'll have accomplished something major with your leadership. I hope that's where you're going."

"Gaon, have you ever read a word or a phrase as familiar to you as breathing, whose meaning you thought you understood, and therefore you no longer paid it much attention? Then one day you look at it, and the word, the sentence pops off the page with a meaning you missed, something you should have seen all along, something exalted, more profound? After that moment it starts to inform your life, shape your opinion, and touch your actions.

"In that speech, I tried to get Israel to think about what they're praying for when they fulfill the prophet Jeremiah's command to pray for the welfare of the city where we live. If this is the first flowering of redemption, we're the gardeners. How shall we best tend this garden of ours?

"I know it's not the Garden of Eden, but still, I'm trying to stir in this whole people Israel, not just the Borisovers, a renewed sense of *kavanah*, directed intent. Without the intention of the soul, what you speak of cannot happen, and my hope cannot occur. I want to release the energy of their good inclination. I believe that most people have that *yetser tov*, but they're concerned so often with the trivia of living that they have neither the time nor the energy to free it. When people free that energy, historically it happens in spurts. It is not a phenomenon of the long haul, and too often it's the leader who wants power who releases that good intention and harnesses it to his own ends, too often, wicked ends. With so many political parties and their politicians seeking power in Israel, we must be wary as we proceed."

"No, Nachum, it is not *we* who proceed. It is you: you, the Rebbe. And it is you who must be wary of the hidden agendas of others. And we who must be wary of the hidden agendas with which you may ally yourself, as well as the hidden agendas that you personally possess, for they may even be hidden to you."

"Gaon, I can't argue with what you're saying. I ask God each weekday in our prayers for knowledge, understanding, and wisdom. For all of us, may they be granted."

They *benched* and parted, but still friends, and still teacher and student, or student and teacher.

CHAPTER TWENTY-FOUR

Five days later in Brooklyn on the festival of Shavuot, Nachum, Dina, and family celebrated the giving of the Torah. The atmosphere in the Borisover synagogue remained normal in one respect, the celebration of a major Jewish holiday. But on this Shavuot the friction of hot and cold clouds of conflict within the Borisover ranks imitated the original thunder and lightning at Sinai. Those who warmly favored recognition and living with the State of Israel collided with those who retained, against their Rebbe's words, a coldly non-Zionist messianic position.

When the time came for Nachum to address the throng of his Hasidim and fellow travelers, he spoke in a slightly Hebrew-accented English about a verse that preceded the traditional Torah reading for the festival, the Ten Commandments, "And the Eternal came down upon Mount Sinai." (Exodus 19:20)

Nachum used chapter 10 of Maimonides' *Guide of the Perplexed* as his launching pad to advance the idea that the giving of the Law at Sinai was for God a *yeridah,* a descent. God "deigned" to give the commandments at Sinai in an attempt to use the Jewish people to reach humanity. But for us, we who stand at Sinai every Shavuot, we participate in an aliyah, an ascent, a going upward, drawn toward heaven by that fateful moment in our history, our ears open to hear the echo of the words just revealed.

Our time, Nachum concluded, reshapes aliyah and *yeridah* into purely physical terms. Today aliyah signifies going up to Israel. Many Borisovers have made aliyah, witness the growth of Kfar Rachel and the movement's presence across the State of Israel. *Yeridah* means leaving Israel to live in another land. *Yordim,* those who have left and their descendants by the hundreds of thousands, live in America and elsewhere.

"From this Diaspora shul, I call upon Borisover Hasidim to open their doors to *Yordim,* their children, and their children's children. Invite them in. Teach them of a different kind of aliyah, an upward spiritual momentum, and help them to know, honor, and live their sacred heritage. To this Diaspora shul I say, never forget that you must be leaders in aliyah of the spiritual order, following the path of Moshe Rabbenu, to climb high in Sinai moments like this Shavuot, bringing the Law down to earth for the sake of Heaven itself. Your physical aliyah will always be welcome in Israel, but spiritual aliyah is demanded of us no matter where we reside. Shavuot invites us all to relive Sinai, to go up and accept the Torah, and with it, to reshape this world of ours toward its fullest possibility."

Nachum's words dispelled the stormy clouds of controversy swirling about him in Brooklyn, letting his American leadership understand that no, he would not cease speaking of the State of Israel, but yes, they and all Borisovers, all Jews played a unique role in building a heavenly Jerusalem on earth no matter where they lived. In that respect, Eretz Yisrael counted as just one more mundane place awaiting complete redemption. Nachum led with a workable compromise. And besides, wasn't his task as Rebbe to move them in old-new directions?

CHAPTER TWENTY-FIVE

10 Kislev 5783 – Sunday, 4 December 2022

Nachum asked Dina, "How does it feel to go to the mikveh? I mean, what's the ambience like? Is it something you dread, something you're neutral about, enjoy, what's it like?"

"Why do you ask now, Nachum? I've been at this for ten years, and now you want to know?"

"At least you have a track record to report on," he joked. "It comes down to this: I think I'm in a position to make some changes for the sake of Borisover Hasidic women, but I don't want to bring up the issue if one doesn't really exist. What do you recommend?"

"Nachum, you know I'm on the Pill. It's pretty straightforward that way. I had some trouble at the outset, spotting, but it settled down, and I've been fortunate that it worked so well. If you're talking about the experience at the mikveh itself, some mikvehs are more spiritual than others. Most of the time it's pro forma. You go, you do what you have to do. The mikveh lady says 'Kosher,' and you're good to go."

"Doesn't sound too inspiring or too threatening."

"It could be more of a spiritual experience. First of all, the Chief Rabbi has not required that women be inspected at the mikveh since 2013, but some rabbis still demand it. What for? Instructions are clearly marked. Inspection never feels pleasant, my friends report.

"Let me tell you what the whole experience *could* be like. Remember that time we traveled to Los Angeles visiting some of our Borisover installations there? You were giving a talk, one I'd heard a few times, so I went to that Jewish museum between the city and the Valley, the Skirball. I took the kids with one of the local moms and her children.

Hanna Liora and David had a fun, but worthwhile time at that museum, and while they played at one display, I asked the other mom if she knew a mikveh in the area. She directed me to the Jewish American College up the street. I told her no, that it's not Orthodox. She leaned over and in a quiet and confidential tone of voice she said, 'You've got to see it. Go.'

"She watched the kids, while I drove up the hill and went to the mikveh at that school. Nachum, I don't think we have one like it in Israel. The lighting is subtle, low and warm. They surround the mikveh with candlelight. The glow bounces off the water and dances in your eyes. Imagine a mikveh spotlessly clean, not a speck of dust, not a trace of mildew, with towels thicker and more luxurious than any 5-star hotel and water that caresses the olfactory glands, mikveh deluxe.

I took the full treatment just to see how they did it. Modesty and dignity marked their approach. Somehow, when the mikveh lady called 'Kashér,' in Modern Hebrew, as someone who grew up in Israel, I felt renewed. When they say 'Kosher,' with the Ashkenazic accent à la Borisov, it makes me feel like a piece of meat. Nachum, if you could replicate mikvehs like that one, women would swoon to be Borisovers. Add a spa and a women's gym with exercise classes and day care, and observant Jewish women would line up at the door."

He said, "I imagine that's something we could manage financially little by little, and it's certainly worth the effort. Still, the women you know who dip themselves regularly, they must have some complaints, yes?"

"Beyond the condition of the mikveh? Sure. Regarding the spotting I suffered when I started taking the Pill, the question is, does it have any halachic consequence or not? Does it make me *niddah*, a menstruant? That affects our intimacy, whether I can use the mikveh, and so on. Do you know what the textbooks tell a woman to do in that instance?"

Nachum responded, "Obviously: consult your rabbi."

"And how do you think a young woman, any woman feels about walking into her rabbi's office to talk about spots on her panties?"

"Not so good, I suppose."

"You suppose? Come on, Nachum. You know how difficult that would be. You've no idea how many times the textbook tells the woman, consult your rabbi. What woman wants to invite a man who's not her husband into her sex life, her private bodily functions? It's not easy, let me tell you. If you could fix that issue, you'd accomplish a huge mitzvah for all of us of the fair sex.

"Do you have any idea where women really go with their questions? Sometimes they ask another woman who's an old hand at family purity issues, because the same problems of *taharat hamishpacha* arise again and again. The mature women at the mikveh have some answers. Or, there's another solution.

"For years *yoatzot*, advisor women trained in the laws of *niddah*, have answered questions over the internet and over the phone. They consult with leading rabbis for responses to queries whose answers aren't so obvious. It's a project of the *Dati Leumi* National Religious Orthodox here in Israel, but Jewish women around the world have bought in. Of course, Borisovers don't opt into the *Dati Leumi* approach. Haredi Jews in general won't touch it. Me? I think it's terrific. You get rabbinic answers when you need them, and otherwise you receive sound advice from women trained in specific Jewish law by experts."

Nachum countered, "I'm aware of the program. Even the Modern Orthodox have doubts about these *yoatzot* advisors, complaining that they tend to make things more stringent to play it safe."

"You make a good point, Nachum, but why be stubborn? You could try out the idea with a supervisory board to judge how the *yoatzot* are doing. You'd make a lot of young Borisover women very happy. Get the Gaon to create the training and the supervisory board. If the Gaon will do it, his stamp of approval will sail through almost every Black Hat storm imaginable. You'll have observant women flocking to Borisov, particularly if you upgrade our mikvehs."

"What, Dina, me stubborn? You make a lot of sense. Let's see what I can do." Nachum smiled, the couple kissed, Nachum nibbled at Dina's lips, and then they kissed again more deeply. "It's getting late. What do you say?"

She smiled a bit wantonly. "Mmhmmm."

The next week at Kfar Rachel, Nachum summoned the Gaon to tea in the late afternoon. They exchanged niceties for a few minutes, reviewed the latest decisions from some of the halachic courts in Israel, and then Nachum came to the reason for the meeting.

"Gaon, my wife has been informing me about women's reality in regard to family purity matters, and it's not pleasant."

"Rebbe, I already see where this conversation is heading. My wife gave me an earful when she regularly visited the mikveh. It's the 'consult your rabbi' problem, right?"

"Exactly. Gaon, the *Dati Leumi* have these *yoatzot* advisors who handle questions from women on a confidential basis. They do it by phone, by internet. Rabbis give the *yoatzot* training in specific Jewish law on the subject, and the counselors in turn agree to refer difficult questions to rabbis for answers. The program sets women at ease."

The Gaon said, "For us, the question is, how weighty are the disadvantages?"

"Once again, it's true confession time. Dina minimizes the disadvantages, and since she's the one regularly using the system, I have to listen to her. She's convinced that if you personally designed a program of education for our Borisover *yoatzot* advisor women, and if you personally created a supervisory panel to track questions and answers, we could experiment with the arrangement. In a matter of months we'd know whether it's working for us or not. To be fair, I have to add that I'm aware it requires extra work by you, and we would arrange for compensation."

"I have my doubts about the system, and there's no need to re-hearse them all before you today. But my doubts aren't sufficient to say we shouldn't give it a try. I can put some of our halacha teachers to work writing curriculum and maybe even get a peek at what the *Dati Leumi* have already prepared. The curriculum writers should also get extra pay. And then there's the supervisory panel. Oh, and you haven't mentioned setting up the hotline and website. Do you have the money for that? How do we get the *yoatzot*? That's another question."

"Gaon, you get the curriculum written, set up the supervisors, and I'll get the volunteers to learn with us. In the meantime, I'll push all the buttons at our communications department to arrange a start-up date within four months from now."

"Rebbe, you must be joking. Four months?"

"Why not? We're not reinventing the wheel. Others have it up and running. Let's try to move it along."

"No promises, but I'll get on it tomorrow morning."

"Just to encourage you, Gaon, I've spoken to our Brooklyn center about revamping our mikvehs. A few days ago we hired an architec-tural firm to pore over the plans of every mikveh we own. They're tasked to propose revisions, redesigns, redecorations that will make the mikvehs at Borisov into an experience more sumptuous, pleasing, healthful, and more spiritual than ever before. They will be veritable spas, attractive and enticing to visit. The architects also have only four months to set forth their new plans."

"Rebbe, how can I refuse? You're advancing a vital mitzvah. Espe-cially knowing my doubts, I thank you for asking me to be involved."

Steakiah 443 again, this time on the Sonol gas station side, on the road to Yerushalayim and Kfar Rachel. Nachum slowly fiddled with the gas cap of his car, then selected a grade of gasoline as he inserted the nozzle in the vehicle. Another car pulled up from the other direc-tion. The driver made his stop parallel to Nachum's on the other side of the pump. The two identified each other, and one spoke.

"What's the problem?" the Director demanded.

"No problem, just a heads-up. I'm calling a private conference at my home regarding women's *niddah* issues. We're making some changes at Borisov in that regard. Plus, I have an unusual Torah interpretation I'm floating to catch their reaction. I have a fairly long list of rabbis to invite. I wanted you to know, just in case it might create a problem for you."

"No problem for me. In fact, there's one rabbi I want you to invite: Yosef Gruber. Do me a favor. See that he's there. It could work out well."

"He's already on the list," Nachum said.

They completed their fill-ups and drove off.

CHAPTER TWENTY-SIX

Genesis 49:4 "unstable as water": Rabbi Pinchas said, "You acted like those who break their legs when they recklessly jump into shallow water.[50]

L iron Megiddo, son of Oded and Tova, seemed a positive choice for the presidency of Israel. Active in Israeli politics, he served from time to time in the Knesset in middle of the road parties whose names shifted with national issues. Members of Knesset who knew him recognized his balanced views and often counted upon him as a swing vote in a crisis.

Megiddo practiced law for many years, but his true love bore a literary timbre. He wrote imaginative poetry with a classical base and a subtly nationalist bent. He penned rhapsodic essays that captured the Israeli soul and found their way into print through quality magazines and newspapers. Not everyone understood his verse, but they admired his style.

For fun, he wrote lyrics for songs. Even in middle age, he could be viewed in some musical videos as an extra. His wife told him to stop the practice, which she described as both unseemly and politically incorrect, so he desisted from any more cameo appearances on YouTube but continued composing lyrics for some of Israel's best singers. First and foremost, Liron Megiddo, even as a "golden-ager," possessed a palpable presence that the public adored.

The press welcomed a president who eschewed the usual stuffed shirt image. After all, the papers wrote, our president must be in touch with the people. Yes, he signs treaties and those Knesset bills that pass the Israeli parliament, but the president's ear should hear the people's needs and desires clearly. He must be sufficiently amiable, sensitive, and good-hearted that the people know he cares. Liron Megiddo gave the appearance of being the first president of Israel in many a year to possess all these qualities.

When rockets flew once again into the north from Lebanon and Israelis dived underground into their bomb shelters, Megiddo commandeered a limo, headed to Haifa, and joined them. The press called him Israel's First Secretary of Sympathy.

During rush hour on the morning after an Arab attacker seriously wounded riders of Jerusalem's light rail system, Megiddo and his wife went to the Mount Herzl stop, boarded a tram, and rode over the Calatrava Strings Bridge and through downtown Jerusalem all the way into Arab East Jerusalem until the last stop, Heil Ha-Avir. He chatted with riders, gave up his seat to a pregnant woman, and could be seen waving at pedestrians from the train window. Photos along the length of the route situated the president throughout the city, including the Damascus Gate area of the Old City. The gesture drove Shin Bet to the wall trying to protect the president and his wife, but the effort significantly raised Israeli spirits.

And when Israel confirmed another, more extensive natural gas field off its shores, it was Liron Megiddo who helicoptered out to sea to visit the exploratory platform and to congratulate its workers, the bulk of whom were Texans who knew no Hebrew. At the rig he offered to reporters his entirely unsolicited opinion that the price of electricity in Israel ought to plummet because of the abundance of fuel in Israeli waters. The populace kvelled with joy.

In early December of 2022, all began to go sour for Liron Megiddo. Transients, refugees, and foreign workers marched through Tel Aviv to demand equal pay and protection of law. They smashed store windows on Dizengoff, and police chased them back to the area around the central bus station, where they disbanded and melted into the neighborhood. A reporter from *Maariv* overheard President Megiddo while he spoke to a friend. The president referred to Israel's *KOOshi* problem. The reporter noted that among most Hebrew speakers a felt linguistic difference exists between *KOOshi* and *kooSHI*, the distinction being something akin to the N-word versus the Biblical word for Ethiopian. Left wing Israelis and Israel's Ethiopian Jewish populace took Megiddo's words as an insult and began to turn against him.

In early 2023, Liron Megiddo exercised his power to pardon jailed offenders. The president freed a scion of one of Israel's six richest families. He was jailed for conspiracy to bribe a judge in a case whose positive verdict regarding licensing fees would have turned the middle-aged man's millions of shekels into billions almost overnight. One clever headline writer for *Yedi'ot Aharonot*, playing on the similarities of the Hebrew word for president, *nassi*, and the verb "to be married," *hinassei*, claimed that the president was married to moneyed interests. Subsequently the press learned that the freed prisoner subsidized the publication of the president's literary works.

A former Israeli High Court judge slammed the president's insult to the nation's system of justice. "What facts changed in this situation to cause the president to favor this fellow with a pardon?" the judge demanded, and then answered his own question: "Nothing has changed except the mind of the president, which seems to go mushy when his work is published."

The prime minister then met quietly with Megiddo to admonish him for impolitic and imprudent use of his power. The president replied simply that the Basic Law of the State of Israel exempted him from having to supply evidence as to his decision.

Yet another insult to his office occurred shortly after the controversial pardon when Liron Megiddo unceremoniously and without warning left Israel, rumored to be on a visit to his aged aunt in London. The prime minister called a special meeting of the cabinet. In front of each member of the inner circle he placed a copy of the Basic Law regarding the president. In yellow marker, he highlighted the words, "The President of the State shall not leave the territory of the State save with the sanction of the Government."

"I have received no missive from President Megiddo stating that he wished to depart from the territory of the State of Israel, nor did he verbally ask of me leave to do so. Having left our country without permission of the government, he violated the Basic Law and deeply insulted the very democracy for which his position stands. We cannot brook a president's flouting of the Basic Law which governs his position, no matter what personal stake he might have in this London jaunt of his. Twenty members of my party brought a complaint to the House Committee regarding this negligence on the part of the president. The House Committee met late last night, demanded the president's immediate return to Israel, and summoned him to meet with them next Sunday.

"Just to remind you of procedure, the House Committee shall hear the circumstances of this violation, and if three-quarters vote to ask Knesset for his dismissal, then Knesset must also bring a vote of at least three-quarters of its members in order to remove him from office.

"I take this breach of procedure seriously. It shows contempt for high office. Our democracy has suffered an indignity of major proportions. Public office bears with it public responsibility to carry out the law. We must have a president, and currently, according to the law, the Speaker of the Knesset is acting president of Israel. I have notified the Speaker of the Knesset, Hammud ad-Darazi, a Druze, of his temporary presidency, so historically he becomes the second Druze to hold this position.

"Obviously I must inform the press of this embarrassing situation. If any of you have insight into Megiddo's reason or excuse for leaving without notice, please let me know. In the meantime, we have sent him electronic messages and emails, but without reply. Honestly and just between us, I fear he may have lost his mind. Questions?"

There were none, and the meeting ended abruptly at 11 PM with knots of Knesset members conversing heatedly as they left the residence of the Prime Minister.

Liron Megiddo returned to Israel seven days later, enough time for newspapers and television to raise an immense outcry at his disdain for proper national procedure. When he came before the Knesset House Committee, he carried a sheaf of handwritten notes, which he beguilingly waved at them.

"By way of explanation, would you care to read these?" he asked, as he shuffled through the papers, a beatific look of innocence and sanctimonious importance on his face.

The chair of the committee demanded to know what he was waggling at them.

"These," the president said with amour-propre, "constitute a set of the finest poems I have ever written. I traveled secretly to the Lake District of England for inspiration, spent a week in quiet isolation under the region's spell, and now I finally understand what animated Wordsworth, Coleridge, and Southey to become the great poets they were. The lakes' serenity bewitched me, as well. They create a feeling of tranquility so lacking in our daily struggle here."

The chair of the House Committee of the Knesset responded, "And this is your reason for leaving Israel without prior notice and permission?"

"Yes, of course. The writing of poetry requires privacy and hours dedicated to its unfolding. What could be more important than one's art?"

Shortly thereafter, the House Committee recommended the president's impeachment to the Knesset, which also voted 80% in favor. Hammud ad-Darazi remained the temporary president for six weeks while the prime minister combed the nation for the perfect candidate.

In the meantime, Megiddo's newly released jailbird friend paid for the publication of the Lake District poems. Although ultimately most copies of the book became recycled paper, *Yisrael Hayom* obtained permission to publish a few stanzas on the editorial page, only to mock them in the day's editorial. However, one professor of literature at Hebrew University, while carefully condemning the former president's unstatesmanlike actions, extolled the oeuvre of Liron, son of Oded and Tova, as a much-needed revival of romanticism in the Hebrew poesy of our time.

CHAPTER TWENTY-SEVEN

A student came to Rabbi Joshua and asked, "Is the evening prayer compulsory or optional?" Joshua said it was optional. The student then inquired of the Sanhedrin's president, Rabban Gamaliel, who said it was compulsory. The Torah scholar sputtered, "But Rabbi Joshua told me that it was optional!" Rabban Gamaliel responded, "Wait until the heavy halachic hitters arrive."

When they arrived, someone put the question: "Is the evening prayer compulsory or optional?" Rabban Gamaliel answered, "Compulsory," and challenged the Sages, "Does anyone disagree?"

Rabbi Joshua replied, "No."

Gamaliel said to Joshua, "I heard that you deemed it optional. Stand up, Joshua, and I'll get the informer to testify against you!"

Rabbi Joshua stood, but objected, "It would be my word against his."

Rabban Gamaliel remained seated, expounding Torah, while Rabbi Joshua was constrained to stand. Soon all in attendance began to shout, "Stop!" and grumbled, "How long is Rabban Gamaliel going to continue insulting Rabbi Joshua? After two earlier insults, here he insulted him once again. Let's depose him!"[51]

12 Adar 5783 – Sunday, 5 March 2023

J ust before the Fast of Esther and before Purim, Nachum Aviam Steinitz, the Borisover Rebbe, sponsored a conference on *taharat hamishpacha*, family purity. His purposes for the symposium were multifold.

He wished to present a paper that might provide a near-revolution in the area of family planning and wanted criticism from rabbis of a stature equal to his own. He also hoped that his solution might be hailed in some quarters as a great advance. If so, it might carry to everyday observant people in Israel, which could build momentum towards ends he sought for the ultra-Orthodox.

Assured that the *yoatzot* program would soon be in place, Nachum also wanted a worthy setting to announce forthcoming sumptuous improvements to the Borisover mikvehs and the group's new women counselors for questions about *taharat hamishpacha*. The conference, set at the edge of Purim when Jews read the Scroll of Esther, offered him a podium from which to push reluctant halachic leadership toward amelioration of women's Jewish life, inspiring his influential rabbinic guests to openness about matters that pertain particularly and very personally to women.

Nachum knew that many rabbis forbade any public mention of sexuality issues, deeming it a violation of the Torah prohibition against *gilui arayot*, exposing the nakedness (Lev. 18:6ff). Nachum banned the press corps to assure all invitees of privacy. He conditioned attendance of his yeshiva colleagues on their acceptance of a nondisclosure agreement. As a result, a number of scholars acquiesced to take part.

Moreover, Nachum desired to create a situation where he could appear as a leader of the Israeli religious right, as the Director suggested. The symposium did not require him to get in bed with any political party, but it might polish his image with a number of rabbis and Knesset members representing right wing religious points of view.

The conference presented a risk to Nachum, since its results and reactions to it could not be foreseen. If negative, the Borisover Rebbe's acceptance by his religiously right-wing peers could drop precipitously. He felt impelled to take the chance by conviction and by years of careful comprehension of traditional texts. The Director of Shin Bet also approved the risk during a brief sunset meeting in the pedestrian tunnel between Jerusalem's Giv'at Klor Garden and Rehavia Park, verdantly situated in the Valley of the Cross below the Israel Museum.

"Our whole project is a gamble," he said. "Might as well start taking risks now."

Sixteen halachic decisors, *poskim*, attended the assembly, a group small enough to gather around the dining room table of the Steinitz home. They arrived at 9:30 AM and schmoozed over continental breakfast for half an hour. The most likely opponent of change, Rabbi Yosef Gruber, arrived at the last minute. Most attendees wished Rabbi Gruber had agreed to offer a paper, since the ultra-Orthodox world considered him the supreme authority on the subject of the menstruant woman, the *niddah*. Rabbis usually called Gruber "the Yazuv Zov" because of his immense compendium of all halachic considerations of non-menstrual flow, a book called by that very name and based on Leviticus 15:25. He possessed a contentious personality and seemingly unlimited memory for law relating to family purity.

Once the Yazuv Zov greeted all in attendance, Nachum seated the group and set forth the ground rules. Half the scholars brought papers to deliver. Nachum divided the schedule to allow a general question period at the end of the day.

When the second presenter concluded, the third speaker declined to read his paper, fearing it would only repeat what the previous rabbi offered. Maybe the day would be a tad shorter.

Presenters engaged the group in profitable discussion and listened to kindly criticism of their thinking. After lunch and two more speakers, Nachum arose to contribute his comments.

"I have an announcement," he began. "Out of shyness or embarrassment, for centuries young Jewish women have sought the counsel of older, more experienced women on matters of *niddah*. It has all been private and ad hoc. Now the same occurs on the internet, and our own Haredi and Hasidic women are among the questioners.

"To create educated responses and anonymity of inquiry, women today can refer to *yoatzot*, trained female counselors who answer women's halachic questions about *niddah*. The counselors are women schooled to understand halacha about matters surrounding use of the mikveh and so forth. When the problem exceeds their ken, they refer to a rabbi and transmit his answer to the questioner.

"That program can largely be found among those who wear the knit kipa, the *Dati Leumi*, but also among the *Haredi Leumi*. Their wives demanded female consultants, since it embarrasses a woman to appeal directly to a rabbi for an answer on a matter regarding a woman's body and relations with her husband. Those who wear the black hat have no such advisory program, at least not officially.

"Among the Borisovers we are now selecting women to become *yoatzot* who will learn halacha from our own people. Our well-known Talmud giant, the Gaon of Kfar Rachel, organized a team to write curriculum and will draw a supervisory panel from our most learned rabbis. We'll soon have a corps of *yoatzot* available in North America and in Israel. They will be on trial, their counsel monitored by our supervisors, who expect them to refer difficult problems without naming the woman involved. If the results are satisfactory, the program will continue. The corps of supervisors will also continue, never fear. We'll maintain high standards.

"In addition, we have raised funds to restore and vastly improve our own mikvehs, but that is a story for another time. Later, I'll be glad to answer questions."

Buzz around the table continued for a minute. Most faces seemed dark and unaccepting, particularly the visage of the Yazuv Zov, who threw threatening glances at Nachum and could be heard to mutter to the rabbi at his right, "He cites the *Haredi Leumi*!? *Dati Leumi* wear sandals. *Haredi Leumi* wear their sandals with socks. Both are tref."

Nachum went forward undaunted, commanding silence. "Today I want to propose a revised understanding of the Torah's first commandment, *piryah v'rivyah*. The commandment to be fruitful and multiply, *p'ru ur'vu*, comes to us from the beginning of Genesis, when God said to humanity, 'Be fruitful, and multiply, fill the earth, and subdue it; and have dominion over . . . every living thing that moves upon the earth.' (Gen. 1:28)

"This command God gave to all humanity. Abraham was yet to exist. The Torah had not been given at Sinai. Therefore we take it as a general command to the human race. The earth being empty of people, the need existed to fill the earth with human beings.

"When we received the Torah, the command became specifically aimed at Jewish males, with the co-operation of Jewish females, of course. Since *p'ru ur'vu* now aimed only at the community of Israel, its raison d'être shifted to building up our own numbers. This approach to the mitzvah we have taken ever since. Torah requires us to have how many children? Beit Hillel say two, a boy and a girl. Beit Shammai say two boys suffice. Talmud endorses Beit Hillel.

"If we need only replicate ourselves, why do we insist that Jews continue to have more children? Tradition offers many reasons. For example, if one of the two children died, Rabbi Yochanan says in the Jerusalem Talmud that the fulfillment of the mitzvah ceases. Having more than two children insures that the mitzvah stays fulfilled.

"Another reason is to speed the coming of the messiah. Talmud *Yevamot* 62a teaches that 'The son of David will not come until all of the souls in heaven (in the *Guf*, the treasury of souls) have been born.' Since every child born to our community hastens the coming of mashiach, a couple should try to have as many children as possible. These are some of the reasons that we go beyond the minimum of two prescribed by our rabbis.[52]

"Let's return to the source of the mitzvah, the Torah verse, Genesis 1:28. Three parts of the verse describe the commandment: 1) be fruitful, 2) multiply, 3) fill the earth. The original commandment to humanity then mutated into a commandment for Jews. In 2023, we are now reaching 8 billion people on earth, of which we Jews might be 14 million. Surely the command to fill the earth can't mean that we should fill the planet with Jews, not unless we take it as a command to convert billions to our faith. It must mean something else.

"When the mitzvah changed into one for Jews only, the meaning of 'ha-aretz', the earth, also evolved. Fill *Ha-Aretz* becomes a commandment to fill Eretz Yisrael, the Land of Israel, with Jews."

At this point, Nachum paused to drink from a glass of water. It gave him the opportunity to track the reaction of all those sages of Torah present. To Nachum, it appeared that they followed his reasoning, and positively so. He put down his glass and carried on.

"I have a critical, crucial question for you. Why does the traditional mitzvah ignore the last part of the verse? *V'chivshuha ur'du* – after being bidden to be fruitful and multiply and fill the Land, we are told to subdue it and have dominion over it. What happened to those last two words? Are they forgotten?

"Rashi makes *V'chivshuha* into a command to 'subdue *her*,' that is, the husband should propitiate his wife to incline her toward lovemaking. Today's biblical scholars translate it as 'subdue it,' that is, subdue the earth. We have paid little attention to these two final commands because when the mitzvah originated, the Land stood virtually empty of Jews. Today the seven million Jews inside Israel probably number twice as many as in the height of our ancient days.

"The latter part of the verse may have gone unheeded because of high infant and young adult mortality. Large families provided a survival mechanism. But now? When people have two children, those children will likely live, and father and mother will have fulfilled their Jewish obligation. They'll also be able to feed and educate them much better than the seven kids of the typical Haredi family, and after two children, a mother can return to work to help support her family.

"With around 60% of Haredim living below the poverty line, plainly the current practices of Haredi and Hasidic Jews breed destitution. Please show me where in the Torah, written or oral, a law requires poverty and glorifies it over sufficiency.

"*V'chivshuha* – This command challenges us to take the measure of our accomplishment. Have we subdued the Land? Areas in the north of Israel could easily accept more population, especially if we include the Golan. Do you have Hasidim ready to move there? What about Israel's Negev desert, a harsh, hot, unforgiving environment and unlikely to be well-settled for a long time, except perhaps for purposes of agriculture or natural resources. Are we developing many Haredi farmers?

"Central Israel? We devour good farmland for housing and build apartment blocks on virtually every available hillside in central Israel, destroying a natural environment we cherish. People cannot afford housing in such an intensely settled area.

"How much more population the triangle from Yerushalayim to Tel Aviv to Haifa can take, I don't know, but I say that *'v'chivshuha'* is modified by *'ur'du'*, 'have dominion.' The proper exercise of dominion requires consultation. We need to consult demographers and ecologists to learn what is healthy for this land of ours for the fish, the birds, the animals, and us, too – every living thing in the Land, because we want our children and their children to inhabit *Ha-Aretz* in a wholesome and productive Jewish environment. God gave us this little piece of earth, this Land of Israel to manage it, and if we spoil Israel, who will set it right? As the Midrash says, 'Take heed not to corrupt and destroy My universe.'[53]

"In regard to having to produce a male and a female, or even two males, in an age when parents can select the gender of their child, we need to oppose that option. Parents must accept the children that God gives them. My colleagues, if we do not play the gender selection game, for every family with two girls, some other family will have two boys, and it will all even out in the end. Because China's government permitted parents only one child, families constantly selected a boy, and China developed a shortage of females. We Jews dare not come to such a situation. If we allow nature to take its course, the number of boys and girls will be nearly 50/50, the goal of Beit Hillel's dictum. Let's talk about the balance of the sexes within the family of all Israel, not within a single family.

"If you argue that every birth hastens the messiah, I have to ask, how many souls are in the treasury of souls? One tradition teaches that an infinite number resides there. Since the mashiach will not come until the last soul leaves the treasury, mashiach will never come because infinity means no end to the number. Why promote this ancient and unprovable idea? Anyway, we have better ways to bring the mashiach that do much more for the world, ways like repentance, deeds of love and kindness, and tzedakah.

"My Borisover Hasidim can have as many children as they like, but I intend to inquire of Israel's experts, and if they advise that we have, indeed, subdued the land, and the proper management of the country now requires smaller families for the long haul, I am prepared to advocate that Borisover Hasidim consider limiting their family size to two offspring, and we'll provide the means for them to do so within halacha."

The Yazuv Zov arose from his seat, a nasty scowl written across his face. "The meaning of Maimonides' 212th commandment of the Torah has not changed in over 800 years. Who are you to rewrite the work of the greatest mind in Jewish history since Moshe Rabbenu received the Torah on Mt. Sinai?"

"Sir," Nachum said, still standing at the head of the table. "Did you not hear me? I quoted a source much earlier than the Rambam, a source that comes from Sinai itself, the book of Genesis. The text of Genesis speaks for itself, does it not? Why do you avoid the rest of the command? Can you answer that question?"

The Yazuv Zov responded, "Is it not enough that you're prepared to trust vital halachic decisions about family purity to women who, of course, have no ordination, no decades' long study of halacha, no familiarity with the intricacies of *niddah* law? Next these *yoatzot* of yours will want to become rabbis. You are a troubler of Israel with those plans alone. But to rewrite the traditional understanding of the first commandment in the Torah? You are nothing more than an *apikoros*, and as a heretic, you deserve to be put in *cherem*, barred from contact with any responsible, halachically observant Jew. Certainly, we rabbis should not have anything to do with you, nor with your Hasidim!"

The other rabbis present held their peace. Some nodded their heads silently. No one contradicted the Yazuv Zov.

"What is it you intend to do about your threats, Rabbi Gruber?" Nachum demanded.

"I intend to call a press conference for the Fast of Esther, tomorrow morning at my yeshiva after services. The Jewish press corps will be invited to hear my condemnation of you, and after the press conference, I'll form a beth din to meet after Purim. We'll deal with your *apikorsus*. We must stop you before your heresy threatens the whole body of Torah."

Nachum stared the Yazuv Zov down. "Do as you please, Rabbi Gruber. But if you call a press conference, you'll have violated our agreement to hold this meeting privately. Why do you not keep your word? And will you air matters of sexuality in public? That is not seemly, sir, and precisely the reason why we made this gathering private.

"As to my interpretation of 'be fruitful and multiply,' you know that you cannot make or retain a law which Israel finds impossible to observe. So, Rabbi Gruber, we'll see whether our people will ultimately follow your interpretation or mine."

"Don't worry about the folk, *Mister* Steinitz," the Yazuv Zov sneered contemptuously. "Worry about where Borisov will find its next Rebbe. Worry about whether the Borisovers will be any more acceptable than," the Yazuv Zov spat profusely upon the table, "than Reform Jews." And with those stinging words, the Yazuv Zov dashed from the room, slamming the door on the way out of the house.

The other rabbis present said nothing to Nachum. They quietly gathered their papers and departed without a thank you or a good-bye. Unable to look Nachum in the face, they shuffled head-down as a group through the dining room into the vestibule and out the door.

Nachum knocked on the door of Dina's personal home office and opened it. He kissed the mezuzah and spoke from the room's verge, "Dina, what happened today, it's a tragedy. Things could not have gone more badly. The Yazuv Zov condemned the *yoatzot*, condemned my Torah interpretation of *p'ru ur'vu*. Tomorrow he's calling a press conference to destroy my reputation. He plans to put me in *cherem*, along with all the Borisovers."

Dina arose from her desk chair and wrapped her arms around her husband, pulling him tightly to her. "He'll do what he has to do, Nachum," she whispered. "Now you do what you must. Call the Director. Go up Azza Street to the Kings Hotel, use a pay phone, and call the Director. Do it now."

Nachum kissed his wife and left the house for the Kings Hotel, where he sequestered himself at a pay phone in a corner as far from the lobby as possible. He called the number the Director gave him, and after a long series of rings, he heard simply, "What is it?"

Quickly Nachum explained what transpired at the conference.

"Who is threatening to destroy you?"

"The Yazuv Zov."

"What's his real name?" the Director demanded impatiently.

"Rabbi Yosef Gruber."

"He's the mikveh expert, right, the one all the women have to turn to regarding . . . you know."

"*Me'ah achuz*. The one you told me to invite."

"Not to worry. We've gotten very close to him, and he's acting in character. Attend his press conference yourself. You might learn something. Seriously – do it." The Director clicked off abruptly.

CHAPTER TWENTY-EIGHT

The Fast of Esther, 13 Adar 5783 – Monday, 6 March 2023

Nachum Aviam Steinitz, the Borisover Rebbe, occupied a bench at the Yazuv Zov's synagogue. All present recognized him, and no one would sit near him. The morning prayers went pro forma.

Everyone but Nachum seemed to know the next destination, downstairs to a reception hall where no food was served on account of the fast, and seats were arranged in a semi-circle around a podium with a microphone attached. Reporters already awaited the Yazuv Zov and his announcement. It wasn't a large crowd. What great announcement could a Torah authority on menstruation and birth control make at this point? The Voice of Israel and the *Jerusalem Post* were there, as were *Arutz Sheva* and *Ma'ariv. Yated Ne'eman,* the Haredi journal, had a presence, along with some neighborhood giveaway news sheets serving Orthodox areas. The Yazuv Zov planned it that way, having no real use for the general press but wanting to make at least some splash outside his usual arena.

A number of police were also present. Nachum thought them unnecessary, but maybe the Yazuv Zov feared that Borisovers would attend with the intention to riot and attack him for his statements and planned excommunication of their Rebbe and all his Hasidim. Nachum, however, hadn't told anybody about the meeting. Wasn't confidentiality the meeting's original premise?

After a few minutes, the Yazuv Zov appeared and strode to the podium. He blew into the mic, found it in operating condition, and began.

"Yesterday I attended a meeting held at the home of the Borisover Rebbe, Nachum Steinitz. At the meeting, that man discussed his plans to teach women how to help other women with problems related to *taharat hamishpacha* and to provide classes for these *yoatzot* so that they might know more about halacha, becoming women counselors to advise other women on matters which require reference to a rabbi."

Nachum knew that wasn't precisely what he'd said. The Yazuv Zov skipped the part about the supervisory panel and about teaching the *yoatzot* to refer difficult problems to rabbis, while keeping the identity of the inquiring woman private.

"My thirty years of study and experience tell me that I must condemn this elevation of women into an area of Torah which requires rabbinical knowledge. But it gets worse. The Borisover Rebbe spoke of a new understanding of the mitzvah of *p'ru ur'vu* which would lead the Torah True observant family to limit family size to two children only, two children regardless of sex, and which might also lead to use of halachically unacceptable methods of birth control in order to accomplish this unholy goal."

Nachum noted that the Yazuv Zov once again skipped important parts of his presentation and made his birth control statement seem extra controversial. The man played fast and loose with his words.

The Yazuv Zov went on. "The Rebbe believes he defends our women of valor, our observant Jewish women. He believes he is sensitive to women's needs and their privacy. He believes he is opening doors for women to participate more quickly and readily in the society of Ha-Aretz. In fact, his proffered changes offend religious Jewish women and the Torah. We must react against anyone who disrespects the role of women in our Torah observant society. We must levy sanctions against a man who would embarrass and destroy women's true role in our unique Jewish world. We must also sanction the group that affords such an *apikoros*, such a heretic, the reins of leadership. Therefore, today I . . ."

A captain of the national police stepped into the circle and stood immediately in front of the Yazuv Zov.

"Rabbi Yosef Gruber, I have a warrant for your arrest."

The Yazuv Zov looked shocked and befuddled. "What are you talking about? I'm about to conclude an important press conference here. What could I possibly have done to deserve this ill treatment?"

In sotto voce the captain of police said simply, "I don't want to embarrass you any further. Come with me now, and we'll lay out the charges at the station."

"No!" the Yazuv Zov shouted. "Do you know who I am? Do you know what I do? Who do you think you are?"

"I do know who you are. You're a big-time expert rabbi on mikvehs and such. And I know what you do. You set up small secret cameras in all the mikvehs you control, and you masturbate while watching the pictures of naked women stripping for the mikveh. That's what you do. Who do I think I am? I'm the captain of the police who is arresting you for years of violations of the sacred privacy of women. You're a voyeur hiding behind a veil of halacha, and you're coming with me."

With practiced effortlessness, the captain of police grabbed one wrist of the Yazuv Zov, slapped a handcuff on it, whirled the rabbi 180° around and captured his other wrist. Two bulky police officers seized the Yazuv Zov by either elbow and escorted him from the hall, and as they did so, the captain of police announced officiously, "This press conference is over. If you want more news, the arraignment of Rabbi Gruber will be this afternoon."

The press scurried out to file their stories.

"As water" (Gen. 49:4): Our rabbis said, You have sinned through water [semen]; so let the one who was drawn from the water, Moses, come and bring you near to God. As water is poured from place to place, so have your sins been expiated through My depriving you of your distinction and privilege.[54]

And all this came to pass at the time of year when Jews drink in excess and children parade through the streets in costume, when Esther is cheered and Haman is jeered, that is, Purim. The plot which the wicked Yazuv Zov hatched to destroy the innocent Rebbe and to continue the subjugation of the women of Israel was exposed at the hand of the Israeli police in a fortuitous manner, for close are the relations of the police to Shin Bet. The Yazuv Zov, indicted for untold counts of video voyeurism, a type of sexual assault, dwelt at home on bail, but so ashamed was he of his sinful acts that he did not depart from his home to celebrate Shushan Purim in Jerusalem. He marked the day with excessive drink, just as he also marked many another day thereafter. Later, after his trial, conviction, and a sentence of ten years in prison, no one ever again referred to him by the name of his book, the Yazuv Zov, though the strictest *niddah* decisors still refer to their private copies of his work to this day. They abominate his name but they love his Torah. Haredi libraries, however, removed his book from their shelves.

What of the other fourteen rabbis, those who slunk wordlessly from the Steinitz residence when the Yazuv Zov brazenly attacked the Borisover? One rabbi called Nachum to say he disagreed strongly with Nachum's approach, but he disagreed even more vehemently with the actions of the Yazuv Zov at the Borisover residence and thereafter, and certainly he rejected the disgusting voyeurism of the *niddah* expert. Anyway, the caller did not want to question how Nachum led his Hasidim. That was not his business.

Another rabbi from the conference, Asher Atsbani, called in a timid and fearful voice to offer his belatedly considered assessment that Nachum made a breakthrough interpretation of the Torah, but that Atsbani himself did not have the chutzpah to teach it at his yeshiva lest it destroy his influence in the eyes of rabbis whom he could see over his right shoulder. Still, someday he might speak out.

The rest of those rabbis said nothing, did nothing, acted as if the event never occurred.

The Borisover Rebbe, who dared to make his interpretation by a classical rabbinic method, associating nearby commanding words of the Torah to an already existent traditional mitzvah, *p'ru ur'vu*, caused a stirring of independence among the female population encamped with the Black Hats. The streets of Mea Shearim, B'nei B'rak, and elsewhere buzzed with news that an important rabbi, Nachum Steinitz, the Borisover Rebbe, advocated his discovery that the Torah actually foresaw conditions calling for smaller family sizes, though he had not officially declared it. Many of those women heard this as permission to visit secular doctors in secrecy, obtaining a prescription for the Pill. Many others began covertly to ask questions of *yoatzot* from the *Dati Leumi* side of Orthodoxy. Many more called their Borisover friends to learn when the Hasidim foresaw the launch of their female halacha counselors. They were told to wait until Yom Yerushalayim 5783, not far off.

Rebbe Nachum, for his part, assembled a group of scholars from Israel's finest universities. What kind of scholars? Orthodox scientists, experts in the geography, the climate, the flora, the fauna, the demography of Israel. The Rebbe wanted to know, have we subdued the Land? And if not all the Land, what part has indeed been subdued so that we must learn to manage it before we destroy it. And how do we manage ourselves appropriately to do so? To Nachum the questions cried out for answers that came not only from ecology, but from an understanding of tradition. He waited with impatience for his advisory group to report.

Throughout Israel and North America, speaking engagements for Rebbe Nachum poured into Borisov Central. The Rebbe refused them all. The less he appeared, the more he was in demand to be seen. The less he spoke, the more people spoke about him as the key rabbinic actor of Yerushalayim.

Shortly after morning prayers on Yom Yerushalayim, 28 Iyar 5783, that is 19 May 2023, Rebbe Nachum cut the ribbon at the new Borisover headquarters on Jerusalem's King George Street. Closing the block to traffic for the overflow crowd created a bottleneck of unprecedented proportions, with cars and buses lined up all the way to the Talpiyot industrial area. The Plaza, Kings, Waldorf, David's Citadel, Panorama, and King David hotels abounded with Borisovers and their sympathizers. Nachum's Hasidic leadership from Kfar Rachel and from Brooklyn stood at his side to applaud the moment. The city fathers of Yerushalayim were there, too, along with some members of Knesset and the new Israeli president, Yair Johnson, who briefly added congratulatory words. Female city council members and other women sat in a separate position on the stage erected over the broad entryway to the building.

At the ceremony, the Rebbe announced commencement of his *yoatzot* advisor program for women. The press and all women present received cards bearing the new *niddah* advisors' logo and communications co-ordinates. The cards also promised forthcoming inaugurations of model mikveh spa-gyms in Kfar Rachel and New York, with others to open soon thereafter.

The dedication ceremony, gala but unusually brief, honored the right of the city to carry out its own remembrance functions that morning, and besides, it was *Erev Shabbat*.

CHAPTER TWENTY-NINE

Come and listen: Rabbi Eleazer ben Ya'akov said . . . a Jewish court may designate a punishment not derived from Torah and carry it out. Why? Not to transgress the Torah law but to protect it by putting a fence around the Torah.

We've an example of a man in Hellenistic times who rode a horse on Shabbat. The beth din convicted him and stoned him, not because the Torah prescribed that punishment but because the times demanded stringency. There's another example of a man who had sex with his wife under a fig tree, and they brought him to a beth din, which flogged him, not because the Torah prescribed that punishment, but because the times demanded it.

The severity of a punishment may differ from Torah law as an extraordinary measure to curb lawlessness.[55]

2 Iyar 5783 – Sunday, 23 April 2023

When the prime minister of Israel chose Yair Johnson, son of Sender and Michaela, to be president, the public breathed a great sigh of relief. Johnson's family came from Sweden before the Six Day War and went immediately to Kibbutz 'Idit in the Jezreel Valley, where later Yair was born. He grew up watching the kibbutz movement decline in power and success, so after *Tsahal*, Hebrew University, and a respected master's degree in political science from Washington, D.C.'s Georgetown University, he became active in the Likud, promoting Israeli capitalism. A politician through and through, ever near the top of the electoral list of his party, ever serving in Knesset, Johnson knew all the names and personalities of those who mattered to Israel's present and future, and he knew how to treat the greats of the past.

As Israel's ambassador to the United Nations, his barbed speeches clothed in wooly eloquence navigated Israel through often choppy and sometimes stormy seas of international relations. Coming home after a number of successful years at the U.N., he briefly served as chair of the executive committee of the largest Jewish charitable organization, JAFI, the Jewish Agency for Israel.

When the prime minister put forward Johnson's name for president of the State of Israel, Knesset approved his appointment with hardly a debate in committee or on the floor of the parliament. After the foolish, arrogant, and oafish egotism of Liron Megiddo, the entire nation felt that a scion of the midnight sun had come to shine on them for their every season. At last they had a president whose feet were on the ground and whose head understood the craziness of Israel's political life well enough to avoid its pitfalls and to exploit its possibilities for the general welfare.

As a corollary to the accession of Johnson to the presidency, most newspapers mined their files for biographical material already prepared. They proceeded to fill pages with photos of the new president during his illustrious career, scattering details of his long life of public service throughout their articles. They featured pictures of the new president greeting the crowds at Yom Ha'Atsma'ut Independence Day parades. *Haaretz* did much the same, but also took the time to assign Dov Kimberg to examine the record of the new president's work more carefully.

Typical among top journalists, Kimberg began every major story as a cynic. His ruling precept might be stated as, "T'ain't no one that good." He believed that everyone filed something under a heavy rock, and no way did they want that information uncovered. He imagined himself the lever that could uplift the stone and simultaneously remove and view the hidden dossier.

The reporter pored through years of Knesset records, checking on which committees Johnson sat, listing major contracts that arose during his tenure on those committees, looking through personal data open to view – revelatory statements meant to demonstrate that Johnson complied with Israeli tax laws, for example. After a week of interviews and backtracking through years of public records, Kimberg conceded to himself that perhaps Johnson was the real thing, an honest public servant. The reporter went back to his boss to say that Johnson's trail never yielded much worth pursuing, and maybe the country at last could claim a president it more than deserved. His boss agreed that if Kimberg couldn't find anything at all in a week of hard digging, he wasn't likely to unearth a story for the paper.

"Tell you what," Kimberg's editor said, "Think of some angles that don't leave a trail. Maybe one of those unmarked paths will actually lead you to a find. Let me know in a couple of days."

Dov Kimberg drove out to Savyon, where Johnson owned a house. Savyon, a suburb at the top of the mark, boasts homes that look like they belong in America's finest neighborhoods. Situated on large lots, they're often difficult to see, hidden behind fences covered with greenery. You might think you were in Scottsdale, but for the Tel Aviv humidity creeping uphill. The reporter supposed that a high-ranking politician could own a place in Savyon after decades in Knesset. Still, it would be a reach, a long reach. Maybe a reach that would reveal one of those latent trails.

Kimberg didn't expect the neighbors to be talkative. Probably all the owners of large homes in Savyon wanted their privacy and gave each other the same courtesy. At least he'd get a sense of the president's taste. That might be worth a different article, or material to hand over to the Israel real estate editor.

The house was easy enough to find. You almost didn't need an address – just drive around Savyon until you came across a place crawling with guards. Kimberg didn't think they'd suffer his driving twice around the block, so with journalistic aplomb, he parked his car directly in front, pulled out his camera, his ID, his business card, and walked over to the driveway. Before he got there, a guard accosted him.

"It's forbidden to park here," he stated, glowering at the reporter.

"I'm from *Haaretz*. We're doing a story on President Johnson's life. I want to get a picture of his house, just the outside." He handed the guard all his credentials. The fellow grabbed them, scanned the words and phoned his supervisor, repeating the office telephone number to the person on the other end of the line.

"Just a minute," the guard said. After a short wait, Kimberg got the go-ahead for two quick camera shots of the house from the point where street and driveway meet.

"Thanks," the reporter said, snapped his photos, returned to his car, and drove away.

At the office, Dov Kimberg loaded the photographs onto his computer to view them with the large screen at his desk. Elegant house: large, two stories, white stucco and glass, imposing entry, all in a kind of re-imagined Bauhaus style, very Tel Aviv, but much bigger than anyone could afford inside Tel Aviv's crowded city limits. The home presented itself as an expansive property of impressive design, certainly worthy of the president of Israel. But it wasn't government property: it belonged to Yair Johnson. How did he come to purchase it?

Civic records were open to the public, and Kimberg did the legwork to uncover them. After collecting all the records on paper that he wanted, he laid them across his desk, the picture of the house still on his computer screen, the picture of a costly residence paid for by a long-term mortgage in US dollars. Over the years of the mortgage, the new Israeli shekel, in circulation since 1986, grew in value against the dollar, which made it cheaper to pay off the loan. Johnson did a lot of speaking abroad, and those fees could help retire the mortgage, too. But a number of building permits appeared in the records, as well: general improvements, a swimming pool, kitchen upgrade, bathroom re-dos, two additions toward the back of the place, and they added cost.

Then it struck Kimberg that maybe Johnson owned other properties. With all those years in Knesset, wouldn't Jerusalem be a likely locale, and maybe a country home? As he prepared to do another computer search centered on those ideas, he noticed on the screen a pile of construction material at the far end of the drive, nothing huge, but a sign of some work to come. Using his mouse, he zoomed in on the material. He saw labels, but he couldn't make them out. He downloaded his two photos to a USB stick and took the stick up to the photo lab.

"I've got a picture here I'd like you to blow up for me," he told the woman in charge. She loaded the photographs onto her computer, split screen.

"What do you need?" she asked.

"See that pile of stuff at the end of the driveway? I want to read the labels, find out where they originated, where they were sent, what company brought them to Savyon, whatever you can discover."

She said, "That'll be tough, but I've got some strong enhancements built into my computer for this sort of problem. Let's see." She centered on what looked like the clearest label and magnified it, then hit a couple of function keys, and the letters became legible. "Kadima Construction Co., Caesarea. That's who received the goods. They came from . . . let me add magnification . . . from Akko Building Materials Co."

"Can you read any more?"

"I'll try. I'll send you a text with the answers," she said.

Kimberg thanked her and returned to his desk, where he began to research the projects for which Kadima Construction had filed permits. Currently they were building a condo in the vicinity of Hashalom train station in Tel Aviv. He remembered the controversy over the land use permit. It took four years to clear it through two city councils – pretty quick, actually. He punched in some data and searched it.

Johnson endorsed the project. What else belonging to Kadima Construction did he endorse?

It turned out that Johnson's list of endorsements for Kadima projects went back many years. How many years? Kimberg checked the dates of the Savyon building permits and pursued those as a base for his research. Every major venture started by Kadima coincided with home improvements for Johnson. His only evidence, which was, after all, tangential and circumstantial, remained the label on the supplies sitting in Savyon. For all he knew, whoever was working on the Johnson home bought the supplies from Kadima, overstock that the firm didn't need. Kadima's name could be found on none of the permits over the years.

A text arrived from the photo lab with nothing to add. He delved further into the construction permits. The contractors seemed to be individual workers, but the work required certain specialties: plumbing, heating, air conditioning, electrical. Where were the registration numbers of the professionals? He found them at the end of the form and traced the names that corresponded with the numbers. None of the individuals who were the supposed contractors came up: only Kadima Construction. The names on the permits represented employees of Kadima, not freelance builders. Kadima did all the work in the past, probably was doing some small job even now, and the reporter suspected there would be no bills to show. The construction company received its payment in Johnson's aid and endorsements, and all contracts were probably verbal.

Kimberg searched for other real estate that Johnson might own. He turned up one in Jerusalem, one in the Galilee. Kadima worked on the Johnson pied-a-terre in the German Colony of Jerusalem, as well as on the family's country home high in the Galil, which appeared to have been built completely by Kadima at a massive discount. Johnson spent just enough to show that he paid something for it. Once again renovations or new construction coincided with the timing of projects approved for Kadima.

Kimberg visited his editor and laid the whole story before him.

"Are you ready to publish on the Johnson real estate connection to Kadima Construction?" Kimberg asked.

The editor said, "I'm ready to be the first to publish the story, but not yet ready to say 'go'. We have a bunch of 'in connection withs' right now. What can we say? It appears that the president's house in Savyon had an addition built in connection with construction of La Tour de la Plage in Netanya. It appears that the president remodeled his pied-a-terre in Jerusalem in connection with the Har Ka'ur project. It appears that the president built his house in the Galil in connection with Haifa Landing Condos. We'd have to ask Mr. President for the receipts, the checks, some proof of paid purchase, and since, with one exception, we have none to show, he'd blow us off and deny, deny, deny. He'd say, 'The head of Kadima is just an old friend of mine. Can't a man have friends in the business world?' Anyway, he knows he's in a position of impunity.

"The workers will offer nothing to help us. They want to keep their jobs. We'll write a fussbudget editorial about the whole thing, make a stink, and people would forget it the next day. Or they'll say, that's Israel. I think we need to go quietly to the Israel Attorney General with what we've found and blow the whistle. The AG's query gets a response. His summons must be answered. You've given me what we need to push this along, and it's commendable work. Write the story up to the moment and save it. There'll be a new assignment for you tomorrow. But don't worry. *Haaretz* has the ear of the attorney general. I can talk to him."

Secure in his righteousness, Kimberg's editor stood before the attorney general's investigator like a prophet. He laid bare the sins of President Johnson of Israel. In turn, the investigator, like a judge on the bench, subpoenaed the president's testimony, demanding an account for the questionable connections.

The president acted like the biblical Samuel, both judge and prophet. He did not wait for the privacy of a courtroom or a commission hearing to make public his defense before all Israel. He turned the questioning around: "Here I am. Testify against me before our people. Whose money have I taken? Whose palm have I greased? Whom have I defrauded? Whom have I oppressed? From whose hand have I received any bribe which might blind my eyes? Tell me, and I'll make it right."

The polls vindicated the president, which led him to claim, "The people are my witnesses today. They hold me guiltless."[56]

Only then did Dov Kimberg publish his damning research in *Haaretz.* Thereafter the attorney general's office confronted Yair Johnson for an explanation of his costly home improvements. Despite his impunity in office, the president could no longer avoid the judgment of the nation.

Responding to the president's public self-defense, the attorney general came before the nation to make his case. He did not tip his hand until the end of the broadcast, when he produced two retired workers sent by Kadima Construction years before to work on the president's Savyon home. They testified that Kadima employed them, Kadima paid them, and to Kadima alone they reported. Kadima peeled them away from a major project, quietly using the company's supplies to improve the Johnson home.

The prime minister sat with the president to review his violations of trust, and finally to compel his resignation. Since the president cannot be prosecuted for any crime while in office, the process of justice required the resignation as an essential step. Johnson, red-faced and ashamed, vacated his office, and once again the Israeli public saw the acid of dishonor eat through the veneer of both popularity and public service that covered the presidency, only to reveal corruption in high and distinguished places. To some, the demand for Yair Johnson's resignation seemed too harsh. He had no offshore accounts. He took little in comparison to others in governments past and certainly extorted less than he could have. Wasn't bribery the way of the political world?

The prime minister, however, promised more than the resignation of the president. He promised a full and thorough prosecution according to the law, and because Johnson was the second president to fall in less than six months, a hard-nosed court made an example of him, sentencing him far longer than anyone expected: ten years. But he was, after all, the president of Israel, and many said, he should have known better. Many others said, this will put an end to shenanigans in high places. Still others said, he'll be out in five or less. And all agreed, the State of Israel faced a staggering ethical crisis.

Why do you think your way is hidden? Have you not known and heard? Do not pervert justice or show partiality. Do not accept a bribe, for a bribe blinds the eyes of the wise and twists the words of the innocent. Follow justice and justice alone, so that you may live and possess the land the Eternal is giving you.[57]

CHAPTER THIRTY

Rabbi Ishmael son of Rabbi Yochanan ben Beroka said: the one who learns in order to teach should be afforded enough means to learn and to teach. The one who learns in order to practice should be afforded sufficient means to learn, to teach, to observe, and to practice. Rabbi Zadok said: Do not make the words of the Torah a crown by which to exalt yourself, nor a tool with which to earn a living.[58]

23 Iyar 5783 – Sunday, 14 May 2023

One week after Yair Johnson resigned the presidency, Nachum Aviam Steinitz, the Borisover Rebbe, called a press conference in Kfar Rachel. He teased the press with a promise of unprecedented changes to the world of Borisover yeshivas. A few journalists attended, mostly from the *Dati*, the Modern Orthodox religious side because the topic would probably not magnetize the attention of the secular masses.

Nachum ascended the podium in full Borisover Shabbat dress. He wanted photographic impact as well as verbal, and the fur *shtreiml* worn in the midst of summer certainly created a photographic attention-getter. Despite feeling overheated, he smiled at the small group and spoke.

"My friends, we meet in Kfar Rachel, a distinct part of the State of Israel because it is home to so many Borisover Hasidim. Our yeshiva, our adult *kollel*, our schooling for young children – Israelis consider them among the nation's finest. We intend to maintain their integrity, but we also intend to maintain the integrity of the Jewish nation where we live.

"During the last two years, we have quietly raised funds to bring about important adjustments to our requirements regarding the education of older youth and adults. In the coming months, you will see the opening of the Rebbe Emanuel Davidson Technical School. Rebbe Emanuel studied engineering and knew how to apply its principles to everyday life. As Rebbe, he always possessed a practical bent. The Rebbe Emanuel Davidson Technical School will teach the trades and will graduate Hasidim as welders, electricians, plumbers, carpenters, cabinet makers, auto repair people, but also as website builders, programmers, computer and cell phone installers and repairers, and the like. I must clearly state that we are tapping the proven skills and benevolence of ORT Israel to help us with this exciting project. We shall borrow their extensive experience in the operation of technical schools.

"Why create the Rebbe Emanuel Davidson Technical School? In the next few years, standards for entry into our yeshivas and our *kollel* will stiffen. No one will study rabbinics and halacha who is not concurrently either learning a trade or attending university, practicing a trade or working a job, or demonstrating a wholehearted attempt to find employment. Toward the latter end, we plan to expand the employment office in Kfar Rachel. Please note: We shall expect all our students to serve in *Tsahal* like any other Israeli, so that high school graduates from Kfar Rachel and other Borisover schools will not begin their technical or university studies until after their army days or after other recognized public benevolent service equivalent. We'll exempt those unemployable because of disabilities, but we'll rely on the welfare bureau to certify them.

"What about women? Women, too, will be expected to serve in the army in order to gain later entrance into our teachers' and other study programs for women. We'll expect unmarried women and married women without very young children to learn an employable trade or skill or to attend university. Our training programs will offer day care, as well.

"Why are we doing all this? My first reason resides in Mishnah *Avot* chapter 4, mishnah 5. 'The one who learns in order to teach should be afforded enough money to learn and to teach.' For those who want to become teachers in our schools, provided they acquire marketable skills, we plan to support them in their studies until graduation, along with the usual state aid.

"If a person is only studying Torah for its own sake, *kol hakavod*, we honor him or her. Their learning is for the sake of Heaven. But we bring another part of the verse to bear upon such a person: do not make the Torah a spade to dig with. As Rabbi Zadok said in the Mishnah, don't use the Torah as a way to make a living, a reason to draw welfare checks. Hillel gathered wood, Hiyya was a carpenter, Shmuel of Talmudic fame dealt in silk, Maimonides served as physician to the Sultan Saladin. Like our rabbis of old, those who want to learn, must also have a trade, a craft, a profession, or a job.

"Regarding those who want to learn in order to teach, observe, and practice: we take that to mean that they wish to teach by their *modus vivendi*, by letting their very way of life demonstrate to the world the goodness and worthiness of the Torah's truths. Because they want to make Torah felt in the world, they must work in the world, hold a job, and be visible to Israeli society, studying in their spare time. For these reasons we have established our Technical School and changed our study requirements.

"There is another important reason. Many among the Haredi community wear their black hats like a crown, exalting themselves because they spend their lives in holiness, learning Torah. The Mishnah teaches us not to think so egotistically. Because of that prideful attitude among Haredim in Israel, many receive public assistance, and only 55% of males work, with a loss of billions of shekels to our economy. They believe that a 45% rate of unemployment is fitting and proper for the sake of Torah. We do not. We agree with the Torah, 'By the sweat of your brow shall you eat bread' (Gen. 3:19). We agree with Rabbi Eleazar ben Azariah,[59] *Im ein kemach, ein Torah*. If there is no bread, there is no Torah.' We hold with Rabbi Ishmael in the Talmud[60] that study of Torah must be combined with a worldly occupation. The Borisover Hasidim want to bring the ultra-Orthodox level of employment up to the same level as the general public's.

"Why must we choose one commitment over another: more Torah, less work; or more work, less Torah? Let word go forth from Kfar Rachel that Borisovers are contributors, not takers; taxpayers, not welfare recipients. We want the weekly pride of a paycheck to become a major part of Hasidic and Haredi life. We are willing to work as hard as we study. Indeed, let it be said of us that we study Torah as hard as we work. *Im ein Torah, ein kemach*. If Torah is lacking, what good is income? *Tsricha!* Both are necessary in equal share. Israel and the whole Jewish people will be the better for our initiative, better physically, better spiritually."

Nachum fielded questions, stayed on message, brought the reporters to view the site where the Rebbe Emanuel Davidson Technical School was arising, and showed them large billboard drawings of various workshops and training laboratories. The religious press greeted the news on back pages with tiny write-ups, not wishing to disturb status quo. The *Jerusalem Post* and *Yisrael Hayom*, however, put the news on the front page, which caused other dailies to pay attention. They called Borisover Central in Jerusalem for press releases and copies of the Rebbe's speech, and they put the news in their inside front pages two days after the event took place. Kol Yisrael gave it a few seconds on the news in the evening. *Arutz Sheva* put it at the top of the website's opening page. *Yated Ne'eman*, Haredi daily, took the advice of their rabbi advisors and did not report it.

The American press, however, ballyhooed the move, calling it a breakthrough in ultra-Orthodox practice in Israel which would return Haredi Jews to the days when the State of Israel began, a time when nearly every Black Hat worked. The amount of attention the Borisover Rebbe's robust move achieved in America prompted the Israeli press to take a second look at his policy change. The dailies used feature articles, exposing the public more thoroughly to the plan and showering the Borisover Rebbe with editorial praise for his actions to "normalize" life among his Hasidim. In opinion polls, Nachum Steinitz began to receive acknowledgement from the public as the man to watch in Israel, the Rebbe who loved labor and looked after women's rights and needs among his flock.

Then Nachum gained permission from the military to wear his old Israeli reservist's uniform for interviews and at the induction centers where his first new Borisover draftees, men and women, received their welcome into *Tsahal*. Mercifully, it still fit. His captain's insignia glinted in the sun as he posed for photographers surrounded by a few Hasidim at each location. The Israeli press had never before seen a full-blown Hasidic Rebbe in such uniform, for Nachum never served as a chaplain, but as an everyday soldier, and such were his insignia. Those images of Rebbe Nachum made him the talk of the nation, an overnight sensation, a rebbe with spirituality who played his part in Israel's physical survival.

Leaders of the Hasidic and Haredi camps disagreed with Nachum's stance. First, they condemned him for putting on the uniform, since it required him to abandon "Jewish" clothes. Then they condemned his exclusion of yeshiva students not intent on attaining gainful employment, since study of Torah trumped any other occupation.

In response, Nachum donned his captain's uniform to appear on television for an interview to answer charges that he had abandoned "Jewish" clothes. On Israel Broadcasting Authority's Channel 1 news, Nachum did not mince words.

"As leader of the Borisovers, I'm happy to wear the traditional Rebbe's costume. But let's be clear about Haredi and Hasidic clothing. Lithuanian Haredim simply wear dark suits, white shirts with no tie, kipas and black hats. In the past, they attired themselves in light color suits, too. Their look is, in the main, western. Other Haredi groups wear clothing styles that originated little more than 200 years ago. When we consider the Jewish people's 3800-year history, what's so old about that? In fact, when so-called "Jewish dress" began, you couldn't tell a Haredi Jew from anyone else in the East European street, except for headgear and tzitzit. Similarly, Hasidim wear clothing reminiscent of their early rebbes, widely fashionable 200 years ago. What's so Jewish about that? Probably the fact that Jews assert its Jewishness today.

"Right now, whether my colleagues among the ultra-Orthodox like it or not, I am wearing the most Jewish costume in the world, the uniform of *Tsahal*, which I have received special permission to don again, since my reservist's days are complete. What clothing is more Jewish than this uniform? Those who wear it defend millions of Jews from destruction, from bombs and rockets, from invading attackers and from terrorists within. Those who wear it defend our State of Israel with their lives. I honor them all, past, present, and future. I thank them, and I want my Hasidim to be among them and proudly wear *Tsahal*'s uniform.

"How two-faced it is for some of my colleagues to condemn my wearing of the uniform of *Tsahal* while they accept *Tsahal*'s defense of their families. Some of my co-religionists are anti-Zionist. Some are non-Zionist, yet they live here and accept welfare checks from a government they do not recognize. I challenge them to match our initiative. I challenge them to close their yeshivas to all students insufficiently educated to support themselves or their families. I challenge them to condemn these groups' lack of education for useful trades and lack of secular subjects like mathematics and English, as well – the academic inadequacies that keep their people in poverty. Precisely because Haredi and Hasidic poverty is endemic to our country, I challenge Black Hat leadership to make honest labor the key that opens the door to Torah study, never again to approve handouts from the State of Israel."

The host of the program asked Nachum, "Do you think any of them will pay attention to your challenge?"

"I doubt that their leadership will turn around. But isn't that exactly what *teshuvah* is, turning around in repentance for the errors of the past, changing our ways, walking the right path? The Haredim of Israel in 1948 were largely working people. Only the change in policy encouraged by Ben Gurion, which provided handouts from the government for yeshiva students, altered the situation by incentivizing unemployment. Shortly after his government instituted that giveaway to yeshiva students, Ben Gurion himself did verbal *teshuvah*, regretting the fact. Records at his Sde Boker archive prove it. Now we have a society of welfare dependents who claim to be religious. They have made the Torah their spade to gouge a living, however poor, from the rest of the citizenry. It's not too late for Israel to change, but the day of reckoning is coming soon."

"The day of reckoning?" asked the interviewer.

"Yes, the day when Israel tears itself to pieces over the demands of a minority that grows ever closer towards majority status and requires everyone else to sustain their way of life and to defend them. Exhausted by high taxes, a part of which pays for tens of thousands to have more children and study Talmud, the dwindling non-Haredi majority will amplify their objections to this unfair system. Those with skills who can relocate may do so. The country will not be able to bear such civil strife.

"We are coming to a Yom Kippur moment. *Chatanu*. We have sinned, we who have approved the taking of these handouts, and we who so eagerly took them. And *pashanu*, we have sinned, we who failed to guard carefully the policy of the nation and continually permitted the government to send those payments. That means we're all implicated. National policy must change. If national policy won't change in this regard, at least the Borisover Hasidim will make sure that our group's policy does *teshuvah* and returns to sanity and Jewish tradition regarding the need for gainful labor."

At these words, cheers echoed through the streets of Tel Aviv and Haifa, Rishon Lezion and Modi'in and in every non-Haredi home across the land. The internet and airwaves resounded with the name of Rebbe Nachum, at last a real Israeli Rebbe, even a man worthy of high office, or so said many. And the Haredim, the rest of the Hasidim? Hardly a word. Their tradition prohibited them from watching television.

CHAPTER THIRTY-ONE

As Nachum departed the television studio, a reporter stopped him at the door.

"Excuse me, Rabbi Steinitz." It sounded more like Rab-bah Stah-nitz. Nachum immediately detected an American southern accent.

"Yes?"

"I'm Travis Benson, a reporter for the Arkansas *Quotidian*, the main newspaper in Little Rock. I'm here with a group of evangelical Christians touring Israel – Christian Zionists, all of us. We do our utmost to support Israel through thick and thin. Anyway, our group is staying at a hotel not far from the studio. Flipping through channels in my room I saw you on TV. You've become a highly recognizable face."

"Yes? Well, how can I help you, Mr. Benson?"

"I understand you've just started requiring your followers to serve in the Israeli army in order to continue their Jewish studies. Is that right?" Producing a small notepad and pen, he stood poised to write.

"Yes, that's correct. Jewish oral tradition teaches that those who study Torah should also earn a living, as did our rabbis even at the time of your savior, Jesus."

"That's right," Benson said. "He was a carpenter. Well, we can get a lot of the news about your proposed changes straight from Associated Press, but you're wearing an Israeli army uniform, and I'd like to get some background on that. I think our readers would be fascinated by that human-interest material."

"What would you like to know?"

"Rabbi, what did you do in the army?"

"I held the rank of captain with a small team of specialists serving below me."

"Right, but what did you do?"

"They called us 'tunnel specialists.'"

"Tunnel specialists? What does that mean?"

Nachum didn't expect this encounter with the American press, and he wanted to get home, yet he didn't want to treat the reporter discourteously. He took a deep breath and continued. "We were stationed in the Jerusalem area and ordered to explore for possible tunnels dug for illicit purposes, and if we found them, we were commissioned to destroy them."

"And who would dig these tunnels?"

"Honestly, Mr. Benson, tunnels around Jerusalem might originate with either Arabs or Jews. For example, fanatical Jews who want to rebuild the Temple might construct a tunnel to smuggle explosives under the Dome of the Rock in order to blow it up. The State of Israel recognizes the sanctity of the Dome to Muslims, and we try to protect it. On the other hand, a tunnel might be the product of hostile Arabs attempting to smuggle arms or explosives into a part of the city."

"Did you ever find and destroy any tunnels?"

Nachum paused. Though perhaps a serious omission, no bond of secrecy had ever been imposed upon him. If he answered truthfully, the news could easily stir anger on either side of the divide between Jews and Arabs in Jerusalem. If he dissembled and said no, others who served with him and knew the truth could inform the press and call him a liar. He decided to reveal an instance placed early in his years of service, shaping and downplaying the story as an obscure, old example.

"Mr. Benson, let me tell you a memorable tale from a couple decades ago, at the outset of my military service. We were exploring the east side of the Old City walls, looking for evidence of misbehavior. On the east side you'll find two gates. Of the two, one is open, while the other gate stands totally closed, mortared shut since the time of Saladin. That's the Golden Gate, or what we Jews call the Gates of Mercy or the Gates of Repentance."

"I know about the Golden Gate. Jesus went through it on a donkey."

Nachum waved him off and continued, "Yes, well, down the hill in the area of the Golden Gate and the Muslim cemetery outside it, we found evidence of earth being moved, and we located a hidden tunnel entrance. We excavated inward, and to our surprise, this tunnel's physical location traveled well below the cemetery, well below the currently visible wall and closed gate. As the archeologist Warren reported, another, older gate existed below it, probably from Herod's time. This they used to call the Shushan Gate, and it was once the main entrance to the Temple area. Someone or some group drilled or exploded through the ancient Shushan Gate. The tunnel did not provide easy passage, but I donned a helmet with a light attached and made it through on my *tochas*, leading several members of our group forward to see where it would lead. My compass told me it headed straight for the Dome of the Rock, toward the southwest. At the end of the tunnel, still about 100 meters from the Dome of the Rock, the excavation ended. We found tools abandoned there which we seized and sent for criminal analysis. The police took over the case. We guarded the entrance until we could destroy the tunnel properly the next day, and since then, the area lies under strict camera and electronic surveillance."

"What a story! Rabbi, who built the tunnel?"

"We have no idea."

"Why do you think they were constructing it?"

"Possibly to destroy the Dome of the Rock, possibly to smuggle arms into it and distribute them to the faithful or massacre visitors to the Dome."

"Do you think they were Jews?"

"A handful of Jews are bent on destroying the Dome of the Rock to replace it with what they call a third Temple, but the vast majority of

Israelis condemn them and consider the State of Israel itself, as General Moshe Dayan did, our Third Temple. The tunnel builders could have been Jews, yes, or they could have been Arabs trying to create an international incident and immediately cause a war by arousing the entire Arab world militarily against Israel, falsely portraying the cataclysm of a ruined Dome of the Rock as the work of Israeli Jews. Or, as I said, perhaps they planned to distribute arms or to use them in an attack on visitors to the Dome. No one knows. Since our destruction of the tunnel, the government takes every step to prevent a future calamity emanating from that area. Have I answered all your questions?"

"You sure have, Rabbi. Thank you for your time."

CHAPTER THIRTY-TWO

The following day, Rabbi Cohen, communications assistant to the Rebbe, flashed him an SMS during a time designated as Nachum's study hour. "Shin Bet wants to talk to you."

Nachum put down his Talmud and went to the office door, opened it, put his head out and said, "Give them an appointment whenever they want. Who argues with Shin Bet?"

When the Director of Shin Bet called at the Rebbe's office, Nachum beckoned him in, shook his hand and the two sat at a small table in the corner of the room.

"Coffee, Director?"

"No thanks, Nachum, but we do need to talk. You're a brave man, but you may have put yourself in danger."

"How so?"

"On television you challenged your Haredi colleagues to match Borisov's new standards. With the educational and social changes you're creating in Borisov – requiring *Tsahal*, job training, employment, and so on – someone out there might take umbrage at your challenge, might consider you a *Rodef*, a pursuer upsetting their holy way of life. Remember, that's what Amir considered Yitzhak Rabin, and then he killed him."

Nachum started to play with his *peyot*, curling and uncurling the hair dangling at his ears. "But we are Hasidim, frum Jews, you know? We daven, we study, we do mitzvot down to the nth degree. What could be the complaint? What I said on TV the other day?"

"Exactly. You are the *Rodef* destroying the welfare of the most pietistic Jews in the Land. You condemn them for their most obvious faults, and you've upset many. We see it on the web where they talk to

214 · LEIGH LERNER

one another, and if Black Hats are speaking on the web, it's just the tip of the iceberg. You should worry. *I* should worry."

"Listen, Director, what I said, what we're doing, I believe in its importance. We've raised a ton of money for the new trade school. I've got all my Talmud teachers on side. We'll pay them temporarily, even if classes diminish to nothing while we get the project up to steam. The whole country will soon see how serious we are about positive change."

"You consider it positive. I consider it positive, but Nachum, many Haredi and Hasidim do not. So . . ."

"So I need increased security now?" asked Nachum.

"I wish it weren't true, but yes, you do."

"They're going to have to look like authentic Borisovers. You know that, don't you?"

"We can do it. I'll send some extra people this afternoon. If they need adjustment in their clothing, let them know. We'll keep the new bodyguards on duty until this blows over. But realize, added security is going to limit your travel somewhat."

"That's just it, Director. It's not going to blow over, because I'm not done playing the prophet and challenging our Haredi and Hasidic society. I should receive a report pretty soon from my ecology and demography scientific team. If the scientists say it's necessary, I'll advocate family planning full force. And there'll be more, I'm sure."

"You're a gutsy guy, Nachum. If ever we put into effect the plan you and Dina signed onto years ago, you'd probably be saying these things anyway. More power to you. We'll protect you as long as necessary, so let's talk now about the plan.

"We've just lost two presidents. One acted stupidly. The other acted stupidly and greedily. A president of Israel must model ethical behavior, and the Prime Minister knows it. We can't afford further ethical difficulty in the president's office, and the *Rosh HaMemshalah* is working hard to find a paragon of virtue.

"Nevertheless, who could have predicted this political mess? Like the Americans say, three strikes and you're out: if we lose another president to an ethical brouhaha of any kind, the office itself could be destroyed from lack of public trust. I'm here to put you on notice: make sure your nose is clean, because if the next prexy goes, we're activating the plan."

Nachum's brow furrowed. "After all my chastisements of the Haredi and Hasidim in Israel, do you think the plan is still workable? My colleagues in black often reject me and condemn my words."

"Nachum, hand me a list of your biggest enemies, and I can probably give you a list of their biggest sins, maybe even with photographs. One way to keep fanatics in check is to cut off their *beitzim*, you know what I mean? To do that, we do watchful waiting. We know a lot more than we tell. It's our job."

"I'd hate to use that kind of stuff. We're all human. We all make mistakes."

"Right, Nachum, we all make mistakes, but these guys have power, and when they make mistakes, it affects more lives than their own or their immediate family. And they purport to be pillars of God's society on earth. Don't get me started. Just send me your enemies list. Give me the list via the special number I gave you. Call from a pay phone at the Plaza Hotel across the street. In the meantime, let Dina know that circumstances have altered and we've escalated to a yellow alert. Tell her that we're intensifying the guard on her and the kids on a 'round the clock basis. It may get in the way of their normal, everyday life, but we have to act to protect all of you."

"She'll be OK with the increased security, but since it impacts the children, well, it could be a little tense at home for a while until everyone accustoms themselves."

The Director added, "One more thing. You present yourself on the media with strength. The public recognizes you, and most stand fully in favor of your efforts. You don't need more exposure right now. Take care of Borisov, enjoy your family, think about a trip to the States, think about it seriously. A couple of speeches, a Shabbat in Brooklyn, with R&R to get away from it all. Every Israeli needs an offshore vacation from time to time.

"Anything you need to tell me, Nachum?"

"Me? The matter of my family's security has always been in your bailiwick. Now we can talk more readily – no more meetings at a gas station in Modi'in. You're welcome here anytime. I'll make Rabbi Cohen aware of that fact, and in a few hours he'll see new bodyguards and understand your presence as entirely a matter of safety. As for the news that I'm a disturber of the status quo, it's already in print and on the air. I think that's what brought you here. No, nothing to tell you. Just be well, and keep my family healthy, please. Thank you for your help and concern."

Are not the results of Rebbe Nachum's initiatives written in the annals of Borisov? How Borisov-affiliated women received the right to free membership in a growing chain of exquisitely clean, luxurious mikvehs, all with spas, women's gym, and exercise classes including Pilates and yoga, as well as day care; how the new spas added to the spiritual experience and physical health of Orthodox women; how especially younger women gravitated to them, looking for a wholesome and inspiring experience; how the Borisovers promoted their literature at the mikvehs so that women awaiting their turn for the ritual bath studied the opinions of the Borisover Rebbe regarding key matters of change: recognizing the State of Israel and the need for Haredim to participate in its defense, the importance of Haredi employment, the availability of woman to woman counseling, the Rebbe's Torah interpretation regarding smaller families that he backed with traditional texts and the long-awaited scientific evidence from his council of environmentalists. Indeed, the more women read, the more they pushed their husbands to taste and enter the life of Borisov. The magnitude of the response surprised even Nachum.

The movement toward Borisov put fear in the hearts of other rabbis, and fear produced competition, if not outright liberalization. The timorous Rabbi Asher Atsbani, for example, saw the writing on the wall and discovered his backbone at the same time. Previously, his most audacious decision reaffirmed the right of Jews to dispose of nail clippings in the toilet, opposing strict interpreters who maintained that Jewish law demanded burial of such waste.

Atsbani surprised the halachic world with a major responsum to endorse Rebbe Nachum's interpretation of "be fruitful and multiply," permitting ultra-Orthodox couples to limit family size to two children of either sex.

Despite the efforts of many to retain their followers, Borisover synagogues popped up everywhere like the red cyclamen of the Israeli spring, obtaining ever greater attendance. Their education programs for women filled to capacity and constantly sought ever larger venues. Young husbands followed the wives' initiatives, demanding entry into Borisover yeshivas. Though the requirement to study secular subjects and serve in *Tsahal* at first put them off, one by one, they bent down and listened to their spouse's admonitions, and as the momentum developed, ultra-Orthodox demography slowly began to shift. Employment grew. Army draft numbers rose, and youth service corps ranks started to swell.

It was all because of the women, and because Dina advised and inspired Nachum Aviam Steinitz, the Borisover Rebbe.

CHAPTER THIRTY-THREE

Shim'on Toledano made "start-up" a household term in Israel. After starting up several software companies in Silicon Wadi around Tel Aviv and Herzliya, he turned to Technion University's expertise and began exporting innovative security and graphics chips from Israel. A famous internet search engine purchased two Toledano companies for nine figure amounts.

Committed completely to Israel and its development, Shim'on Toledano encouraged American and European firms to open Israeli branches in order to take advantage of the talent offered between Tel Aviv and Haifa and arising in Jerusalem. Well-known international tech names took their place beside Israeli logos on squat manufacturing plants as well as office towers whose lights burned late into the night with engineers writing code. Featured time and again in Israel's business journal *Globes*, Toledano grew to be known as an original thinker, and despite his non-Yiddish, Moroccan background, journalists couldn't help referring to him as a mensch.

It seemed natural to Toledano to grow businesses, and insofar as possible, never to cast off his employees, regardless of their redundancy. Since he constantly created new initiatives, he regularly transferred to another start-up the capable people whose work became unnecessary in their current position.

Toledano knew how to select the best upper level staff, often former *Tsahal* officers who had commanded others. They, in turn, proved good judges of character. He did not overload his companies or his executives with employees, making sure that operating executives managed about the same number of persons they once commanded in the army. That's how he responded to the Peter Principle, challenging but never overloading a staffer's proven abilities. Anger, impatience, negative thinking – all seemed foreign emotions and attitudes to Shim'on Toledano as he rose in business success.

Late in his career Toledano sold one of his companies, a crucial mobile phone app, for over a billion US dollars. After the shareholders finished dancing in the streets and the executives cashed in their cheaply bought stock and the newspapers grew weary of more articles about Toledano, the start-up master sat at his desk twirling a pen and wondering what next. He had amassed more wealth than any man needed in several lifetimes, provided a living for thousands of Israelis, and played the start-up game so well that his life work provided a living lesson to a few thousand others who were laboriously emulating his management style and his joy in technology. What next for a man in his early sixties?

Toledano called his wife Chava. "I need a break," he said wearily. "I can't see the next step. Let's relax a bit and think about shaping a new vision for tomorrow. What would you like to do?"

Chava said, "I'm ready for a cruise, something slow and easy, no particular destination. Let's pamper ourselves. Why don't we rent a yacht for a week and do some Greek islands?"

He agreed and phoned his agent to arrange for a charter jet to Chania, Crete, where they did a day of touring, then boarded a yacht to go from island to island toward Athens. The azure waters soothed his angst, the slap of the waves against the yacht became a melodious background for contemplation and lovemaking, while the food and wine on board gave both Toledanos the opportunity to draw closer and consider their future. They decided that he needed something new, and she wanted to be at his side as he strode toward that horizon. They listed three options for the course of the coming years and planned to actualize their first choice when the vacation ended.

Upon their return to Tel Aviv, Shim'on Toledano let the prime minister of Israel know that he wanted to see him, and soon. The two met in Jerusalem the following day at the prime minister's residence, where Toledano offered himself as a candidate for the presidency of Israel. Somewhat stunned, the *Rosh HaMemshalah* suggested that the start-up master might become bored in such a ceremonial position.

"I suppose that's possible," Toledano said, "but I don't think so. I can put my talents to good use for Israel here and abroad in a benevolent and formative way. How long since the country made a business person into the president?"

"How long? Never. You're right on that score."

"Don't you think it's about time, especially in light of our reputation as 'Start-up Israel'? As for party affiliation, you know I stand with you. I've backed the party financially for many years. Regardless of your decision, you can count on my continued support. I'm only indicating that we're like-minded politically. Mr. Prime Minister, I can do the job, and do it well. Think it over."

The prime minister reviewed a shortlist of candidates with political party leadership, coalition partners, key citizens whose opinions mattered to him, and with both the Mossad and Shin Bet. Shim'on Toledano emerged from scrutiny as his foremost candidate. Once vetted by Knesset, the appointment came swiftly, greeted with minimal skepticism by a twice-burned public, although perennially anti-business commentators sneered at the choice and fulminated against it.

For Toledano, the presidency of Israel came as a refreshing, invigorating change. Decisions rotated more around his agenda than a balance sheet or the measure of technological competencies. He met people across the Land and from beyond, fulfilled his duties of state easily, and used his executive's reputation as a springboard to improve Israel's commercial status worldwide, all with government approval. His wife Chava relished the change in their lifestyle and the opportunity to entertain somewhat effortlessly due to the enlarged social staff that she enjoyed. Time for family also expanded because the Toledanos held tight rein on their schedule. In many ways, the presidency assumed the character of a busy retirement for the couple.

4 Shevat 5784 – Sunday, 14 January 2024

Seven months into Shim'on Toledano's presidency of the State of Israel, his wife Chava suffered a paralyzing stroke. At Hadassah Hospital in Ein Karem, Chava's physicians administered blood thinners as part of her treatment, but internal bleeding set in, requiring withdrawal of the medication. Then a further cerebral incident occurred, putting Chava into a coma. The president visited her daily together with his adult children, hoping for signs of reawakening. None appeared. In the meantime, Toledano carried forward with his schedule, albeit with a diminution of time for meetings and of his role as a dinner host, which he found an onerous task without his wife's presence.

Chava's absence proved itself a profound void in his life. He missed her wisdom, her joie de vivre, the canny, down-to-earth balance she brought to his personality, and the intimacy they shared both intellectually and physically. He felt his nerves fraying and considered resignation of his newfound national role.

The loss of Chava from what amounted to the president's stage, his official residence in Jerusalem, also caused deterioration in the oversight of housekeeping. Toledano noticed it and asked the staff supervisor to look more carefully after the orderliness of the house and to make a small addition in personnel for that purpose. The supervisor added Valeria Bercovici to the night shift.

A few years before Toledano's accession to the presidency, Valeria Bercovici came to Israel from Moldova. Site of the infamous Kishinev Massacre in 1903, Moldova also saw the tragic destruction of its Jewry during the Shoah. At thirty years of age Valeria joined 75,000 other Moldovan Jews who had made aliyah. After learning Hebrew and entering the job market, she quickly discovered that her lack of university education and her accented speech left only housekeeping and care giving as honest work alternatives.

Valeria made a living in Israel the hard way, working two jobs. As a housekeeper, she began at 8 AM, while her care giving functions lasted from 4:30 to 10 PM. She committed her best efforts to both positions. Employers held her in esteem. Fourteen-hour days stole the youthfulness from her once timeless face, a visage that echoed the warmth of a Fayum portrait, with straight nose, full lips, and large, sad, liquid eyes reflecting an inner thoughtfulness and warmth. She managed to keep her figure, though her work made it more muscular.

On one of her Shabbat days off, Valeria met a sweet man – big, burly, and kindly, a laborer at Machaneh Yehuda Market who hoped someday to have his own food stall. He recognized her suitability as a wife and mother and asked her to marry him. She accepted willingly, partly because she found herself at marrying age with no other prospect. Though unready to set a date, he presented her with a simple engagement ring, a thin band of white gold with a diamond chip that received undeserved adulation from her friends. Valeria knew they admired not the ring, but rather her engagement to be wed.

When Valeria learned of an opening in housekeeping at the president's residence, she applied immediately. Once hired, she quit her old night job, found caregiver work for the daytime, and took up the task of maintaining Israel's president in neat, clean, and elegant style during the evenings. With attention to the minutest detail, she competently completed the simple, unchallenging duties assigned to her.

By knowing the law about a murderer, what can we infer regarding the case of an engaged woman who is raped? It's the other way around: you can learn about the case of a murderer from the case of the betrothed woman. Just as it is legal to save the life of a betrothed woman by doing away with the man attempting to rape her, so we are permitted to dispatch the one attempting murder.[61]

One early evening in March, near the end of dinner hour so as not to inconvenience the president, Valeria entered the presidential chambers to turn down the bed. She needed only to prepare the bed for sleeping, as well as to fulfill a brief schedule of tasks to refresh the room. As she worked, Shim'on Toledano wandered in. He closed the door without noticing Valeria's presence. He clutched a handkerchief and sobbed into it while he sat on the edge of the bed, head bowed. Valeria cleared her throat to gain his attention, excused herself for disturbing his privacy and began to leave. The president looked up with tears in his eyes.

He said, "No, please complete the cleaning as usual."

He wiped his eyes again and watched the fulfillment of her few evening chores, then broke once more into weeping.

She came to the bed to turn down the covers. He continued to sit by the pillows, drying his eyes, blowing his nose.

She asked, "Do you want me to turn down the sheets?"

"Uh, no. That's alright. Sit here a minute," he said, pointing to the foot of the bed, "and tell me about yourself. You're relatively new in the building, and I know nothing about you."

Valeria wasn't sure whether she should follow his lead. He pointed to the foot of the bed again. "Sit," he choked out the words, "Sit and tell me about yourself. It will take my mind off my sorrows."

She sat, leaving some distance between them.

Reading her name tag, he said, "Valeria. You're Russian, right?"

"No," she said, "Moldovan."

"Chisinau?"

"Yes, that's where I'm from. I've been here a few years. Mr. President, there's not much to say. I didn't need to deal with the famous Moldovan anti-Semitism anymore. Israel is more prosperous than Moldova, that's for sure, but either way, it can be a hard life. I work a couple of jobs to make ends meet, and I like working in this place."

"You do good work."

"Thank you. What about you? How are you managing with all the troubles of the nation and your own problems, too?"

He broke into tears once again, sobbing violently.

"Forgive me," he said, his chest heaving. "It's my wife. I'm sure you know. She's in a very bad state, and I've never faced this kind of loss before."

His profound misery, his deep melancholy touched her heart. She found herself unthinkingly moving closer to him and encircling him with her arms, rubbing circles gently on his back, trying to comfort him. At first he continued to shudder while his tears fell on her dress. She could feel the moisture. Then his moaning changed. He kissed her neck, her ears; he muttered, "Oh, Chava."

Valeria tried to pull away. He drew her closer.

"I need you," he said.

She managed to put a few inches between herself and the president, waving her engagement ring before his eyes. "No! Stop!"

Oblivious to her importuning, he carried on. She lifted her hand, and as she did so, quickly she used her thumb to turn the diamond on her ring towards her palm. She whipped her hand against his cheek, dragging the ring across it in a downward motion, letting its jagged facets and pointy mount tear at his face. He began to bleed. When Shim'on Toledano put hand to jowl, he felt the blood – warm, moist, and sticky. When he saw it with his own eyes, his nerves snapped. His wall of calm and kindness, the inner barricade of his composed attitude, crashed down like a building in the midst of demolition. Uncontrollable rage scorched his sangfroid. His innards raged at the wound he'd just suffered, at his wife's pitiable fate, at his lack of Chava's stabilizing presence. He felt overpowered by a fury that demanded physical expression.

Though Valeria's work made her strong, Toledano's regimen of weight lifting made him even stronger, despite his age. Grimacing, he grabbed her by the forearms, leveraged her to the bed, and pinned her with a knee. Then he struck a telling blow to her head, pulled up her dress, ripped off her panties, and raped her. Enervated, he collapsed on top of her.

Valeria used the opportunity to shove him aside. The punch to her head dizzied her. Despite her uncertain steps, she somehow navigated to the door, yanked it open, and escaped into the hall. As she wiped away blinding tears from her eyes, she steadied herself with a hand on the wall that led to the employees' dressing room. There she showered and put on her street clothes. She applied ample make-up to cover the rising black and blue welt on her forehead. She needed time to think. She phoned her supervisor, who had gone home for the night, and excused herself on account of illness.

At home, with her emotions revved over the red line, Valeria sensed the urgency for calm. A warm bath helped. She sat in the tub, at first scrubbing herself over and over. Then she lay quietly and considered her alternatives. If she wanted to prosecute, even this very bath was washing away the evidence of her rape claim. Not so smart. A bump during her work could have caused the black and blue mark on her head. The scratch on the president's face could be evidence of a struggle, or maybe by tomorrow he'd claim he'd cut himself while shaving. Besides, if she blew the whistle, her working days for the government and maybe for anyone else were finished.

The man was in his sixties, she thought, not likely to make her pregnant. If she let the whole thing drop, stayed away from the president's person, and continued to do her work as if nothing happened, she'd have her job, her paycheck, and her benefits as usual. In the future there would be other presidents, but she'd still have her daily work and a future pension. If she took that course of action, she needn't speak to her fiancé about the rape, either. Resolutely she determined to forge ahead under status quo ante.

CHAPTER THIRTY-FOUR

Simeon and Levi are brothers; their swords are weapons of violence. Let my life not be joined to their council; let not my reputation be linked with their faction; for in their anger they slew men . . . (Gen. 49:5-6)

Whenen Valeria missed her period, she fretted a bit, then comforted herself with the fact that she missed periods before, especially when under a lot of tension and working at full tilt. When she missed her second period, the game changed. A pregnancy test proved that she was with child, and it had to be the president's. Her fiancé carefully used a condom when they made love. Besides, with advanced genetic testing she could prove paternity without an invasive test. A little checking on the internet showed that if she gathered ten hairs from the president's bathroom, she'd have enough genetic material to get a profile of his genome within .3% accuracy. When the pregnancy became more advanced, a blood sample from her would also yield information about the baby's genes. She could easily demonstrate genetic heritage.

Once again lolling in the bath, Valeria conceived a plan. The president stood among the wealthiest men in Israel, with a reputation to maintain and a position that required public approval. She must confront the president privately, demand hush money as support for herself and the child, and then she would promise to leave him alone. She could quit her work altogether and live comfortably for the rest of her life, with or without her fiancé, as she chose. Once she determined her course of action, over a period of a week or two she cautiously gathered 20 hairs from the president's sink and shower. Still she waited, letting the president think that nothing was amiss, that she chose not to act, allowing him to slide calmly into life as usual. One night, more than three months into her pregnancy, Valeria withheld her arrival in the president's chambers until she knew he had just entered the room. She walked calmly through the doorway, closed the door, but kept hold of the handle, ready to flee.

Valeria spoke clearly and with sufficient volume to gain attention. "Mr. President, I am pregnant by you. I am going to carry your baby to term, and I'll let the world know that you're the father unless you arrange support payments sufficient to keep both me and my child well-sustained for the rest of our lives. I'll expect an answer tomorrow night."

Immediately she turned heel and darted into the hallway.

Shim'on Toledano paced his room, anger and fear seething in his gut. He could not let this young Moldovan nobody ruin him. He picked up the receiver of his telephone, and immediately an operator responded. "Send Levi Dalfon to my bedroom," Toledano demanded.

Levi Dalfon was the sole bodyguard on the president's staff who had worked continuously for Toledano during the last ten years. All others were state appointed, but in taking on the role of president of Israel, Toledano insisted that he wanted his most trusted security aide to join him. Citing Dalfon's long affiliation with Toledano, his proven efficacy as a bodyguard, and a flawless security check, no one objected.

When Dalfon arrived, he immediately intuited the president's agitated state of mind. "I can tell something's wrong, Shim'on. What's eating at you?"

Toledano turned on his clock radio, upping the volume of some classical music, then whispered in his aide's ear, "Levi, I'm being blackmailed by a chambermaid, Valeria Bercovici. She claims I'm the father of her baby and wants hush money. I cannot afford to have word of this situation get out, and the nation cannot afford another scandal in the presidency. This woman shows every possibility of spilling her story all over the press. I need her to vanish. I need you to arrange to have her suffer an accident, something with a natural appearance to it, and I need it fast."

Levi Dalfon promised, "This will all be ended within the week," and he left the room.

The next night, before she could say a word to him, the president passed Valeria in the hall as she worked. "Don't bother me," he said.

Dalfon followed Valeria back to her apartment that same evening, obtaining her address without inquiry at the office. He returned early in the morning to watch for her departure and noted the time, 7:30 AM. He also saw several others leave the apartment block before she did. Gaining entrance would be a snap. Dalfon reappeared the next day at 6:45 AM dressed as a laborer carrying an electrician's tool case. When one individual left the building, he edged through the doorway and climbed the first flight of stairs, looking for a likely place to plant himself. At the top of the stairs he noticed an electrical outlet. Seating himself before it, and keeping easy hands-free access toward the stairway, he began to unscrew the plate over the outlet. One person walked down the stairs wordlessly. Another greeted him with "*Boker tov.*" To that "good morning" he responded, "*Boker or,*" and continued fiddling with the outlet cover, turning his head slightly only to scout for Valeria.

So it went with each passing occupant. Close to 7:30 he verified her person coming towards him, her shoes clacking on the steps. He turned his head away from her and looked closer at the pretended job. As she passed to the landing where he sat, she turned and extended her foot toward the final flight of stairs. Dalfon twisted around, his forearm purposely nudging and pushing against the inside of her knees. Valeria's legs buckled. She tumbled down the stairs head first. By the time she reached the bottom, she was unconscious, maybe dead. Dalfon intended to give her a final whack on the head as he left the building, planning to aim it where a contusion would hide the evidence from the blow of his boot.

Then Levi Dalfon heard the echo of a door opening from just down the hall. He threw the screw driver into his tool box, gathered it up in his arms, and flew down the staircase. With only a moment to spare on his way out of the building, he kicked Valeria one vicious blow to the stomach and another to her head. The oncoming apartment dweller appeared at the edge of the stairwell, saw Valeria's body, and called 101 for an ambulance. Magen David Adom arrived speedily. With lights flashing and siren blaring, skilled paramedics drove Valeria to the emergency room of Hadassah Hospital in Ein Karem.

Valeria sustained broken ribs, battered legs and hips, cuts and contusions, as well as a concussion. The medics wanted to watch for further symptoms from that trauma and from possible internal bleeding. She also miscarried. When she finally awakened, a nurse at her side asked what happened. Valeria remembered little and couldn't understand how she tripped and fell.

"It happens," the nurse replied. "You rest. We'll talk later. Let me know if you have pain, and we'll manage it for you."

"I have a horrible headache, and my sides are on fire." The nurse injected pain killer, and Valeria slept.

CHAPTER THIRTY-FIVE

L evi Dalfon visited Shim'on Toledano in his quarters. Again the president turned on the radio, and again, the whispers. "It didn't quite go as planned," Dalfon muttered into the president's ear. "She's still alive, but the baby is not. My sources at Hadassah tell me that she miscarried in the accident. I think you're out of trouble."

Toledano said in hushed tones, "*Halevai*. From your lips to God's ears. At least the provable cause for blackmail disappeared, but Levi, I've always counted on you in the past for positive results. I hope this one doesn't go south." Toledano shook his head worriedly, and Dalfon took it as a signal to leave.

The following day, Valeria, still suffering from a headache and wincing with each breath, rang the nurse, who informed her how to self-administer painkiller. When she delicately told Valeria that her baby was lost, Valeria began to weep. The nurse sat at her side and tried to hold her without causing further pain. As Valeria's tears lessened, the nurse added, "We have the tiny fetus. We need to know what you want to do with it."

Valeria tried to gather her senses. As if through a fog, an inner light shined on the question. "I want you," she said, "to scan the genome of the fetus before we decide the next step. I'll pay for it if I have to. It's critical. Then I'll take the fetus with me and bury it later."

"I'll see that you get the analysis."

"If I can have that report when I leave the hospital, along with the fetus, I'd appreciate it, and please wrap and cover it carefully as part of my personal effects. I have a fiancé, and I don't want him to know about the miscarriage. It's extremely personal."

The nurse nodded sympathetically, "I understand."

Valeria finally felt well enough to call her fiancé on her cell phone. Deeply disturbed at her disappearance and her injuries, he arrived in short order, spending evenings with her thereafter. He patiently and gently tried to help her recall what happened. Did she wedge her shoe between some boards? Was someone in a hurry behind her? That question brought to mind an electrician sitting by the stairs. She related the fact to her fiancé, who suggested that maybe the electrician moved and accidentally pushed her. She wasn't certain.

Valeria's fiancé brought clothing and necessities in a small suitcase from her apartment. On the day she left for home, she placed in the valise a parcel given her by the medical staff. It included her copy of the genome of the miscarried fetus, a bottle containing the fetus itself, which was not much larger than a thumb, and prescriptions for strong painkillers. Her fiancé accompanied her to his apartment and tucked her in bed.

Absent from both her jobs, Valeria spoke to a social worker about arranging disability payments while she recovered. When she felt able to move about, she went to an internet long distance phone shop where she thought her call would be untraceable. She called the reporter Dov Kimberg at *Haaretz* and told him she wanted to give him a story that would make his report of the Yair Johnson debacle look like a minor political skirmish. Kimberg, in the midst of an assignment, made an appointment for the following week.

2 Av 5784 – Tuesday, 6 August 2024

At the appointed hour, Dov Kimberg rang the bell of Valeria's Jerusalem apartment and entered to the jangle of the electric lock's raucous buzz. He climbed two flights of stairs, walked down a dismal, shadowy hallway and found Valeria at the door. They introduced themselves, and she showed him to a chair. Valeria sat across from Kimberg on a battered brown sofa, used furniture on its fourth or fifth recycle.

"You're the journalist who caught Yair Johnson red-handed, right?" she said.

"I'm the guy," he replied with a grin.

"I followed your exposé in *Haaretz* – memorable and important reporting. I think people trust you now. That's why I called you."

"OK, so why don't you tell me what this is about?"

Valeria detailed her story to Kimberg. He listened and took notes, all with a poker face that revealed not a whit of emotion.

"I suppose you have some proof of this?" he asked skeptically. "I mean, why should I believe you?"

"I'll give you three reasons to believe me, and two of them you can take with you to test the truth of what I've said. First, here's the fetus that I miscarried." She raised the bottle for him to see. He blanched. "I'll be keeping this for a while yet," she continued.

"Second, here's the genome of the fetus, done by the lab at Hadassah Hospital. They keep a copy of it there, too, and I scanned a file of the results, as well. You can take this one with you." She handed him the sheet with the genome on it.

"Third, in this envelope are ten hairs culled from the sink and bathtub of the president of Israel, from his own bedroom. You get *Haaretz* to make a genome from them and have an expert compare it to the genome of my baby. Shim'on Toledano will be found there, believe me."

"Alright, let's say the hairs are his and that he got you pregnant. How can you prove rape?" the reporter inquired.

"Maybe I can't any more. I told you I scraped my engagement ring along his cheek while yelling 'No.' Look for a fresh scar on his face and ask about it. But you tell me, why would a woman engaged to be married give herself to the president of Israel without protection? My fiancé uses condoms. I don't take the Pill. I know: it's circumstantial. But why would I expose myself to ridicule and controversy if I wasn't telling the truth?

"Then take it a step further. He's married. His wife is in a coma. He's a national figure, and the presidency is in crisis. The mere fact that he got me pregnant speaks to his contempt for all the values for which the presidency should stand – intercourse with an engaged woman while his wife is – what? Dying, suffering, in a coma? How low can you go?

"At work, I'm on my feet all day long. I don't fall. With my accident, I think somebody pushed me, but who? All I remember is an electrician working on the landing. It could have been an accident. So, Mr. Kimberg, what do you say?"

Kimberg paused, then said, "Maybe you planned to extort money from Toledano by coming onto him and getting pregnant by him. Maybe that's still your plan."

She spoke in acerbic, angry tones, "Is it extortion to expect a father to support his child along with the mother of that child whom he raped and whose life he interrupted and hindered while his unacknowledged offspring grows? Would support be too much to ask, do you think?"

"Well, not if you put it that way. But your innocence is not readily proven, and I still don't understand why you didn't go to the police."

"How could I do that? I washed the bastard clean off me after he attacked. I decided to leave well enough alone, steer clear of the man, keep my job, keep myself employable. I'm an uneducated *olah* from Moldova. I need the government job I have, as lowly as it may be."

"What about the electrician? Do you think he was for real or there to do you harm?"

"I don't know. Can I go to the police on the basis of that suspicion?"

He said, "Hmmm. Maybe. Let me see what I can dig up. At this point, I think you've handed me enough to work with. If I have something to share with you, give me your phone number so I can be in touch. I hope you make a good recovery, and I thank you, Valeria, for opening this story. Let's see if it goes anywhere." After they traded contact information, the reporter departed for Tel Aviv with the evidence Valeria provided.

While Kimberg waited in Tel Aviv for genetic testing of the 10 hairs, he thought through Valeria's words. As for Toledano, make-up covers scars, and no males wear more make-up than politicians, which Toledano had become. He doubted that he'd find a recent picture of Toledano with a new scar.

The electrician held a key to solving the puzzle. Was he really an electrician? Kimberg knew the date of the accident and where the electrician stationed himself. He dug through Jerusalem city records, found the owner of the apartment, and called his office. In turn, they referred the reporter to the building manager. Kimberg telephoned him. Electrician? No, the man said, electricity in the building functioned well, and besides, he'd probably repair a simple outlet himself.

Late in the day he collected the genetic report. Fearful of phone taps, and possessed of confirming data from analysis of the genomes, Kimberg went back to Jerusalem to talk personally to Valeria at her flat. He told her immediately that the lab test could verify her contentions. If in fact the hairs belonged to the president, then the baby resulted from him.

Valeria responded angrily. "What do you mean '*if*'? I collected that evidence during my work at his residence."

"So you say," Kimberg answered. "Listen, I'm inclined to believe you because circumstances demand it. Neither the owner nor the apartment manager summoned an electrician the day of your accident. In fact, the management hasn't required an electrician for some time. If there's a connection between the president and that man at the electrical outlet, then you have a strong indication of your story's truth. But I have another idea."

"What's that?"

The reporter leaned closer to Valeria. "Do you have a friend who cleans the president's room on the morning shift?"

"Sure. Aviva. We meet in the dressing room virtually every day between shifts. Well, not lately, of course, but I have her phone number. We're friends."

"Call Aviva. Tell her you want her to check the pillow and sheets, the bathroom sink, shower, or surfaces. We're looking for remains of hair, saliva, urine, blood, cast-off skin. Things like that. Maybe he throws his socks in a bin. At the end of the day socks show lots of skin cells. Tell her to take one home with her. With a good sample, we can run the genome test again, but this time with DNA collected by someone else. If she says yes, tell her I'll meet her at the Kings Hotel, and she can pass it to me. That's close to the president's home."

"What else should I do?" she asked.

"Call the police now and ask them to come here because you want to report a crime. Let's see if we can catch the fake electrician."

When the police arrived, Valeria and Kimberg put the case of the accident on the table for them to consider, including the fact of the bogus electrician.

"I fell because someone pushed my knees," she said. "At first it seemed like an accident, but now I believe it was purposeful. It must have been the so-called electrician. I'm asking you to go downstairs to the landing and check for fingerprints on the outlet cover plate located there, not a lot to ask. If you can identify prints from it, maybe the passers-by in the building can identify his face."

The policeman called the station to assign a fingerprint expert to Valeria's building. Kimberg waited and watched while, with gloves on, the detective carefully unscrewed the plate, deposited it in a clear plastic baggie, labeled it, and took it with her. "If there's something untoward, we'll be in touch with the Bercovici woman," she said, taking Valeria's number.

The next day, Valeria hobbled to a hotel in her neighborhood, found a phone booth, and called her friend Aviva at lunch hour. She explained what she needed and begged her friend to gather shreds of the president's hair or skin, or take a sock. Valeria could hear Aviva sigh hesitantly, and then she agreed to help out in the morning. She'd be in touch.

Valeria called Kimberg. "I heard from the police," she whispered. "The only fingerprints on the outlet cover belong to Levi Dalfon, one of the president's body guards. The government has his prints on record because of his position. They asked whether I was acquainted with him. I told them yes because of where I work. Now they're bringing him in for questioning. Also, police are knocking on doors here, asking if anyone remembers an electrician at work on the landing the day of my fall. Maybe they'll discover some witnesses."

"Where is Dalfon going, Central Police Station in Jerusalem?"

"Yes."

"Thanks for the tip, Valeria."

Kimberg contacted a correspondent in Jerusalem to wait at police court to learn if criminal charges were laid against Levi Dalfon.

Aviva absconded with a used sock and notified Valeria, who SMSed a number to Aviva. In turn, Aviva arranged to pass the material the next morning to Kimberg at the Kings Hotel, 7:30 AM. He directed her to look for a man with a Yankees baseball cap.

Said Shimi bar Hiyya to Rav: People say that a camel in Media can dance on a barrel. Here's the barrel, here's the camel, and here we are in Media, so where's the dancing?![62]

4 Av 5784 – Thursday, 8 August 2024

Dov Kimberg left Tel Aviv early to avoid rush hour traffic jams on the way to Jerusalem. Aviva arrived at the hotel lobby on time, quickly identified Kimberg's Yankees cap, and handed him a plastic bag. Returning to Tel Aviv with the evidence, Kimberg waited impatiently at the laboratory for test results. Two hours later, the lab, though unaware of whose DNA they analyzed, certified Aviva's collected evidence as a corroborating match for what Valeria claimed was the president's DNA material.

In the meantime, the police determined that Levi Dalfon possessed no electrician's license and could offer no reasonable excuse for sitting uninvited on an apartment staircase landing to fiddle with an electrical outlet, save to bide his time for some foul purpose. Several apartment dwellers remembered seeing the electrician, and late in the evening, two identified Dalfon in a line-up. The Jerusalem prosecuting attorney threatened an indictment against Levi Dalfon for aggravated battery, but he didn't believe he could make it stick. He decided to hold Dalfon over Shabbat, hoping that more questioning might yield deeper information.

Dov Kimberg hastily pounded out another blockbuster investigative story on his computer keyboard, his report capable of bringing down the president of Israel. Once again he went to his editor, and once again the editor held up his hand with a "go slow" signal.

"If we get an indictment on Dalfon, we'll go to press," he promised.

CHAPTER THIRTY-SIX

5 Av 5784 – Friday, 9 August 2024
Little Rock, Arkansas

Newspaper reporter Travis Benson found his Israeli adventures so fascinating and religiously uplifting that as a committed evangelical Christian he felt impelled to take his story on the road, arranging lecture dates in one church after the other throughout America's south central states. In his many speaking engagements, he extolled Israel as the first flowering of Christian salvation as well as Jewish redemption. These lectures and his rigorous newspaper reporting assignments consumed his daily schedule. Nor did he want to rob evening time from family in order to write his planned feature about Rebbe Nachum Steinitz, whom he interviewed outside the Israeli TV studio.

When his wife and children made a week-end visit to Benson's mother-in-law in Shreveport, at last he sat down to craft his piece about Rebbe Steinitz. He borrowed ample material from the files to trace the Rebbe's career from secular Jew to leading religious leader of a vast Hasidic sect. He saved the story of how Nachum discovered and entered the tunnel at the Golden Gate for last, considering it a delectable morsel of reportage to cap his story. In reviewing his notes, one word troubled him.

Benson counted a few Jewish friends in Little Rock. He picked up the telephone at his side and dialed the number of Brian Warshawsky, whom he knew from college days.

"Hey, Brian, it's me, Travis . . . oh, I'm doing fine, and you? . . . Good, good . . . family's OK? . . . Great. Listen, I have a translation problem here, and maybe you can help. I did an interview of this Jewish leader in Israel, and he mentioned something about a . . . let's see . . . a *tokas*. Do you know what a *tokas* is? . . . A what? . . . Are you sure? An ass? You're positive!? . . . OK, well thanks for the help Brian, and give my best to Cheryl, OK? . . . OK, take care."

Travis Benson did, indeed, conclude his article about Nachum Steinitz with the tunnel story, how as a young captain in the Israeli army Steinitz discovered a tunnel under the "new" Golden Gate and through the ancient one; how he did not walk across the Muslim cemetery, forbidden to any messiah, but traveled well below it, underground and through the ancient Herodian Golden Gate, thus quietly and secretly making him the first man in 2000 years to pass through Jerusalem's Golden Gate on an ass, perhaps fulfilling the prophecy of the prophet Zechariah (9:9), "Rejoice greatly, O daughter of Zion; shout, O daughter of Jerusalem; behold, your King comes to you; he is just, and victorious; humble and riding on an ass."

The Arkansas *Quotidian*, conscious of its extensive evangelical readership, prepared the article for the Sunday religion section, but also put it on the wire for use by other newspapers across the country. Several, including *The Mail* of New York, also included Benson's article in their Sunday edition. *The Mail* moved Benson's tunnel story higher into the piece to grab the interest of their many Jewish readers. The *Jewish Reporter*, however, with substantial Orthodox readership in Brooklyn, published it as received in their Monday issue. Israeli papers translated the article, and a number readied it for print on Tisha B'Av.

CHAPTER THIRTY-SEVEN

7 Av 5784 – Sunday, 11 August 2024

Dov Kimberg appealed to his editor even before the boss could finish his morning coffee.

"There's no indictment yet on Dalfon, and they'll probably release him. That's what I hear."

"Ergo," the editor stopped to take a sip of java gone stale, "your story must wait."

Kimberg grew irate. "No! Boss, it's just the opposite. If you release the story, you give sufficient evidence to hold Dalfon and bring down the president. Don't wait another minute."

Kimberg's editor took a draught of cold coffee, considered the proposition, and said, "OK. You're right. Push the send button. Turn it in . . . fast. To hell with these presidents. It'll be tomorrow's front page."

In commemoration of the ancient fast day, the ninth of Av, *Yedi'ot Acharonot* and *Yisrael Hayom* printed an opinion column by Nachum Aviam Steinitz, the Borisover Rebbe. Using only those two dailies, he reached 75% penetration of Israel's weekday newspaper readership.

What Tisha B'Av Means to Us

by Nachum Aviam Steinitz, The Borisover Rebbe

Tisha B'Av arrives, a mournful fast, the day we lost both Temples of Jerusalem. For 2000 years we have lived without the Temple, without its sacrifices. Now some Jews seriously study how to reinstitute sacrifices and rebuild the Temple. They are grossly in error.

Rambam (Maimonides) teaches two opposing views about sacrifice. His Mishneh Torah *law code foresees sacrifices in the messianic time.[63] Later, his* Guide of the Perplexed, *declares the opposite: 'For I did not command burnt offerings or sacrifices. I commanded them, Obey My voice, and I will be your God, and you shall be My people.'[64]*

Rambam holds that sacrifices originated as idolatrous customs ingrained in the folk. God permitted them to continue, hoping we would wean ourselves from them and someday snuff out our craving for pagan observances.[65]

Which is the real Rambam? The Mishneh Torah *he wrote for everybody, including the uninformed multitudes from whom he feared attack. The* Guide *he wrote for the few enlightened Jews of his age.*

Maimonides agreed with Rabban Yochanan ben Zakkai, who saved the Torah after the destruction of the Second Temple. When a colleague bemoaned the loss of atoning sacrifices, ben Zakkai rebuked him: "We have another atonement that is its equal, 'I desire loving-kindness and not sacrifice.'"[66] Talmud concurs: "While the Temple stood, the sacrificial altar atoned for Israel, but now our dining tables atone for us."[67] Every Jewish home is a mikdash me'at, *a small Temple where we offer prayers – sacrifices of our lips, and where we develop the ethic whose loving deeds require sacrifices of our time and substance.*

Why do learned people vainly plan reversion to pagan customs? To prepare for the messiah, they say. They must know that when Elijah sent Rabbi Joshua ben Levi to the gates of Rome, where the messiah was caring for lepers, Joshua asked him when he would come. "Today," he said. Returning to Elijah, Rabbi Joshua protested that the mashiach lied because he did not come "today." Elijah explained that mashiach quoted Psalm 95:7, Today, if only you listen to God's voice.[68]

In Talmudic times, the messiah who waited to be called from the depths of human suffering symbolized the people of Israel seeking redemption from oppression.[69] Ours is a different age: we needn't

wait for an individual messiah to return us to our Land. We are here!
If there is oppression, we Israeli citizens cause it, not some foreign
power.

Why should we fast on Tisha B'Av? Because our vaunted prayers
have failed to inspire actions that foster true redemption, particular-
ly in the State of Israel, our Third Temple.

Hillel used to say, "Be of the disciples of Aaron, loving peace and
pursuing it."⁷⁰ If we seized land near the Dome of the Rock or de-
stroyed the architecturally wondrous Dome itself to build a Temple,
would that be the pursuit of peace? No, the pursuit of peace requires
us to make all Yerushalayim into Ir Shalom, *a city of peace, a temple*
of peace.

May the day come speedily when we live at peace with our neigh-
bors, an age that is as if the messiah had come. Remember: "My
house shall be called a house of prayer for all peoples."⁷¹ Any future
Temple will not burn sacrifices in imitation of pagan cults. It will be a
beacon of inspiration for all – all Jews, all humanity. All deserve the
right to enter it in peace: a place of prayer and study, of justice and
mercy, of friendship and human kindness, an exemplary place for all
men and women of every race, nation, and belief. That day of shalom
waits to be born in the holy tomorrow for which we pray, and to-
wards which our fast should impel us.

Many, including the Director of Shin Bet, thought Nachum's expo-
sition too scholarly, but the write-ups by the press distilled his
surprising editorial into a few sentences, and by the end of the day, all
Israel knew that their own Israeli Hasidic Rebbe, Captain Steinitz,
shot words like arrows to hit targets of retrogressive religion. He
stiffed the small group of Temple Mount fanatics; he sliced through
the accumulated messianic irrationalism that weighed like ugly fat on
the body of Orthodox Judaism; he suggested that any future Temple
become a temple of unity, a meeting place for the minds and hearts of
all humanity; he turned the messiah idea on its head by moving it

from a single person to the endless search of the people of Israel for shalom. The Borisover Rebbe made headlines in all Israeli media.

The rabbinic advisory council of *Yated Ne'eman* parried Nachum's thrusts by keeping their ultra-Orthodox readership in the dark. That council underestimated the reach of the internet and free newspapers. While some members of ultra-Orthodox sects who read Nachum's words spat upon them and threw the newsprint on the ground, many more took home their free copy of *Yisrael Hayom* wedged inside their Talmud to read and reread the inspiration of the Borisover Rebbe.

8 Av 5784 – Monday, 12 August 2024

While Israel's dailies reviewed the Borisover Rebbe's editorial as news, *Haaretz* trumped them all with its revelation that President Toledano impregnated a chambermaid whose baby failed to survive an apparent attack upon her person in her apartment building. The attack seemed connected to actions of a long-time bodyguard of the president. The injured woman, engaged to be married to a worker at Machaneh Yehuda market, was recovering from her wounds and claimed the president raped her, but because she feared for her job, she kept the matter private until after she was attacked. Even if the police failed to prove the bodyguard guilty of a crime, the newspaper held all the genetic proof it needed to accuse the president of a major impropriety in office.

When Kimberg's story broke, Jerusalem's prosecuting attorney immediately connected the dots between the president, the once-pregnant but unnamed housekeeper, and Levi Dalfon. Once again Dalfon refused to talk. When the prosecutor slapped the newspaper story on the table directly in front of him, Dalfon demanded his lawyer's presence. Citing Dalfon's long connection as a muscle man for the president, the newspaper clearly revealed a motive for his actions, and an indictment for aggravated battery with intent to kill followed.

Regardless of the possible commission of a crime by the president of Israel, under the Basic Law his position protected him from criminal prosecution during his term of office. The prime minister of Israel read the newspaper headlines when he arose and swore out loud. That morning, the directors of Shin Bet and the Mossad did the same. All pulled from their most highly classified document file a single red dossier, "Mossad Messiah Action File." The three met by secure telephone and agreed that the country stood at the point of readiness for change, and the time had come to initiate the plan for the Mossad Messiah.

The prime minister of Israel then telephoned Shim'on Toledano. "Shim'on," he said, "you saw today's *Haaretz*? I won't ask for your demission, only that you cease all presidential function save the required signing of laws. You'll be prosecuted when your term ends, which will be soon, if I can help it, so get yourself a lawyer. I want your signature on a democratizing effort that we are endorsing tomorrow. I'm sure you'll want to lend your name to it, or we'll find a reason to call the House Committee together now, and we'll toss you out of office and into the hands of the prosecuting attorney this week." The president agreed without even asking to view the text.

CHAPTER THIRTY-EIGHT

He rides on an ass (chamor) *so that he'll become separated from material things* (chomer).[72]

Tisha B'Av, 9 Av 5784 – Tuesday, 13 August 2024

The tunnel article by Travis Benson about Nachum Steinitz, the Borisover Rebbe, broke in Israel on Tisha B'Av, the fast day commemorating the fall of both Temples of Jerusalem. *Yisrael HaYom* and *Yedi'ot Acharonot* tucked the article into their back pages. So also did the Haredi journal *Yated Ne'eman*, seeking a favorable piece to reach the large Borisover audience. At first, few people read it or cared, but the internet rapidly magnified the effect of the article. Email after forwarded email plucked the tunnel story from the end of the article, how the Borisover Rebbe, when he was Captain Nachum Steinitz, led the way on an ass underneath the "new" Golden Gate/Gates of Mercy and onward through the original Herodian gates, a messianic sign. At Tisha B'Av's early morning services, one Black Hat told the next that mashiach already arrived years before, and nobody knew it. Silently hidden in the uniform of *Tsahal*, the uniform of an Israeli army captain, the mashiach has been in Israel all along. Today he wears the *shtreiml* of Borisov. See today's *Yated Ne'eman*. Read Zechariah 9:9.

Haredim, Hasidim of every sect and stripe ballyhooed the news. Mashiach, Mashiach, Mashiach. Mashiach, the Borisover Rebbe. Their rabbis and rebbes sought to calm the fervor, but failed. It grew exponentially minute by minute, until it burst upon the streets after

Shacharit morning services, streets where other news greeted the nation.

Simultaneously on the Ninth of Av, a full-page advertisement appeared in every daily paper in Israel, repeated regularly on television, on social networks like Facebook and Twitter, mobile phone SMS, and as a pop-up on the Israeli internet. Posters emblazoned telephone poles. Placed by the Committee for Democratic Realignment, the advertisements proposed political changes. Because the country suffered a loss of confidence in its system of government after three failed presidents, and because decades of petty coalition compromises too often blocked the best interests, or even the inalienable rights of the whole nation, the Committee advocated:

1) Creation of a run-off election to peel away the smallest minority parties from the ballot, forcing their leadership into larger mainstream parties and diminishing the number of parties in Knesset.

2) Consideration of elections within districts, as opposed to elections by national party list.

3) Affirmation of the Universal Declaration of Human Rights, already signed by Israel years before, as a Basic Law of the State. The UN endorsed Israel's legitimacy. Israel should live by the UN's Declaration of Human Rights. Both were born in 1948.

4) Complete the Basic Laws so that Israel at last finalizes its constitution.

5) Abolish the Presidency of Israel as an office and, in accord with the hope of Bar Kochba, the ancient rabbis, and the yearnings of 2000 years, replace the president with a constitutional monarchy, the chief of state being a king or queen who is a possible descendant of King David and who swears to uphold Israel's Basic Laws. The monarch rules for life, but must be prosecutable for crimes in office and replaceable by his or her heir or another probable descendant of David. The monarch may speak at the opening of Knesset, must sign Knesset-passed laws and treaties, calls party leaders to form a government, and

acts as ceremonial head of state. Otherwise, the monarch has no power.

The Committee then called upon the people of Israel to join in massive demonstrations at the end of Tisha B'Av for the purpose of demanding the democratic realignment of the nation. A list of locations for evening rallies followed the advertisement. After the rallying call Israelis found names of one hundred makers and shakers, including the prime minister, several opposition leaders, the Borisover Rebbe, and surprisingly, the president of Israel, Shim'on Toledano.

The public had never before heard of the Committee for Democratic Realignment.

10 Av 5784 – Tuesday night, 13 August 2024

The rallies held across Israel could be divided into three types. In religiously observant areas, the predominant banner and placard offered to participants was "*David Melech Yisrael Chai veKayam,*" David, King of Israel, is alive and well. Crowds of Black Hats so exceeded expectations that police could barely manage them. Haredim and Hasidim alike chanted fiercely, Mashiach, Mashiach, Mashiach, Borisover Rebbe Mashiach, Nachum Melech Yisrael. They formed a black and white tidal wave that flowed through the streets, seemingly hypnotized by a supernal craving for the messiah and a renewed kingdom of Israel.

In Arab areas where any interest could be prompted, the signs read in Arabic and Hebrew, "Make the Universal Declaration of Human Rights a Basic Law." In secular Jewish areas, signs recalled the fact that three presidents in a row had desecrated the office. Placards echoed the popular Passover song, declaring, "Presidential Shenanigans – Dai, Dai, Dayenu! (Enough, Enough, It's enough for us!)", while other more serious posters shouted, "Stability, Democracy, Rights."

Crowds forming for the rallies found themselves funneled through particular routes which allowed police and military to make security checks. Officials tolerated no backpacks and looked under many thousands of untucked shirts for hidden threats on that hot evening. All rallies began with singers conducting the people in popular or religious pieces. Leaders then walked the people down main streets guarded by police, with the marchers spilling into central squares or parks of the cities where the different streams of demonstrators often merged – religious Jews with secular Jews and Arabs, Sephardi and Ashkenazi, Sabras and Jews of every stock, status, and state of origin. Police were omnipresent in the squares. Speakers, it was later discovered, all gave the same short discourse, exhorting the nation toward democratic changes and the elimination of the presidency and its unusual powers, powers of pardon and of impunity.

The orators said, "Better a hereditary and limited monarch with a tin crown than a president with clay feet." "Give our courts a declaration of rights to protect us all from the intrusions and abuses of government." "Give Knesset the best of the major players, not slivers from the minor ones." "Israeli government needs strong foundations and clear limitations. Complete the Basic Laws." "General strike tomorrow." "No more presidents. Give us a king." Finally, they all chanted, "Strike, strike, general strike." "David Melech Yisrael." In some Haredi quarters, the lyrics changed to "Nachum Melech Yisrael."

After the short speech, crowds were told where to find more information on the web. They were bidden to meet and greet their neighbors standing around them and given time to enjoy the moment. Rallies closed with the singing of the national anthem, "Hatikvah." Israel's elders reported that it felt like the first night of national unity since the reunification of Jerusalem. Hundreds of thousands of Israelis in attendance went home feeling excited about the possibilities for change, ready to share their experience with friends and neighbors, all carrying word of tomorrow's general strike.

At the end of an exhausting eighteen-hour day, satisfied with the results of the plan and doubly happy to feel the enthusiasm of the Haredim and Hasidim for the new Davidic monarchy, the *Rosh HaMemshalah* picked up the phone and dialed the number of Rebbe Nachum Steinitz.

"Nachum, it's me, the Prime Minister."

"It's midnight, Mr. Prime Minister. I hope everything is *b'seder.*"

"*B'seder gamur*, completely fine, but only now have I the time to ask: did you really ride through a tunnel under the Golden Gate on an ass?"

"No, Mr. Prime Minister, on *my* ass, my *tochas*. I told that reporter from the States exactly that, but he mistranslated it."

"It's too good to be true. Listen, Nachum, if anybody else asks you about it, tell them you mistakenly revealed a state secret and can no longer speak of it. Not a word. That's an order straight from the *Rosh HaMemshalah.*"

Nachum laughed out loud. "I understand. Good night, sir."

"Good night, Nachum, and good work."

10 Av 5784 – Wednesday, 14 August 2024

Flush with the previous day's stories about what the Committee for Democratic Realignment accomplished, the media sought to uncover deep background. None of the fourth estate penetrated past the Committee's blue-ribbon board of trustees to find anything untoward or suspicious about the group, at least not after one day. No single leader emerged as a spokesperson. News from the committee seemed to arrive like bubbles floating up from sources at impenetrable depths. Nevertheless, the general strike proceeded in well-organized fashion, providing the media with another full day of unusual news.

All trains – to Haifa, to Tel Aviv, to Beersheba, and to Jerusalem – all came to a halt. Egged and Dan buses did not run. Arab buses never touched the streets. No planes landed at Ben Gurion. Cruise ships remained stuck in port without debarkation of tourists. Government workers stayed home. Schools shut their doors. All retail ceased except for grocery stores, restaurants, and hotels. After all, the general strike came as a surprise, and the populace still needed to eat. It didn't matter. By afternoon, worried householders depleted the food stocks, which remained unreplenished for lack of deliveries. In Tel Aviv, if they could, people walked to the beach to stroll the strand, swim, and picnic. The hush of Jerusalem approached the quiet of Yom Kippur. A few cars still traveled, but local streets were blocked, filled with neighbors arguing politics, or just chatting while children played ball. Not so the *Kotel HaMa'aravi*, however. There crushing crowds of Haredim and Hasidim took up the chant all day long, Mashiach, Mashiach, Mashiach, Borisover Rebbe Mashiach, Nachum Melech Yisrael. Men danced with men, women with women all the day long, singing, chanting, lifting their arms in thanksgiving for the newfound messiah.

All Israel found itself in a strange semi-paralysis, for some a day of frenzied religious fervor, and for most others the dreamy relaxation of an unexpected midweek holiday.

At the end of the day, when the Committee threatened a further general strike the following Wednesday unless the government acted, the prime minister announced his appointment of a Select Panel of judges, attorneys, and politicians to propose more Basic Laws to complete the Israeli constitution. He stated that he favored making the Universal Declaration of Human Rights into the Israeli Bill of Rights as a Basic Law with fine-tuning to allow for security needs.

The prime minister informed the nation that he understood the message, "Better a hereditary monarch with a tin crown than a president with clay feet." The presidency would continue until the nation re-fashioned itself into a constitutional monarchy based on the Davidic line. He asked the nation for patience while the Select Panel proposed alterations to Israeli democratic forms. In the meantime, President Shim'on Toledano had withdrawn from every official function except the required signing of laws.

The promise of rapid-fire changes to national governance became the evening topic of nearly all Israeli conversation, and as along as the process lasted, every Israeli touted at least three opinions, all correct.

CHAPTER THIRTY-NINE

One year later
10 Av 5785 – Monday, 4 August 2025

Weary of argument and desirous of a long vacation, the Select Panel completed its tasks before Pesach, 5785/2025. The prime minister wanted Knesset to pass Israel's new Basic Laws before Shavuot, seven weeks later, but Knesset remained its feisty, obstreperous self and refused, particularly since splinter parties faced loss of their seats in the next election. The nation's leader demanded that Knesset stay in session until it concluded the business of the Basic Laws and the addition of the Declaration of Human Rights. Faced with no time out during the hot summer months, Knesset members seeking to cool more than their heels urged rapid and responsible acceptance of the new constitutional work. The Select Panel's proposals passed Knesset at last, and the body adjourned on the first of August, when many Knesset members fled to cooler climes.

President Shim'on Toledano perforce signed the changes into law, including abandonment of the presidency as an institution. The prime minister intervened with the attorney general to delay indictments against the former president, insisting that until the King of Israel is installed, the nation needed peace and quiet.

Since the ancient kings were limited to "only" eighteen wives, probably half of Israel could lay a tenuous claim to Davidic heritage. Still, in the minds of most, Borisover Rebbe Nachum Aviam Steinitz made the best candidate for king. Nachum's official claim to Davidic heritage derived from the Borisover line. His star as "mashiach" rose ever higher among the ultra-Orthodox, creating acceptance among a population bloc the *Rosh HaMemshalah* needed for successful change. In fact, polls pegged Nachum's popularity as the highest of any rabbi in Israel. A separate poll of rabbis who were not ultra-Orthodox also acclaimed him. A consensus developed that, because the Borisover Rebbe came from a secular background, he could competently balance royal affairs on the tightrope of state and properly conduct the equal reception of men and women together.

The prime minister faced a stony question. Overwhelming crowds of Haredim in the street saw Nachum Steinitz as the mashiach, but how could he get the self-important, self-absorbed, and often self-serving rabbinic leadership of disparate ultra-Orthodox sects to agree to the Borisover Rebbe as the first *Melech Ha-mashiach*, the first anointed king of Israel since Rabbi Akiba proclaimed Bar Kochba the rightful heir to David's throne 1900 years before? Once again, the prime minister sat in his private office contemplating the red Mossad Messiah Action File. Both Mossad and Shin Bet preferred a one-step approach, briefly outlined on a single sheet of paper. The prime minister reviewed the step and exactly what it entailed. Then he summoned his most trusted aide, Enosh Hagarzen.

When Hagarzen arrived, the prime minister explained that he required his help to solicit endorsements for Rebbe Steinitz to become Israel's first king in two millennia. He wanted endorsements from a list of rebbes and rabbis, all ultra-Orthodox, all likely to seek the office themselves or to try to block the nation's first choice. He handed Hagarzen a large envelope stuffed with evidentiary material. The aide opened the envelope. On its first page, he found more than a catalog of rabbinic names. He found an incident from the life of that Haredi or Hasidic rabbi. It amounted to an alphabet of woe.

Advocated collective punishment and genocide against Israel's enemies; **B**locked vaccination of girls against HPV, human papillomavirus, common STI, cause of genital warts and cancer; **C**ynically compared child sexual abuse to having an upset stomach;

Demanded *metzitzah b'peh*, traditional labial sucking after circumcision by mohel, source of STDs in infants; Endorsed and argued for refusal to rent apartments to Arabs contra Israeli law; Falsely reported conditions in kosher slaughter house; Greedily gouged people for signature on official documents; Had affair with woman he was converting to Judaism; Incited followers to destroy ancient churches and non-Jewish property; Justified the murder of Yitzhak Rabin; Killing of wounded terrorists defended; Lectured against homosexuality while secretly being gay himself; Molested children; Nullified conversion he performed, required new conversion, new tuition, said woman's child not Jewish; Opposed Worldpride pro-LGBTQ parade in Jerusalem, backed by riots that followed in Meah She'arim, charges of incitement to murder filed; Physically attacked Women of the Wall's Rosh Chodesh service at the *Kotel*; Questionably practiced faith healing of cancer, patient died; Rape of enemy women in combat approved; Sexually abused women, counseled them not to report him to police; Threw excrement-filled diapers at passing automobiles on Shabbat; Urged disobedience of military orders contrary to halacha; Vilified LGBTQ people as sick or deformed; Wrote halachic document to approve population transfer of all Arabs from Israel; Xmas trees in hotels condemned; Yielded to urges with prostitutes who are, additionally, trafficked women; Zealous for Greater Israel, advised future soldiers to plead "incapable of obeying" orders to evacuate a settlement.[73]

Behind the list Hagarzen discovered an orderly set of documents and photos to substantiate the notation next to each rabbi's name.

The prime minister said, "We have thousands of law-abiding, decent rabbis in Israel, the vast majority now behind our project. This small group somehow attained inordinate power, and I count on you to deal with them, to bring them to our side. I think you know what to do with all of this."

Enosh Hagarzen nodded his assent. "I might need a couple of weeks to visit all these rabbis."

"*B'seder*, Enosh. It's OK. Right after Sukkot, I want to wrap this up in Knesset."

Hagarzen, a brawny man of quiet and decisive action whose threatening eyes and unsmiling lips compounded his sinister demeanor, responded, "No problem," and shook his boss's hand.

Two weeks later, Enosh Hagarzen reported that he visited all the rabbis, and every single spiritual leader wanted to co-operate fully and wholeheartedly with the prime minister. As proof, they gave their signatures to the fact. Hagarzen placed the signed letters before his chief, who scooped them into a red file folder and said, "Good work." Waving the Mossad Messiah file in front of his aide, he added facetiously, "Enosh, so to speak, this is the whole Torah. The rest is commentary."[74]

CHAPTER FORTY

And Samuel said to all the people, "Do you see whom the Eternal has chosen, that there is none like him among all the people?" Then all the people shouted and said, "Long live the king!" Samuel told the people the rules governing kingship and wrote them in a book. Then he laid it before the Eternal and sent the people home. (I Samuel 10:24-25)

8 Heshvan 5786 – Shabbat *Lech Lecha*, Go Forth – Thursday, 30 October 2025

And so it came to pass that in the presence of Dina Ya'alon, Hanna Liora and David Steinitz, and in the presence of the Knesset and High Court of Justice and Chief Rabbis, and before a large group of invited guests, and in the sight of all Israel through live broadcast from the *Kotel HaMa'aravi*, Captain Nachum Aviam Steinitz, the Borisover Rebbe, went forth to become the first King of Israel since ancient days. Many were the representatives of crowned heads from around the world who also attended, including the King of Jordan, an heir to the Dutch throne, and a prince of England. Elected leaders arrived in great numbers from near and far, including the Turkish president, who reminded everyone that it was the Ottoman Turks who finally allowed the Jews to stand at the *Kotel HaMa'aravi* for prayer hundreds of years before. He did not, however, mention the special tax initially required to do so.

For his part, after returning from the mikveh, Nachum donned his captain's uniform with a tallit and a rope-like *gartel* cord around his waist, a traditional way to cut off baser bodily functions from the higher spiritual ones. An honor guard escorted him to a tall, ornate chair, not exactly a throne, but in fact an opulent antique Sephardic *Kisei shel Eliyahu*, an Elijah's Chair used for circumcision ceremonies, symbolic not only of the prophet Elijah's presence but of the age-old hope that he might soon announce the coming of the messianic age. In a unique way, that hope was about to come true.

As the ceremony began, an artificial fountain arranged for the occasion began to flow near Nachum's singular throne. Talmud teaches that anointment took place at a fountain, a symbolic wish for the King's long reign.[75] Then the Chief Justice of the High Court read the Basic Law of the Monarchy for all to hear. He asked Nachum to put his hand on the wooden case of the Abuhav Torah scroll, which had been set to the Ten Commandments. Rabbi Yitzchak Abuhav was a 14th century scholar of Toledo, Spain. Every time he wrote the name of God in this scroll, he immersed in a mikveh twenty-six times, equal to the numerical value of the four-letter Name of God. It took him thirteen years to write the Abuhav Torah, which was brought to Safed upon the expulsion of the Spanish Jews in 1492.

As Nachum touched the Torah case, he swore by God that he would uphold the law. Removing Nachum's military hat, the Chief Rabbis performed unction upon his scalp using the oil as described in Exodus (30:23 ff.) and in the Talmud.[76]

Anointment was no simple matter. To settle upon the proper procedure for the anointment of a "son of David" required speedy and cooperative action. Israel's two Chief Rabbis, nominally in control of Ashkenazic and Sephardic Jewish practice and civil status, agreed that they would rely on a panel of three experts, and if there was total disagreement among the three, the Chief Rabbis planned to draw straws to determine whether the Ashkenazic or Sephardic Chief Rabbi would rule on any unsettled controversy.

The question of anointment necessitated scholarly thought, for at a certain point in history it ceased in the Judean kingdom. In the end, all agreed to require anointment, since the Davidic monarchy was being reestablished.

What would be the recipe for the oil? Torah and Talmud don't seem to agree. The panel recommended using the Talmudic recipe, a concoction of 28.571428% myrrh, 28.571428% cassia, 28.571428% sweet cinnamon, and 14.285716% sweet calamus mixed together in a certain measure of purest olive oil.[77] Because of the extreme perfection of the percentages, a laboratory at Technion cautiously compiled the amounts. Was it a sin to make the amount of oil as large as Moses prescribed in the Torah? They made half the amount. There were questions of solubility[78] which led them to agree that since the first anointment oil had miracles attached to its creation, they would simply work with chemists to obtain the best results possible in 24 hours.

Equipped with an approximation of antiquity's unction of coronation, the Chief Rabbis poured anointing oil in the shape of a crown or a wreath around the top of Nachum's head, rubbed it over his eyebrows and on the bridge of his nose.[79] After anointing Nachum, the rabbis substituted a black kipa for his captain's hat, followed by a simple crown shaped like the crenelated walls of Jerusalem, what ancient Jews called a Jerusalem of Gold, *Yerushalayim shel Zahav*. It was a crown of unrevealed content, but in fact, of a light metal, golden in color only, and padded with blue cloth where metal touched the skin. A cantor chanted verses of Psalm 72, praying for the king's long life and strength. The leaders of the country cried out, "Long live the King!", and the shofar was sounded with a great *Tekiah* blast of an immense and curved ram's horn whose tonal quality surpassed the finest trombone.

The Chief Ashkenazic Rabbi offered the new prayer for the State of Israel which now contained words of supplication for the monarch's well-being. The Chief Sephardic Rabbi offered *Shehecheyanu*, thanking the Eternal for keeping the attendees alive to reach such a day of joy not seen in more than two thousand years.

Israel's prime minister arose and introduced Nachum Aviam Steinitz, King Nachum of Israel, who would address the nation. The immense assembled crowd cheered, applauded, and many in black suits and hats chanted, "Mashiach. Mashiach. Mashiach. Nachum *Melech Yisrael* – King of Israel, Mashiach."

After a long minute, Nachum held his hands high to quiet the crowd and began his address. He said, "*Rosh HaMemshalah*, Members of Knesset, Justices of the High Court, Chief Rabbis, honored guests, my fellow citizens of Israel: You have placed upon my head a royal crown and recreated the Davidic monarchy as a symbol of Israel's ancient heritage. We are a constitutional monarchy, for a full written constitution governs our laws at last, and I shall do my utmost to uphold it as your King.

"I cannot serve all Israel as King while serving as the Borisover Rebbe. Therefore I have placed a learned rabbi in charge of our Hasidim who will tend to the future of the movement.

"Let's be honest with each other. All claims to the Davidic heritage are doubtful and start in Babylon with the Exilarch. No one can say with certainty that he or she descends from King David. The Borisovers have long maintained that their Rebbe descends from David *Melech Yisrael*, and that is part of the reason I stand before you today. But Israel is a free nation of equals where virtually anyone could have become the monarch. I accept this great honor in all humility knowing that fact.

"Today when I was anointed king, I became mashiach."

Suddenly scores, then hundreds of Haredim and Hasidim began chanting simultaneously, "Mashiach, Mashiach, Mashiach, Nachum *Melech Ha-mashiach*." Louder and louder they chanted, until others joined them, repeating and strengthening the tidal wave of acknowledgement received by Nachum after the story of his tunnel adventure came to light.

Nachum raised his hands skyward and spoke loudly into the microphone, "Please, please," silence suddenly reigned. "Yes, I am *Hamelech Ha-mashiach*, the anointed king of Israel. But as Maimonides wrote, 'Do not presume that the king must work miracles and wonders, bring about new phenomena in the world, resurrect the dead, and more. This is definitely not true.'⁸⁰ In ancient days, mashiach meant 'the anointed one,' the proper descendant of David elevated by popular consent to King of Israel by pouring special oil upon his head. In that sense, I am mashiach, and in no other. Israel is a monarchy once again with an anointed sovereign and a constitution the monarch must follow. We now live in *Yemot Ha-mashiach*, the era of the anointed one.

"What will be my role as King? As your Sovereign, I foresee two critical tasks: first, always to be a mensch to our people. You should expect an example of ethical, compassionate, and just leadership from your Sovereign. The law of kindness must be on the lips of Israel's ruler, who shall ever remember that he is monarch of all Israelis, not any particular group or segment, and he must meet them with a loving, caring heart."

As Nachum spoke these words, he placed his hands upon his heart.

"Second, because the monarch occupies a powerful position of leadership, he or she can play the role of the ancient prophet. The prophets comforted the afflicted and afflicted the comfortable. When needed, I shall bring hope. When required by the times, I'll confront the mighty with truth, calling for social justice and a more genuine Jewish spirit. As your King, I'll have the opportunity to speak to Knesset at the beginning of every year, the Throne Speech. In those discourses do not expect a chronology of events or a list of kudos. I'll focus on a single topic of deep import to the people of Israel, and therefore of importance to their representatives. With the conviction of my deepest soul steeped in the traditions of our faith and history, I shall not shirk from speaking Jewish truth to power.

"Thank you for the confidence you place in me and in my family. As we enter together into this new time, I say to you now words based on the Book of Joshua, 'Be strong and courageous. Do not be afraid; do not be discouraged, for the Eternal our God will be with us wherever we go.'

"And may God bless the State of Israel."

Immediately a diva from the opera company in Tel Aviv stepped forward to lead the singing of "Hatikvah," whose words and melody echoed from the *Kotel* into the entire city of Jerusalem and on media across the Land. Nachum surprised a few higher-ups by approving the diva's participation in order to set the bulk of the nation at ease regarding his ability to satisfy both the Orthodox and the *Hiloni* secular citizenry.

Upbeat Israeli music and jubilant dancing then commenced at the three sections of the Wall: the men's, the women's, and the liberals' section under Robinson's Arch, where all could dance together. King Nachum danced at the men's section, but with greater sobriety and modesty than King David showed in his flamboyant and revealing rollick so long ago.[81] The Royal Consort, Dina, danced with the women. Hanna Liora and David Steinitz insisted on mixed dancing with other young people at Robinson's Arch. Shin Bet and the Jerusalem and national police applied all their skill and experience to maintain safety. At the close of festivities at the *Kotel*, they celebrated their success by joining the waning crowd in the last hora.

As the King, his consort, and children returned home, they saw all Israel cavorting in the streets, singing "Mashiach, Mashiach, Mashiach" and "*Nachum Melech Yisrael Chai Vekayam.*"

Celebrations lasted until the dinner hour, and Israelis across the Land came back to their parks and beaches for fireworks after dark.

The *Rosh HaMemshalah*, the director of Shin Bet, and the director of the Mossad returned to their offices and almost simultaneously withdrew the red Mossad Messiah file from its secure niche and fed its contents into a paper shredder, grinding the documents into tiny dots of confetti suitable for use at Purim.

BOOK V

דברים

Deuteronomy / "Words"

CHAPTER FORTY-ONE

Commenting on Deut. 1:9, "And I spoke to you at that time," Rabbi Levi ben David v'Yehudit asked why in Deuteronomy the Torah permits Moses to speak in the first-person. In several speeches he seems to ascribe God's words to himself, saying, "I [Moses] spoke to you." Moses states, "I said," "I say," and "I speak." Don't all such phrases in the Torah belong to God and not to a human being?

No, for Balaam the pagan prophet states, "The word that God puts in my mouth, that I shall speak" (Num. 22:38). Indeed, his discourse points to the days of the Messiah! "There shall come a star out of Jacob." (Num. 24:17)

If the false prophet Balaam can speak God's words from his mouth, then how much the more so Moses the humble one, who knew God face to face, for in his three main speeches in Deuteronomy, the inspiration of the Eternal is found on his lips.

These are the words of Nachum Aviam Steinitz son of David, which he contemplated, wrote, and spoke in the city and in the field during his reign as King of Israel:

I, Nachum, was king over Israel in Jerusalem. By means of wisdom, I set my mind to a thorough investigation of all that is done under heaven; there are troublesome problems that God has given humanity to resolve . . .[82]

11 Heshvan 5786 – Saturday night, 1 November 2025

"Dina," I said, sipping a decaf, "are the kids in bed?"

"Not in bed," she told me, "but in their rooms, still doing their homework."

"So late on Saturday night? There's school tomorrow. And I still can't believe we have two high schoolers in the house."

"More than two high schoolers," Dina winked at me. "A Jewish princess and a Jewish prince."

"You and I are the only two Jews who can officially make that claim," I said, and we laughed, but the joke was already becoming worn.

I fiddled with the papers before me on the table, scratched out a few words, pinched a few more into the space between the lines, underlined a couple items for emphasis, patted the papers and clipped them together. Then, with a flourish, I presented them to my wife.

"My Throne Speech for Knesset feels complete."

Dina laughingly responded, "And obviously you want me to read it."

"Obviously."

Dina accepted the sheaf from me, turned her chair slightly away, and sat reading for a good ten minutes, sipping at her cup of tea from time to time. She faced me and asked pointedly, "Why are you doing this?"

"Well, you know, I said I'd play the prophet, didn't I?"

Dina made a face like, "There he goes again." She shook her head and commented, "Sweetie, you're going to anger a lot of people with this talk. You know that, don't you? Is it really worth it, first royal address out of the bag, to tick off so many MKs, so many communities? Think about it while there's still time to change."

"Let me tell you a story," I said. Dina rolled her eyes upward.

"No, no, seriously, it's a good story. Maybe you know about Stephen S. Wise, a Reform rabbi in New York City in the early 1900's and also a great Zionist. He attended Herzl's Second Zionist Congress.

"Wise refused the rabbinate of Temple Emanu-El of New York because they wouldn't give him a free hand in the pulpit. He started his own synagogue. He called it the Free Synagogue It's still on the West Side today. Wise spoke with such power and charisma that they used to rent Carnegie Hall to accommodate the crowds who clamored for his sermons. Because of those throngs, the congregation went on a fundraising campaign to build a grand synagogue to rival the East Side's Temple Emanu-El, the world's largest.

"While the campaign was in full swing, the steel workers in America walked out on strike. Unions were controversial in those days. One Shabbat, Rabbi Wise told his wife, "Today I am going to light a million-dollar blaze." In Carnegie Hall before a large congregation Wise gave a stirring oration in support of the steel workers, in support of their right to organize and of unions to strike, and in support of fair wages. At the same time, Wise knew that the rich and conservative members of his congregation might renege on their pledges. Many leaders, infuriated by Wise's free pulpit, walked away from Wise and everything that he stood for, taking their friends and their pledges of cash with them. That resulted in a smaller synagogue building, but a congregation that never lost its soul. And a rabbi who never lost his soul, either.

"So, Dina, if I'm going to give Israel what I promised them, yes, there may be a lot of upset legislators in Knesset, but I need to set the tone for what the King of Israel does for our country, and I have to set it now. If I go before them, smile and make nice, I might just as well be a wealthy Member of Knesset from Savyon or Mamilla. I refuse to lose my soul. And besides, what will they do? Fire me? The country can ill afford another failure after the deficiencies of three presidents and the collapse of their office."

Dina pushed the papers across the table to me, saying, "Nachum, I love you, and I knew this was coming. I worry, that's all. Thank God, it's only once a year."

In Rabbi Pinchas's era the rabbis sought to declare Babylon as dough, that is, of less pure descent than the Jews of the Land of Isra-

el. Rabbi Pinchas surprised them by saying, "All countries are as dough in comparison with Palestine, and Palestine is as dough relative to Babylon!" Then he ran off so quickly that the rabbis lost their chance to question him. But when they sat down and examined the genealogies of the finest of Israel, they realized they ought to quit their genealogy project and stay quiet, for many leading families were not so pure after all.

Rabbi Johanan said, "By the Temple! We could reveal the families of impure birth around here, but since the greatest of our time are implicated, we'd better keep our mouths shut and let Elijah sort it out at the end of days . . ."[83]

11 Heshvan 5786 – Sunday morning, 2 November 2025

Nervous? It's impossible to convey the state of my nerves on the day of my first royal address to the Knesset. After a nearly sleepless night my voice felt thready and my legs weak.

Before arriving at Knesset, I mentally reconfirmed my plan: underscore the main points of my coronation talk and give Knesset something to chew on, something to put into the maw of all the political machinations and committee meetings, with the hope that they'd digest the idea and use it to energize the body politic. Otherwise it would come out at the end of the session as – well, a king doesn't use such words, does he?

In my few days as royalty, I'd managed to eliminate any bowing and scraping, curtseying or inclinations of the head or knees toward me. I instituted something new which would put no Israeli to shame, embarrassment, or inconvenience. After all, certain Jews don't want men and women to touch. I devised this approach: when coming before the sovereign, one places hand or hands over the heart, and the monarch then does the same. It caught on quickly, and provided a sense of warmth, rapport, and sincerity. All along the way into Knesset, from the driver to the guards in the parliament itself, we exchanged hand on heart and smiled.

I wore my kipa and crown, and also my army uniform. OK, it was a new uniform tailored for formal occasions, glitzier, and yes, a size or two larger than the old one. I also tied a *gartel* around my waist, as if to say, I want to talk with you about spiritual matters. As I reached the royal throne, Knesset arose and placed hands on heart. I returned their greeting, touching my own heart, as well. As I sat on the throne, all were seated, and at the same time I realized it was that same *Kisei shel Eliyahu* again. Mental note: add a more comfortable seat cushion.

The prime minister's introduction seemed a bit long, but then aren't all introductions that way? I hoped the prime minister wouldn't call me to the podium as "His Majesty the King," but what a surprise when he asked all to rise once again and welcome "*Ha-melech Ha-mashiach Nachum ben David,*" the anointed king, Nachum son of David. Well, it's true I'm the anointed king, and if my great-grandfather had married my great-grandmother, I would be Nachum Davidson. What a turn of events!

As I rose from the *Eliyahu* chair so also arose the entire Knesset, cheering, applauding, making me feel welcome. I thought to myself as I approached the microphone, this text in your hand is all you have. Summon your courage, summon your élan, give it like there's no tomorrow. I indicated that they be seated and began.

"Mr. Prime Minister, members of the Knesset, thank you for your welcome. *Shalom aleichem.* This will be my only speech to Knesset until next year. Therefore, at each annual discourse I must reveal to you what moves my heart as your King."

I rapidly reviewed the coronation speech, outlining my central tasks of providing to all an example of a mensch and fulfilling the role of the ancient prophets as a comfort in difficult times and a challenge to Israel when we miss the ethical mark. Then I turned to the core of my message.

"Several years ago, a foreigner called Israel telephone information and asked for the number of an NGO called Rabbis for Human Rights. The operator responded, 'Sir, there are no rabbis for human rights in Israel.' I was always one rabbi who favored them. Now that I'm king, it clearly remains for me to take the part of the prophets of ancient Israel and defend the rights of the downtrodden.

"One of our Israeli NGOs rated the marriage laws of all the world's nations, every single one. Do you know what rating we received? I am ashamed to tell you. Zero. Zero, 'due to severe restrictions that limit the options for legal marriage and discriminate against certain populations. These severe restrictions on freedom of marriage put Israel alongside countries that are among the worst offenders of violating marriage rights.'84

"Israel signed the Universal Declaration of Human Rights long ago, but we exempted ourselves from the section on personal status – marriage, divorce, and so on. This year we enshrined the entire Universal Declaration of Human Rights into Basic Law. Have you read it? Permit me to quote the document you approved: 'Men and women of full age, without any limitation due to race, nationality or religion, have the right to marry and to found a family. They are entitled to equal rights as to marriage, during marriage and at its dissolution. All children, whether born in or out of wedlock, shall enjoy the same social protection.'

"We base our system of marriage and divorce on the old Turkish *millet* system which gave religious leadership control of civil status for 400 years. In Israel, various recognized faith leaders like our chief rabbinate regulate marriage and divorce. But 300,000 or more Israelis declare that they have no religion, and 9000 Israeli marriages a year take place offshore, civil marriages entered in other countries.

"The Middle East's only democracy keeps a list of at least 4000 names of people whom the rabbinate will never marry. Many are mamzers, halachic bastards not permitted to marry anyone but another mamzer, a convert, or a non-Jewish slave. Are you aware that some halachic authorities advocate slavery as a legal fiction to enable a mamzer to break the chain of bastardy? Oy! That's a long halachic tale you don't want to hear.

"Under halacha, does a mamzer enjoy equal social protection regarding marriage? No. We can't change the Torah. Frankly, as your King and as a rabbi in Israel, I urge us to circumvent that Torah law as we have circumvented others. I'd be happy to testify to a committee how Jews have bypassed many a Torah law. *Et la'asot l'Adonai, heifeiru toratecha,* it's time to act for God by overthrowing this piece of Torah. I would urge rabbis to refuse any evidence of mamzer status, exactly what the Mesorati/Conservative Movement chooses to do, based on their well-written responsum.[85] I urge you to rip to shreds and to forbid all genealogical lists, and especially that list of 4000 names kept by the State. Synagogues and the Chief Rabbinate get money from the State. The State could decide to withhold money from places that promote laws and lists antithetical to our national standard of human rights.

"Do we need to go that far? No. Notwithstanding the halacha, this year's affirmation of the Universal Declaration of Human Rights as a Basic Law requires that the mamzer have equal rights to marriage, and given the current application of Torah law, the way to achieve that is to provide for full civil marriage and divorce.

"Need I add that LGBTQ couples cannot be married within our borders? This issue makes the problem of mamzer marriage look like a sidebar of history. LGBTQ people must go abroad for their unions in order to gain recognition of their marriage when they cross again into Israel, a major factor of inequality in our system that is controversial to many here. Under civil law, no controversy should occur. Gay couples deserve the same protection of law that straight couples receive in marriage, including the right to marry.

"We are told that our children must suffer with some laws because they're written in the Torah. We are told they are inescapable, though as a Torah scholar I differ. However, we Jews made some laws when the State of Israel began, laws that cause people pain. Surely our children needn't suffer with them any longer because Knesset can change them. What did the prophet Jeremiah say? 'In those days they shall say no more, the parents have eaten sour grapes, but it's the children's teeth that are set on edge' (Jer. 31:28). No more!

"The time has come for the Jewish State to assure everyone the equal rights we promise. The Israeli Declaration of Independence intimates, and our signature to the Universal Declaration of Human Rights clearly dictates our responsibility to provide for complete equality in marriage within our civil code of law, for marriage is the cornerstone of the family, and family is the cornerstone of the Jewish people.

"Many rabbis will oppose the change. They want everyone governed by halacha, and I fully understand that approach. To them I say, the existence of civil marriage and divorce will not stop our people from going to their rabbis. If people freely choose to do so, fine. If their option for equality can only be found on the civil side, give them the opportunity to go there and live fruitful, happy lives.

"Many challenges face this Knesset in the coming year to govern our nation justly. Do not view marriage and divorce as a small matter, for they affect every family in Israel. As your King, I respectfully urge you to set this country amongst the most advanced of nations in its legal treatment of marriage and divorce. Every year that goes by without a change puts painful scars and open sores upon the body politic of Israel. Winds of positive change have remade today and uplifted our hope for tomorrow. Unfurl the sails, feel the direction the wind is blowing, and set course for an Israel where every couple can live under the marriage regime that suits their needs, be it religious or civil.

"I wish Knesset a good year. I pray for *shalom al Yisrael*. May all that you do increase the possibility of lasting peace and mutual understanding among us. Thank you."

Throughout my address, no one applauded. All listened respectfully without interruption. No one walked out, and I count that a miracle almost as great as the parting of the Red Sea. As I stepped down from the podium, the entire body arose, a token of respect. Again, no applause, no catcalls, just silence. The *Rosh HaMemshalah* walked up to me and shook my hand, then we both realized he'd broken the new protocol, so we put hand on heart and grinned at each other.

When I returned to my "throne" and sat down, all remained standing, and slowly scattered applause began. It grew and spiraled upward in volume, with a majority of members from the religious parties either applauding lightly, courteously, or not at all. About a third of the religious group, however, not only applauded, but chanted, "Nachum Melech Yisrael." I attribute to this group of Black Hats a certain "tunnel vision" from the Golden Gate story, but how nice to have their support. The prime minister signaled for all to be seated and began the order of the day.

I sensed that my civil marriage issue would meet opposition in the months ahead. Well, I told them what weighed on my soul, and I deliberately selected a topic that would not become too incendiary. If my proposal passed in some effective way, good, and if not, large swaths of our country know their King cares about them and their rights. And there's always next year.

CHAPTER FORTY-TWO

Shortly after my Throne Speech, I received an invitation to a private meeting with the two Chief Rabbis of Israel, Sephardic and Ashkenazic. I recognize that they are powerful men. Their religious courts own jurisdiction over Jewish marriage and divorce, and they have equal power with civil courts regarding personal status, alimony, child support, custody, and inheritance. I possess no such powers, but unfortunately, they turned protocol upside down: if they wanted a meeting with the King, they had to request it of me. I did not respond to their invitation.

A few days passed, and my appointment secretary received a call from the Chief Rabbis' offices asking if together they could meet at the palace. "That's better," I thought, and in conjunction with my office we found a time.

When the Chief Rabbis arrived, the appointments secretary led the way to my private reception area and announced them: Rabbi Benlolo, Sephardic, and Rabbi Hochstein, Ashkenazic. They extended their hands, and I put mine to my heart. They followed suit. After all, the custom of the place is the proper custom. The three of us sat around a table in comfortable chairs, mine just a jot higher than theirs. They chitchatted about the coronation ceremony and the halachic details of it, to me a fascinating mélange of Torah, Talmud, ancient and modern practice. Then they got down to business.

Rabbi Benlolo said, "Rabbi Steinitz, we come to you with serious concerns."

I responded that though I retained my ordination as a rabbi, at this point in history, the proper title of address was "*Melech*," King, or

Melech Ha-mashiach, "Anointed King," for after all, they did co-operate in making it so.

"I realize you're used to speaking rabbi to rabbi with me, but we're in a different era now with different titles to use, Chief Rabbi Benlolo."

He said soothingly, "By all means. Pardon my gaffe, *Melech.* Before we express our concerns about your recent speech to Knesset in regard to civil marriage, let's talk about this term, *Melech Ha-mashiach.* Aren't you being presumptuous to insist on it? You hardly fill the traditional description of the messiah."

I thought, "What unbounded chutzpah!" and jerked my head scornfully. "You think not? Take a hard look at the intermediate prayers of the weekday *Amida,* Chief Rabbi Benlolo. They're about restoring the Jewish Commonwealth under a Davidic king. In that longed-for era, the courts will be Jewish and honest, unlike the Roman courts; Jerusalem, destroyed by the Romans, will be reconstructed; and the descendant of David will return to the throne to lead a community steeped in wisdom and at peace. The descendant of David is the messiah, the anointed one, the king of Israel, just as Rabbi Akiba desired when he backed Bar Kochba and his revolt of 135 CE. Akiba wasn't looking for someone to instigate impossible tricks like resuscitating the dead. Don't be misled by centuries of Greek, Christian, and Muslim influence upon the Jewish ideal of the messiah.

"Our ancient forebears desperately wanted the return of self-rule and their rightful anointed king, the *Melech Ha-mashiach.* That's what they prayed for in the *Amida,* and we pray for it too. We just don't know when to admit that we've achieved some of it. I am, and you assisted in making me *Ha-melech Ha-mashiach,* Israel's anointed king. I suggest you get used to it."

Feeling irate, I carried on. "At a theoretical level, when our rabbis of old described the proof of the messiah's arrival in such a way as to make it thoroughly unattainable, weren't they simply guaranteeing the continuance of their own power over the people, with the promise of an eventual reward for their credulity thrown in? Think about it."

Benlolo winced. I continued, "In ancient days, I mean truly ancient times in Judah and Israel, three sources of power stood in opposition to each other: the king, the high priest, and the prophet. In our own day, the true king of Israel is Knesset, led by the *Rosh HaMemshalah.* Another power center resides with the High Court of Justice, but often their decisions are negated by ministerial or rabbinic inaction, or by Knesset's alteration of the law. You, the Chief Rabbinate, compare to the ancient priesthood, a source of power that shares some prerogatives with the courts, too. Israel has long lacked an official who plays the prophet's role, the gadfly who challenges all other power centers with calls for social justice and adherence to exalted religious and ethical standards, but also someone who consoles the downcast in their bitter lot.

"I have received the great privilege of initiating the shape and form of kingship in Israel, and because the King has the same power as the prophets, the power of ethical persuasion, I choose to emulate them, be it for justice or for consolation."

Rabbi Benlolo turned to look at Rabbi Hochstein, who took a deep breath and said, "We must agree to disagree with this initiative of yours, King. We view your role as ceremonial. Please, let's come back to our joint concerns about your Knesset speech regarding civil marriage. Your thoughts about mamzer status and homosexuality have us deeply worried."

I asked for clarification.

Rabbi Hochstein went on to underscore both Chief Rabbis' opposition to civil marriage. It would become an opening for avoiding Torah law, avoiding rabbinical supervision of civil status, and it would open the door to strange marriages and forbidden unions.

"I understand your concerns fully," I replied, "in that I understand the halachic background from which you arrive at your conclusions. Let's take a bird's eye view of this discussion, as if looking down on the situation from the top of the Tree of Life. As we survey heights that give us not only a broader look at the Land, but of all Jewish time, we view two of today's leading rabbis convinced that Torah law cannot accommodate certain kinds of marriages, for example, between a mamzer and an ordinary Jew. But assessing the full and broad horizon of decisions, Rabbi Benlolo, we find that one of your recent predecessors in the Chief Sephardic Rabbi's chair, Rabbi Ovadia Yosef, a powerful and beloved leader, responded to the mamzer question by showing that it is a status impossible to prove, even when evidence seems clear. From on high, we see that Ovadia Yosef provides you a way out of the problem. Why be so strict with such a workable precedent available? I've mentioned another solution chosen by a different stream of Judaism from your own, also well-founded on traditional halacha.

"When we look down from the top of the Tree of Life, on this issue we see our Chief Rabbis marching off farther and farther to the right, while Rabbi Ovadia Yosef is marching off to the left, or at the very least, down the center. If 'the Torah forbids what is new,' as Moses Sofer claimed, then you, Rabbi Benlolo, the Sephardic Chief Rabbi, should clear away all the mamzer lists and demand cessation to any inquiry about such genealogy. Why? Because you've not only got the Talmud telling you that 'Israel is as dough compared to Babylon' in the matter of purity of descent, but you've got precedent on your side from a notable previous Chief Sephardic Rabbi who would surely say that he stood firmly on hallowed ground. If the Sephardic Chief Rabbi can do it, why can't the Ashkenazic Chief Rabbi?

"As for LGBTQ marriage, let's not talk about other streams of Judaism, just Orthodoxy. I'm sure you'll both agree about the traditional law, *Ein kiddushin tofsin*: Jewish marriage, *kiddushin*, doesn't apply in such a case. But again, if we go up one level and look down from above, wouldn't you wonder why *kiddushin* is the only available type of union? After all, we once allowed concubinage, ages ago. How about arranging a kind of union in which Jewish courts simply keep the issues of gender and sexuality out of consideration? Call it *zivugin*, couplehood, call it whatever, or give it no name at all. You could simply create a special contractual relationship or form of partnership about two people living together and caring for each other in good times and bad, a contract intended to allow two people ultimate responsibility for each other's welfare. If they want a ceremony to celebrate it, that's their business. Let the world make of it what they will. What do you think?"

In one manner or another, both rabbis told me it was unthinkable.

I responded, "Yes, unthinkable to you, but not to others, and that's why civil marriage can offer an alternative. Israel is a democracy that now adds the UN's Universal Declaration of Human Rights to our constitution, whether halacha likes it or not. That's what impelled me to speak about civil marriage. I invite you to undo the 'un-' in 'unthinkable,' without any commitment on your part to make changes."

"Obviously," Rabbi Hochstein interjected angrily, "you're no Hasidic rebbe."

"Let's understand each other," I shot back. "Obviously my present position in life is not rabbinical. I'm the King of Israel, of all Israel, straight or gay, Jewish or not, and what troubles our people must trouble me. To paraphrase Isaiah (63:9), in all their afflictions I am afflicted. Just because halacha disapproves of something does not mean it can't exist within a democracy's positive law. On the other hand, halachists reaching for the highest ethic can, as they have done in the past, arrive at novel and relevant solutions to contemporary problems derived from traditional forms and precedents. I'm sure you'll agree that it has happened over the centuries, and perhaps you might put some of your best minds to work on growing the current halachic ethic in directions that answer present-day problems. After all, 'this mitzvah is not in heaven, so that you have to send someone up there to take it down to us' (Deut. 30:12). It's in human hands. That's a Jewish tradition, right? I'm trying to encourage you to look at halacha through different lenses."

Rabbi Benlolo laughed. "*Melech*, you're as stubborn as we are." Then his voice became grim. "We, however, march with political parties alongside us. They're our troops. They're armed with votes, and we expect them to ride with us into the Knesset fray, joined by allies in coalition. Where are the King's troops?"

I told them I have to rely on *Adonai Tsva'ot*, the God of the Hosts of Heaven. But I added, "My dear Chief Rabbis, I see two possibilities for change that your troops and allies forget. First, a new coalition could arise without your religious parties in it. They might even choose to institute a third chief rabbinate composed of non-Orthodox rabbis who could choose to endorse what your rabbinates cannot or will not.

"The second possibility is already happening. In all fairness, I must tell you that the pollsters note a massive defection of your troops to Borisov, in part because Borisov offers Haredim the possibility of upward economic mobility, smaller families, fairer treatment of women, and a fuller sense of participation in the State of Israel; and in part because of the Golden Gate/Gates of Mercy tunnel story. Gentleman, frankly, your troops in the field are deserting you.

"In any case, you know I cannot intervene in the political process. That would be unconstitutional. Still, you're forgetting two factors. Perhaps most important, don't underestimate the willpower of the people of Israel and their desire to do what is right and what is just. 'If they're not prophets, they are the children of prophets.'[86]

"If Knesset does not see fit to synchronize its laws with the Declaration of Human Rights, a case will come before the High Court of Justice which will eventually force the issue upon the Knesset. The High Court is small, but their well-aimed decisions topple injustice like little David overcame Goliath.

"As for your reluctance to ameliorate some pressing current issues in Jewish law, it's not that you can't believe halacha is capable of meeting the tenor of these times with positive solutions: it's that you don't want to. If you wanted to, you could imagine a Torah that is warm and flowing and healing to this people Israel.

"Thank you for coming to see me," I said, with hand on heart, and I dismissed them.

CHAPTER FORTY-THREE

I, Nachum, was king over Israel in Jerusalem . . . I said to myself,
Behold, my greatness is in the acquired wisdom of all who ruled be-
fore me over Jerusalem. My intellect absorbed much traditional
wisdom and contemporary knowledge. So I set my mind to learn the
difference between wisdom and madness or folly; I intuited that this
was a striving after wind.[87]

One year later
24 Tishri 5787 – Monday, 5 October 2026

As King of Israel, I found almost daily opportunity to meet the
people, and Dina co-operated magnificently to set everyone at
ease, whether at home or on the road. I particularly enjoyed
dropping in on morning services here and there, surprising the minyan of the morning with my presence and sometimes having a shot of
rye whiskey with them afterward. What else but Crown Royal? Courtesy of the King, of course.

I visited some extraordinary places in Israel, among them a home
for terror victims, a children's museum which offers an experience of
blindness, experimental farms in the Negev, and more. The Land is
small, but the people are large of spirit.

All in all, the kingship seemed to imbue a sense of stability in the
Land, even among the most secular. I was in Tel Aviv so often, I finally
proposed that the government find the King a "palace" there, too –
just a house, really, but in Tel Aviv, a house costs like a palace.

Reflecting on my first year as King of Israel, I'm proudest of two
contributions that I made to Israeli life. One I called "*Perush Ha-*

melech," The King's Commentary, a class I gave once a week concerning the weekly Torah portion, *Parashat HaShavua,* and Talmud. Any Israeli could attend, but tickets were required. We apportioned them according to region. One week we'd have a group from the Galilee, then from the Negev, from Tel Aviv, and so forth. We recorded the class after lunch on Thursdays, a Torah reading day. I'd invite all the participants to lunch with the King of Israel and with my Royal Consort, Dina, and then we'd clear the table and study. The TV folks edited it down to an hour presentation in the early evening. We may not have had high altitude ratings, but that didn't stop us from getting flooded with requests for tickets. To prevent scalpers from selling them and to keep me alive, security vetted the recipients, put names on the tickets and matched them to photo ID's at the palace gate.

Dina still kept her marketing savvy. She advised me to vary my dress in order to touch the widest audience. Sometimes I wore my fancy dress *Tsahal* uniform to the class. Sometimes I wore a jacket and tie. Sometimes I looked like a Borisover, and sometimes I wore a *Dati Leumi* knit kipa. I even came like Ben Gurion in an open collar, short sleeve white shirt. Most everyone picked up on that reference. Of course, Ben Gurion didn't wear a crown.

I covered a lot of Torah territory in those classes, and I think the program furthered Israelis' respect for tradition. The program also provided a safe venue for the monarch to connect emotionally to Israelis, as well as a place for them to vent. When we studied the Torah portion *Korach*, one participant broke into tears while comparing her father-in-law to Korach and deploring how he feigned to want blessings for her family, yet if they caved to his demands, the man would control her family life and ruin her relationship with the children. She collapsed into her chair in tears, and I arose from my seat to comfort her, complimenting her on her patience. I took time to speak with her afterward, trying to lighten the heaviness of her heart.

In the same program, a couple of male Jerusalemites strongly defended the biblical Korach, depicting him as a democrat who only wanted Moses to share power with the people. That's been said before, but then they launched into a raucous, angry gripe session between the two of them, grumbling that the new monarchy creates an unelected leader who influences the agenda of Knesset, and therefore of the ministerial bureaucracy beneath it. They worked themselves into a lather over the issue. I rapped on the table for silence, but they stood at their seats and began shouting epithets at me, mostly Arabic curses unsuitable for television, combined with ugly hand motions – quite the scene. When I gave the video crew a time-out signal, two body guards entered and levered the agitated men back into sitting position. I ended the row with a comment that Israel's newspaper editorialists exert at least as much influence as I do, and on an everyday basis. They certainly are not elected by the people but have the ear of Knesset.

Another major contribution, though I made it by the very skin of my teeth, was civil marriage and divorce. Knesset kicked the law around like a soccer ball in play by Maccabi Tel Aviv F.C. They called me to testify before committee several times. Thank heaven the office of the prime minister made all kinds of statistics available to me. When I combined the statistics with the negative halachic possibilities for change given the growing Haredi population, it became obvious that something needed to be done for the secular majority, a diminishing but still large majority, to be sure. That put the fear of God in a wide group of MK's across party lines. They realized that if they did not continue to secure Basic Law rights for the majority now, it could become well-nigh impossible to achieve that goal in a matter of a decade or two.

On the other hand, once the civil marriage and divorce act went into effect, even some traditional halachists felt pressure to liberalize by writing responsa to make changes possible within the halacha, obviating the need for Israelis to utilize civil marriage and divorce. Those responsa kick-started debate in ultra-Orthodox quarters, and we began to discern rabbis who were more open to look leftward and

change, but also those whose right shoulder tic forced them tenacious-
ly to hold their ground. It's good to know all players.

I relate the issue of halachic change to one of the great surprises of
my studies. After years of believing that ethics were the highest expression of Jewish thought, I confronted Maimonides' opinion, which
places ethics just below the knowledge of God, the spiritual life. At
first I thought it was a slap in the face to the importance of ethical living, but after a time, I began to realize that only the knowledge of God
pulls the religious person upward toward newer and higher ethical
goals. Just as in the Torah God regrets particular actions and makes
changes, so we, too, are allowed to regret that we misconstrued what
God may have wanted. Only then do we summon the courage to make
necessary alterations, changes that reflect our current knowledge of
God and humanity both.

CHAPTER FORTY-FOUR

As I came to Knesset for my second address to the national assembly, I wished I'd felt more confident. It strikes me, however, that every year is new, and every Knesset brings different actors. The nation, too, lives through another year's experiences together. Attitudes vary. Hopes and needs shift in their goals. The King's address must change, as well.

Knesset welcomed me warmly on their feet, hands on heart, followed by applause. We enjoyed a rapport, but no political connectedness. I never endorsed any candidates, never showed an inclination toward one party over another, nor showed political favoritism. Favoritism to issues, yes, but to political parties or politicians, no. As Gandhi said, "Hate the sin, and not the sinner."

I kept hands off except when called upon to testify, and then it was as a citizen – a leading citizen, true, the King of Israel, but my testimony came largely from the government statistics office, and I linked the numbers to the facts of underserved populations and pushed hard for laws that provided for the needs of all. I tried to be everybody's King of Israel, and Knesset helped me attain that goal in my first year.

As for the second year and its address, once again I focused on every Israeli, but a lot of my fellow citizens think that term means "every Jewish Israeli." Wherever there's a majority, the minority will be ignored in some fashion. My goal for year two? To make ignoring the minority unfashionable.

The Prime Minister made a brief introduction – yes, truly brief, and all rose once again in respect as I came to the podium. I seated them, concluded the verbal niceties of greeting, and picked up my theme.

"Mr. Prime Minister, members of the Knesset, thank you for your welcome. *Shalom aleichem*. Once a year I have this unusual and treasured opportunity to address Knesset in the Throne Speech, and once again, permit me to reveal to you what moves my heart as your King. I shall be brief.

"In this my first year as King of Israel, I went up and down in the Land. I found goodness, love, and kindness in the soul of this nation. And yet . . . and yet I noted societal practices that obstruct our unity and might even destroy our country, the hope of 2000 years. I am moved to ask the question, 'Are we making strangers of one another?' If so, we must correct our actions, for to make a stranger of one who shares our national life flies in the face of tradition: 'the stranger shall be to you as one born among you, and you shall love him as yourself.' (Lev. 19:34)

"Why does the prophet tell us not to oppress the stranger nor to 'plot evil in your hearts against one another'? (Zechariah 7:10) He knows that when we make strangers of the 'other', it is only human to begin to justify wrongdoing against them and thus break the commandment to love one another.

"Those who call themselves secular, *Hiloni*, beginning with David Ben Gurion himself, created a Jewish 'other' in Israel: Haredim and Hasidim. With an unemployment rate of 45%, worse in Jerusalem, the Haredim are frequently poor, unemployed, and incapable of entering the labor market, let alone a university or trade school. They receive the education their rabbis deem proper, thick with tradition and Talmud. I delight in that curriculum, as you know. But you know equally well that I do not delight in unemployment. I do not delight in generation after generation of welfare-dependent families. I do not delight in the prospect of the State of Israel trying to subsidize whole families of able-bodied persons who, though capable of adding to the spirituality of the State, do so at the expense, the growingly impossible and unaffordable expense of taxpayers. Nor do I delight in the fact that merely 17% of ultra-Orthodox youth can pass our matriculation exams, sadly below national standards, or that Haredi and Hasidic men receive an incomplete general education in comparison to their women counterparts.

"One brush does not paint all. Notable exceptions exist, like one large Sephardic religious school system that teaches English and math.

"When I was the Borisover Rebbe, we stepped away from welfare dependency, and now the unemployment rate of the Borisovers is beginning to drop precipitously as the network of Borisover trade schools expands. Borisovers serve in *Tsahal*. Then, prepared in their high schools with a secular education suitable for Israeli life, they pursue further education. No Borisover yeshiva, no Borisover *kollel* will accept young students who have not showed willingness to serve their country and learn what is necessary to work in this society.

"As a nation we have continued to subsidize welfare payments to yeshiva students, to exempt them from *Tsahal*, to allow their schools not to teach English, math, and more. Do you know what we have done? The majority created a minority. The majority created a Jewish 'other.' The majority allowed this to happen, and though Ben Gurion quickly regretted his yeshiva exemptions and stipends, he never moved to change them. Surely that time of change has dawned.

"Why? Because now *Hiloni* Israelis, the secular, look at Haredi Jews, and what goes through their minds? They think 'parasite.' They feel anger and upset that their children risk their lives to protect these draft-exempt Talmud students that they must pay to support a growing bloc who have turned their spirituality into political power. When they view Black Hats, they see strangers, a threatening 'other' with one hand in the public purse while the other hand tries to steal away human rights in the name of God.

"Then there are the Haredim who make strangers of Jews who observe differently or do not observe Jewish religious rites at all. They crushed the Kessim, priests of the Ethiopian Jews, and demanded the newcomers live a Judaism they never practiced before. They demanded the reversal of the *Tsahal* draft of their young people. They, the ultra-Orthodox who chose to serve in *Tsahal,* walked out of official gatherings when women sang 'Hatikvah,' our national anthem. They consider themselves at the center of Jewish practice and condemn other Israelis who live their Jewishness differently. Too often the Chief Rabbinate supports them in these positions.

"The Turks created the Chief Rabbinate, the British endorsed it, and we inherited it and legally accepted it as if it were God's will. The Chief Rabbinates, Ashkenazic and Sephardic, not only control the practices of our Jewish life, but dictate which groups are acceptable and which are detestable. Reform Jews? Conservative Jews? Their rabbis are not rabbis, their worship is not kosher, their kashrut is tref, and they are to be ignored, rejected, and even spat upon despite the fact that for millions, yes, millions of Jews around the world, including Israel, these liberal Judaisms are their way of Jewish life. The Haredim condemn the 'other', despite the fact that progressive Reform leaders like Rabbi Abba Hillel Silver and Rabbi Stephen S. Wise helped launch Zionism and Israel.

"Those who have received the official state monopoly on God and those who follow them know that theirs is the 'true opinion,' *Orthodox*, and all others worship falsely, or worse, are not even Jews, but strangers who can be disdained and maltreated.

"There is a third 'other' among us. The nation makes strangers of its Arab citizens in two crucial ways. While our Declaration of Independence calls us to 'ensure complete equality of social and political rights to all Israel's inhabitants irrespective of religion, race or sex'; and 'guarantee freedom of religion, conscience, language, education and culture,' we have managed to fund Arab schools with 35- 60% less money than Jewish schools. Also, we do not require knowledge of our second official language, Arabic, on our matriculation examinations. Our children can fashionably swear a blue streak in Arabic but can't carry on a conversation in Nazareth.

"What, then, is our message about the social position of Arabic speakers in Israel? We are saying, to paraphrase King David, we shall not go to them. They must come to us.[88] We are also saying that we who live in a sea of Arabic speaking lands don't care to understand or converse in the language of the multimillions with whom we want to live in peace.

"Our national policies divide us. We require policies that bring us together, religious and secular, ultra-Orthodox and the other streams of Judaism, Arab and Jew. Knesset owns the solutions because Knesset can create and fund them.

"In another generation or two, Haredim will be the majority in Israel. Some years ago we implemented policies to move our ultra-Orthodox toward employment, but the legislation had insufficient teeth, and later governments ignored it, nonetheless. Knesset needs to create tough policies now to bring the Haredi fully into the work force, fully into *Tsahal*, and into the civil society of Israel with full comprehension of their democratic rights and responsibilities. What's the 'or else'? Or else everyone in our tax base who can move away will do so, taking their skills and their incomes with them because they are weary of the current system, a situation that can only worsen unless we take strong action.

"I do not see this Knesset disestablishing the Chief Rabbinates, but I can imagine another new Chief Rabbinate such as was found in Europe before the Shoah, 'New Traditions,' a Chief Rabbinate that has every prerogative of the others in respect to the civil state, but consists of rabbis from liberal traditions. Will you dare to create it? If not, Israel will continue to be the only Western democracy without freedom of religion, since liberal Jews do not have the same rights as the Orthodox.

"Finally, let's equalize educational funding and put Arabic on the matriculation exams to raise a generation that knows how to speak to its neighbors.

"To love our neighbors as ourselves, we need one law for all citizens. Arabs must know Hebrew. Jews must know Arabic. Everyone must try to know English, today's international language. Everyone must have a background in secular studies that meets the needs of our society. Everyone must understand how government works and the rights it promotes. Everyone must serve their country for a time in one useful way or another. Everyone must try to gain skills that will earn them a living.

"We have made the U.N. Declaration of Human Rights our own. We have completed our Basic Laws. Now it's time to get back to the basics of democracy and national unity. Why should we have policies that put us in exile from one another, as if banished upon our own soil?[89] We need to stop making strangers of one another and learn to love our neighbors, despite our differences.

"Thank you for your attention. I wish you a good and productive year in Knesset, *v'al kol Yisrael, shalom* – and peace over all of Israel."

I placed a hand on my heart, nodded to Knesset in acknowledgement of their powers, and left the podium. I thought as I sat down in the breathlessly profound stillness of the Knesset, this *Kisei shel Eliyahu* circumcision chair provides the perfect throne, if only to remind them that the deepest cut was already taken at eight days old, and they shouldn't knife me in the back or the heart.

CHAPTER FORTY-FIVE

In Scripture, the words "it came to pass" introduce unprecedented trouble or unprecedented joy. In the verse, "It came to pass in the days of King Ahaz" (Is. 7:1), what was the unprecedented trouble? Here's a parable to convey the idea.

A slave, allegedly sent to look after a baby prince, was actually commissioned to kill the child. He worried, "If I kill him myself, I'll be liable to the death penalty. If I withdraw his wet nurse, he'll die naturally for lack of nourishment." Just so, Ahaz thought: "Without synagogues or schools, the Holy One cannot, so to speak, cause the Divine Presence to rest upon the world. If I seize the synagogues and schools, the process of Torah will halt and God's presence will die a natural death."

Rabbi Hanina asked, "Why was he called Ahaz? Because he seized (ahaz) the synagogues and schools, and when he did so, Isaiah's disciples began to lament, 'Woe!' That is the unprecedented trouble indicated by 'And it came to pass in the days of Ahaz.'"[90]

In 5787 the Chief Rabbis and their religious parties in Knesset went after me. They condemned me as another Ahaz, creating unprecedented trouble for them, trying to grab their schools and their way of life. They said, next thing you know, like King Ahaz, he'll want to seize our synagogues, too. Seize them? No, but maybe let go of them by ending their subsidies, yes.

My thinking boils down to this: state subsidies empower certain groups and their leaders. In the realm of religion, those who care should empower what they care about, not expecting government to recognize and underwrite official types of Jewish practice like Ashkenazic or Sephardic Orthodoxy and no others. The liberal streams of Judaism largely raised their own funds from day one, against great odds and discrimination. If subsidies ended and people were forced to support religious institutions out of pocket, how would the public react? Isn't a level playing field fairer? I understand some NGOs are bringing suit based on our new bill of rights, and we may soon have answers to these questions.

Meanwhile, the government ought to assure everyone an education for good citizenship: how the government works, every citizen's rights and responsibilities, and in Israel, that's a responsibility of the national government too often ignored for political reasons. *Mipnei darchei shalom*, for the sake of the ways of peace, we need to understand each other's faiths and history. Instead, we hear rumblings of hatred: X religion is idolatry, Y's religionists are *kuffars* who deny the faith, members of Z religion will go to hell. Strangely, certain luminaries of faith darkly militate against mutual understanding, and that militancy must end for peace to arrive in the Land.

On the positive side, the royal Knesset address won me dates on Arabic TV in Israel. I hired an Arabic tutor a year ago and improved greatly, but fluency? No. I prepared answers to pre-scheduled questions with a translator, and that enhanced my media appearance. Maybe it created some unity and goodwill, as well.

Hebrew media also gave me air time, but threats from outside our borders topped the national agenda. I addressed a joint clergy group of all three faiths that meets regularly at the Jerusalem YMCA, and even there, the reception felt lukewarm. No one wants a change in their status quo.

During the question period, one rabbi hit me with, "*Melech*, your name is Nachum. Why don't you concentrate more on *nechama*, on comforting the nation, than on '*imut*, so much confrontation?"

I told him I had a problem. In Ashkenazic Hebrew, the word for confrontation is pronounced '*imus*. Once having read the prophet

Amos, I could never again avoid *'imus*. At least they laughed at a bad pun.

Aside from having to realize that politics-as-usual would continue whether Israel had a king or a president, I can't say that 5787 was a bad year. The populace appreciated that I gave the realm my all, and I loved doing it.

On a rainy day in Adar, just after Purim, the Prime Minister and I met at the royal palace.

"I want to report," he told me, "how goes the unity initiative that you urged last autumn."

"Not well, I take it."

"No, *Melech*, not as well as you hoped. Still, I see progress. I can't get parity, but I can definitely budget more money for the Arab school system. Your point is well taken, and we've suffered a lot of bad press about the issue of underfunding. If Jewish schools get 25% more than Arab ones, you've got to admit that's already an improvement."

"I'll admit it, with only modest satisfaction. But municipalities also provide money, so the ministry needs to follow the funding trail right to the student's desk. Money is like water, following the easiest way down, and often that's not to the students' benefit."

"OK. I'll talk to the education minister about closer supervision, making municipalities toe the mark. Also, I've asked the minister to review what we teach for civics. However, the Chief Rabbinate offices want nothing to do with you since the Throne Speech, while the secular parties are floating ideas for change, but they lack the Knesset members to win the day. We're at a stalemate on that side."

"Other news?"

"Time out on this subject for a minute. Tell me in all honesty, did you plant that Golden Gate tunnel story? Because you won't believe what it's causing."

"Mr. Prime Minister, no, as I informed you when it broke last year, the whole thing is the result of a mistranslation."

"Well, it's performing miracles. We now estimate that close to 33% of young Black Hats have already moved to Borisov, and the numbers keep climbing. Every week, Borisov Central demands more money for schools. The Ministry is giving them school buildings where the numbers have dropped precipitously because of switches to Borisov. I hope they can find sufficient teachers. If the snowball effect keeps up, the number of unemployed, un-*Tsahal*'ed Haredi will plunge steeply in the next fifteen years. *Kol HaKavod*, Melech, congratulations! That tunnel article was a stroke of good fortune. Not even the Mossad could have brought off that coup.

"There's more: sales of the Pill have risen sharply near Haredi neighborhoods. Apparently, the Haredi women buy into your *p'ru ur'vu* Torah interpretation, but they purchase their pharmaceuticals out of the purview of local rabbis.

"Also, a few more yeshiva principals agreed to follow guidelines for secular education in order to prepare students for the army and for jobs. I think that's because their students are seeing with 'tunnel vision,' which forces the principals to act to save their schools. We're making progress with them, but slowly. It's like slogging through Hula Valley swampland. Before we can take each new step, we have to unstick ourselves from the mud we're already in."

I paused to think for a moment and suggested, "If possible, give me the list of yeshivas that are most stubborn about change. Maybe I can find some colleagues to influence them. Maybe I can get some of the early Borisover successes to tell their story."

"Certainly, that might move us forward. I'll ask the minister to be in touch. I favor your proposal, and many other MK's are with me on it. As you know, we're enduring threats from across the border this year, and that takes up a tremendous chunk of my time. I'm not saying you shouldn't count on me, but I am saying that my time is limited. If the King gets a couple of his proposals acted upon in part, he will have accomplished a lot."

"Mr. Prime Minister, on the Haredi side, what if the government substantially upped the family allowance for those who study a trade or attend university? That might leap over the barriers presented by the yeshiva heads."

"*Melech,* that's a strong idea, and probably the best way to ram employability through the Haredi educational system. Will the national budget allow it? Will we be able to create a reliable system that catches the cheats, the ones who falsely prove they're studying a secular subject? I'll put our best staffers to work on a saleable proposal."

I jumped in. "Wait. Legislate a sliding scale reduction on allowances for those who study only traditional subjects, with less and less forthcoming each year. The shekels liberated can help subsidize those who study subjects that lead to employment."

"Those kinds of reductions could cost me my coalition."

"You'd sell the country's future down the river to stay in power?" I asked.

He snapped, "That's an old refrain. Don't you start to sing it, *Melech.*"

Then I asked how the prime minister would react to creating a Royal Commission, experts from all sides to bring a national report and recommendations on preparedness for good citizenship within a certain period of time?

He recovered his equanimity and said, "Royal Commission? Sounds enticing. Create a short-term council separate from the government to assess what we do for citizenship education, bring in best practices, and try to get the bureaucrats to sign onto it for a five-year period."

"Let's do it. We'll both get some names. We'll ask unions, corporations, and professional associations for suggestions, and so on."

Suddenly he looked irritated and responded acerbically, "Something else to fund, right?"

I leaned forward, "Mr. Prime Minister, 'Nothing will come of nothing.' "

"What rabbi said that?" he asked, cynicism in his voice.

"Rabbi Shakespeare – King Lear."

He laughed. Our talk had been heart to heart, so we simply shook hands. Maybe our tête-à-tête will bring positive changes for Israel in the years to come. In the following days, I drew up a list of names for the Royal Commission on Citizenship Preparedness and sent it off to the prime minister, who added his own choices. The teachers and Education Ministry weighed in, along with many others, and we launched the commission between Pesach and Shavuot. Who knows, in a couple of years . . .?

CHAPTER FORTY-SIX

Because of my Borisover Rebbe-ship, my kids were already used to being surrounded by guests and Hasidim virtually all day on Shabbat. When I became King, nothing changed in that regard. Occasionally we'd carve out family time by holding off the guests from some part of the day. I'll never forget one Shabbat dinner alone with Dina, Hanna Liora, and David.

We'd finished all the berachot, even the blessing of the children where one or both inevitably complained, "Oh, *Abba*! Really! I'm 14 already." Or even 17, like Hanna Liora.

We were enjoying our dinner, when Hanna Liora told us what weighed most heavily on her mind. She knew that service in *Tsahal* lay around the corner, and then probably on to university, so she turned to both of us, Dina and me, and asked whether we could talk about her future studies. Naturally, we agreed.

She told us, "I don't really go for all the Torah study I'm doing. I mean, I understand the Talmud, and I read the commentary on the Torah for each week along with the portion, and I get that, too. But I can't say I'm jumping for joy about it. I don't want to hurt your feelings, *Abba*, because I know you love both the written and the oral Torah material, but I have other interests."

I finished chewing on some chicken and said, "My thoughts are not your thoughts, and your ways are not my ways." (Is. 55:8)

Hanna Liora pounced on my words. "There it is, *Abba*. Everything you see, you see through Torah eyes. I don't."

I backed off. "I'm just saying that you're entitled to your own thoughts and feelings. What stands out when you think about your future? When you envision your life here, what excites your interest?"

She explained, "I've got two major agendas, and I can describe each with one word: cityscape and women.

"I love the White City in Tel Aviv and parts of Haifa. I love old Jaffa. The apartments and homes in Rehavia have character. I can walk the winding, narrow streets of the Old City for hours and never tire of them. I hate how we've chopped the tops off the hills and mountains to plunk down so many houses that look all the same, that look like a human desert on top of ancient pasture and agricultural terraces. The population grows and grows, and we cap those hills with concrete to accommodate us all.

"*Abba*, some families in our school have so many kids that I don't know how the parents remember all their names! And then aliyah adds more population. Central Israel is filling up. Ecologically and architecturally, I don't find much that's attractive. Give me the look of Yemin Moshe and its windmill over Har Homa or Ramot any day."

I underscored her words with, "What you're saying about the population explosion, I've got chapter and verse on it in the report that my committee of ecologists finally submitted when I was the Borisover Rebbe. According to the report, having fewer children not only reduces the population explosion, but it's by far the most important thing people can do to fight climate change. Hanna Liora, you're not alone in your opinion."

Dina said, "I doubt that the ecology report talks about architecture."

Hanna Liora tsked with her tongue and turned her head with eyes upward like any Israeli indicating "What are you talking about?"

"I'll bet it does," she said. "Already ten years ago at the Israel Pavilion at Expo Milano we showed the world how to combine farms and apartments with vertical agriculture. Imagine how green the cityscape could be. Har Homa could look greener than it did before we shaved it and plopped down its housing."

I wanted to get back to Hanna Liora's basic theme. "Let me get this straight. You want to be an architect?"

"Or maybe an urban planner, but something like that, yes."

David finally chimed in. "I'm with you, *Abba*. I'll do the Torah thing," he offered. "I'm the best in the class at Talmud, even without your help."

"You like it?" I asked.

"Well, I'm not supposed to admit it to my friends, but yeah, I like it a lot. Take that section from *Ketubot* 22a, the one about 'the mouth that forbade is the mouth that permits.' It's kind of complicated, but it raises a question of whose word you can trust, and with that in mind, I see all kinds of applications – like the news, politics, advertising, relationships. It's good stuff."

I tousled David's hair, dislodging his kipa. I replaced it, patted it down, and gave his arm a squeeze. But I wanted to get back to Hanna Liora. Following up on David, I turned to her and said, "So, dearest daughter, if your mouth and your inclination forbids you from making Torah your central study, it still permits you to become familiar with it, and at the same time to go deeper into what truly compels you. How does that sound?"

"Wait, *Abba*, are you saying urban studies would be OK with you?"

"Only if it's OK with you."

"Of course it's OK with me. What do you think, *Ima*?"

Dina didn't hesitate. "What? Naturally. Study and do what excites you and produces the use of your best attributes."

"But what if I became Queen Hanna Liora? According to the new law, it's entirely possible."

Dina smirked, "Your father meddles in his way. You can meddle in yours."

We all laughed, but that Shabbat we received our first clue that Hanna Liora thought seriously about becoming Queen of Israel and what kind of contribution she wanted to make to the country during her reign. What's more, maybe her cityscape theme would form the basis of my next address to Knesset.

I knew our daughter had more on her mind. "You also mentioned women as a concern. Tell us about that."

Hanna Liora looked downward for a moment, gathering her thoughts. Then she began.

"Women in Israel get a mixed message. On the one hand, the laws are generally in place for our rights. On the other hand, we're earning on average 20% less than men in the same positions. Sexual harassment still exists widely in the workplace, at least according to surveys, and according to the presidential history of Israel's past. Discrimination against women by Haredim and Hasidim has risen. One NGO went to court to assure women the right to sit anywhere they want in public transport. What happened? Black Hat rabbis told their female followers, pay no attention, sit in the back. Bus segregation was a new idea that only came up a few years ago. Then they created their own private transport system, avoiding the legal issue altogether. I'd like to make those situations right for women."

"Here's the big reason I'm interested. If we can stir the nation's women to address major domestic issues, I believe we can change the social landscape of Israel for the better. *Abba*, you and *Ima* discussed the mikveh situation, and your advances are bringing ultra-Orthodox women into Borisover Hasidism. Their husbands follow. Now more are working, more are in *Tsahal*. Borisov integrates Hasidim strongly into the full Israeli society. Women have power they can tap for positive change despite male stubbornness, despite their rabbis. Women's issues matter to me because Israel matters to me."

Dina and I both leaned across to our daughter to give Hanna Liora an embrace and a kiss, and with a lilt in her voice, Dina chimed, "That's my daughter!"

CHAPTER FORTY-SEVEN

8 Elul, 5787 – Friday, 10 September, 2027

The Director of Shin Bet vaulted through the doorway of my personal office to confront me face to face. With urgency in his demeanor he'd never betrayed before, his words hammered out the facts. "Not good news, *Melech*. I'm sorry, very sorry, but Hanna Liora has been kidnapped."

Stunned and shaken, I jumped to my feet. "No!" I cried. My throat constricted, and I rasped, "Something like this had to happen, didn't it?" I slammed my hand down on the desk.

The Director repeated, "I'm sorry."

Unconsciously I clenched my fists and gritted my teeth. I seemed to gasp for air, finally taking sufficient breath to exhale the words, "Tell me what you know."

"Hanna Liora was walking down Eliezer Kaplan Street in Tel Aviv on her way to work in the military area, HaKiryah. As she approached the Journalism Center – there's a mailbox next to it, one of the city's last – a red Israel Post Peugeot Partner van pulled up. A worker with his back to our operatives opened the rear door of the truck, fished in his *Doar Yisrael* bag for a mailbox key, keeping his head down so our men couldn't see his face under his baseball cap. From beneath the hat he quickly pulled a child's mask over his face, turned, and grabbed Hanna Liora as she passed. He hurled her into the back of the truck, leaped inside, and slammed the door shut as the vehicle sped off. A second perpetrator obviously occupied the driver's seat. Our men came running, but too late.

"The van made a fast left, going the wrong way up Dubnov, where the kidnappers had positioned a separate car to block traffic. As soon as the Peugeot turned left down a narrow back street, the vehicle blocking Dubnov moved slightly forward, and all the honking cars behind it moved along, as well. That barricaded Dubnov and prevented our car from following. The driver of the blocking vehicle zig-zagged a getaway on an electric bicycle planted nearby. The van holding your daughter went straight to Ibn Gabirol and disappeared in traffic.

"There are a million closed circuit cams around Tel Aviv. With them we followed the perpetrators briefly, but they abandoned their stolen Peugeot in Ramat Gan, switching to a stolen *Sherut* mini-bus obscured from CCTV by trees and a filled recycling collector box.

"We found the driver of the stolen van, who had a nasty lump on his head. Hit from behind and still dazed, he never saw his assailant. Same for the *Sherut* driver, so we've got his mini-bus ID made, but have they switched vehicles again? We don't know. We sent police an all-points bulletin, and they're scanning the roads.

"Our agents think the captors are Israelis, not Palestinians, and Jews, not Arabs, but we can't be sure. We can't trace your daughter because her cell phone is off, maybe destroyed, and they cut through and discarded her ankle bracelet. Someone found the ankle monitor at a Tel Aviv curb and turned it in.

"We're working with Mossad, poring through every Israeli cell phone call to sort out one that might expose the kidnappers. We're calling in all our chips to find an informer with a clue, but that effort is just beginning. I assume you haven't received any emails or messages."

I shook my head no while biting my lower lip. "I've got to talk to Dina," I said. "Let me bring her here. Stay a few more minutes, please."

I found Dina alone at her office desk working on our mutual agenda. She looked up, started to smile, and saw my distraught condition.

"What is it, Nachum?"

"It's Hanna Liora." I stammered between tears. "She's been kidnapped." I pulled Dina from her chair and clutched her tightly to me.

She reacted as I did. She began pummeling my back, sobbing and trembling uncontrollably, her tears soaking my suit coat. "No! Nachum, Nachum, this is more than I can bear!"

I held her closer, letting her emotions flow through me and joining my own. She wept, we wept together, two parents lost in desperation. Her voice broke as she asked, "Who told you?"

"The Director of Shin Bet is waiting for us in my office. Come with me."

On arrival, the Director offered his sympathies and embraced Dina. He walked her through the story and added, "We're waiting for a ransom note to reveal how much they want or the conditions of Hanna Liora's release. We don't think they'll harm her, not immediately. They want something, but what?"

"If it's money they're angling for, you're aware that the State of Israel doesn't pay ransom. I would certainly push the prime minister to make an exception to the usual policy.

"Maybe they'll demand release of a prisoner. But they might want something else. How that word will come, we don't know. *Melech*, tell your office that you want to supervise the opening of the mail. What we're looking for may come by post. In the meantime, of course you'll cancel all appointments, and please believe that this office, the police, and *Tsahal* are united in looking for your daughter."

My voice uttered its thanks, but my eyes glared at the Director through my tears.

He continued, "Now, two key items. One: publicity. Do we bring the country into this moment or keep it quiet for a time?"

I looked at Dina. She looked at me for a signal, but I gave none. She advocated bringing all Israel into the hunt. I agreed.

The Director then said, "*B'seder*. OK, then the last question, where to start? I have the voice mail you sent of your enemies list. I can reconstruct a file of all the rabbis we persuaded to back you as king.

We'll investigate them and their recent maneuvering. The Yazuv Zov remains in jail, out of the picture, but he may have allies."

"You're starting with an investigation of the ultra-Orthodox?"

He nodded agreement as if that were the single possibility.

"I don't agree with you, Director. Unfortunately, there are plenty of other potential haters out there. The culprits could be disgruntled Israeli Arabs. Or the perpetrators could just as well have come from across the Green Line, or from across one of our borders – Lebanon, Gaza. Borisover Hasidim generally approved my policy thrusts, but some did not. We could be dealing with malcontents among the Borisovers. And what about those weirdos who like to confront me on my TV show? They range from civil service malcontents and the unemployed to Israelis with Jerusalem syndrome who think *they're* the messiah. Have someone go through the videos from the show. You may find a suspect or two."

"You really think so?" the Director wanted to know.

"Why not? The video team can help you."

The Director thanked me. He put his hand on his heart as if to demonstrate the pain of loss and of failure he felt. "I'll be in regular touch. Meanwhile, you've got to watch carefully for a ransom note."

After he left, Dina and I fell into each other's arms and simply held each other as if each was a lifebuoy to the other. We both felt overwhelmed by our recriminations and a horrible foreboding that this was the leading edge of disastrous news to follow.

Dina went with guards to pick up David at school, praying all the while that the terrorists did not go after him, too. She took charge of conveying to David the cruel news. I sat by the phone, TV on, awaiting a public announcement of Hanna Liora's capture. Within minutes of David's emotional return from school, the government press release began, and the nation went into shock. Both Dina and I added to our worries the effect of all this on our son.

After that, we were chained to the telephone, but aside from the Director's situation reports, we had no news.

The mail arrived early. Shin Bet must have pulled strings at Israel Post. We put on "archival" gloves that our office uses not to smudge fingerprints when they open letters, and we began to pore through the mail ourselves, looking for a ransom note or some direction from Hanna Liora's captors for our next step. Nothing, but it was too soon to expect anything in the post.

The ransom note arrived by email in mid-afternoon. An assistant printed it forthwith and brought it to our attention. The note said simply, "If you want your daughter to live to see you again, abdicate your throne and have the prime minister announce it to the nation by 11 PM Saturday night. Then you get the next step.

"Signed,

"[Israel Post Peugeot Partner VIN #VF3LBZHZ3FS3019737]"

Grudgingly I admitted they were clever. They knew that anyone could send a note like this, but once the manufacturer's vehicle identification number on the Peugeot checked out, we understood that only the perpetrators and Israel Post itself could have that exact and very long number on such short notice. I lifted the hotline to Shin Bet and informed the Director of the email's contents. He promised to call back quickly. I hung up and waited.

A few minutes later we learned that the email came from a stolen mobile phone which failed to respond to pings in attempts to locate it. The Director also verified the VIN and asked me what I planned to do about the note.

"Are you joking? There's no choice. I'm trading this kingdom of woe and bickering for our daughter whom we love. No choice." After those words, I saw Dina turn the edge of a smile.

He told me he'd notify the prime minister, and a messenger would come to pick up the abdication letter, but he recommended not to relinquish the throne until the last minute in order to give more time to solve the case. He hoped still to find Hanna Liora and avoid the abdication.

I responded that it would be immediately after Shabbat, about 8 PM. Cutting it too close? No, he explained that the *Rosh HaMemshalah* can have emergency air time at any moment he requests it.

We let staff ready us for Shabbat. We certainly didn't have the will to do it. We took our showers and changed while feeling like actors in a play whose script we deplored, pretending to honor the Sabbath with nothing in our souls but a heavy, corrosive dread. I stayed home and davened with David those parts of the service that didn't require a minyan, and we came to the Shabbat table.

After the blessings, we sat down and stared at the lavish dinner whose aromas, meant to delight, only soured our stomachs further. Dina suggested that maybe the staff would like to take our places to enjoy the meal. "Maybe . . . " I said, equally without appetite. Tears rolled down our cheeks. We daubed at them with our napkins.

"Saving a life puts off Shabbat," I declared. "Let's forget Shabbat for now and stay near the phone to await word of Hanna Liora. We'll focus on saving her life."

Dina looked at David and suggested that we needed energy to meet this crisis. We stayed at table and picked at the meal, a Shabbat dinner with no sense of grace or rest. Silence reigned where usually the sound of engaged conversation filled the air.

At last Dina and I gave up pretending we could eat and sat close to the phone, praying for some word. David went to his room, claiming that he was going to read. I visited him a few minutes later. There was no book in sight.

I sat next to him on his bed. "David, what's going on . . . here?" I patted my chest, telling him I wanted to know his feelings.

He reached up and encircled my neck with his arms. A squall of sobs issued forth, accompanied by a mourner's wail. "It's Hanna Liora. She's my big sister. She watches over me. Now she needs me, and I can't help her, I can't watch over her!" He shed more tears.

"That's not your fault," I said, "not when people plot evil against you behind your back. We do the best we can, and we stick together.

It's got to come out all right. We have the whole country trying to help us."

The doorbell rang. "Could be the chief of Shin Bet bringing some word," I suggested, but I doubted it. Nevertheless, David and I headed for the door, with Dina joining us. We three went to the entryway to see if the visitor carried news of our kidnapped daughter.

Dina's eyes, downcast, noted the first hints – the military boots and the stiff, wrinkled outline of an army uniform, and then the actual visage of Hanna Liora. Mother and daughter ran forward, arms outstretched, drawing each other toward their hearts and holding on for dear life. I heard Dina whisper, "Oh, Hanna Liora, I was so scared." Both held their eyes closed and absorbed each other's love in silence. Then, "Thank God you're here. We were so worried! We love you so much!" And she squeezed Hanna Liora even harder. Hanna Liora wept into her mother's shoulder.

I waited a moment then joined the hugging and kissing, and David brought himself into our circle of happiness, too. There was laughter, there were tears of joy enough to fill a waterworks, and then the sudden awareness that someone else stood at the door watching us, a young man about David's age. He waited quietly, as if comprehending the sacred nature of this reunion.

When our emotions returned to earth, Hanna Liora said, "*Abba, Ima*, can you lend me 100 shekels? I have to pay the taxi outside. Oh, and this is Yonatan Lev. I need to tell you about him. He's the hero."

I ran back to the bedroom to get some money to use on this unprecedented Shabbat. Out on the driveway I paid the Arab taxi driver, tripling the fare with the tip. He couldn't believe his eyes and tried to hand the extra cash back to me, saying, "I am happy for you, happy to bring your daughter home. Everyone in the country knows what happened."

I smiled, "Thank you for your kindness, but keep it as part of our gratitude for her safe return." At that moment, I would have paid the driver anything he demanded, but his reaction simply added to our joy.

Back inside, I told everyone I had to call Shin Bet right away. "I'll tell them our daughter is home, but what else?" Hanna Liora suggested they send someone quickly to do a debriefing. That made sense, and, in fact, we were told to expect someone shortly. I asked Yonatan for his mother's cell phone number to call and reassure her of her son's whereabouts. Yonatan's mother readily approved his spending the night with us.

Yonatan joined us at our table of uneaten food. Dina and I offered the most thankful blessing of our children that we ever experienced.

As we enjoyed the meal, our appetites piqued by the good news, we turned to Hanna Liora with so many questions. She said that Yonatan stood out as the champion of this whole affair, and we should let him unfold his own story of bravery.

Yonatan jumped in. "I live with my mother in Mevaseret Zion because my father and I, well, let's just say we don't get along."

Hanna Liora piped up, "Come on, Yonatan. Tell it the way it is. He thrashes you, so you chose to live with your mother."

Yonatan mumbled, "Yeah, well I guess I can be honest with the King. He beats me, so I keep clear of him. But I have to visit just to keep him happy, like for his family gatherings, or he'll hassle my mother in family court. When I go, I like to bring school books with me because I tell him I've really got to study – big test and all that. He believes in education. I use my homework to avoid him and go home as soon as I can.

"When I returned from school this afternoon, my mom wasn't back from work or shopping. I turned on the TV. Pictures of Hanna Liora and stories of the kidnapping appeared on every channel. I hung out at home and played some video games. Meantime, my mother returned and made dinner for the two of us. On Friday nights she makes me rehash my school week. I told her I've got a test in English on Sunday and needed to review. That was true, but then I said some friends were getting together in a few minutes to study. I'm not sure she believed me, but she said OK. In fact, I needed an excuse to leave the house for a while because last week, after the birthday party that my dad's girl-friend threw for him, I left an important school book at his place. I needed to go there.

"My dad lives about a 45-minute walk from Mevaseret, across the highway in an isolated, forested area. When I approached the house, I stood way back and looked through the windows. Lights were on at the front of the house, but no one could be seen. I decided it would be a mistake to knock and deal with my father if he was there. What if he was drinking? He'd be in a mood to whup me for the hell of it. Besides, I liked the adventure of trying to get in and out undetected. I crawled along the side of the house, thinking to enter through one of the win-dows. They were shut tight, but the back door leads to a hallway through the bedroom area. It was open. The place is so isolated; my dad always waits to lock up until bedtime. I came through the entry-way without a squeak or groan from the door, crawled softly along the hall to my bedroom and entered.

"Hanna Liora was sitting there in the growing darkness. The moon was pretty strong and high in the sky, too, so I could see her hands tied to the chair, the tape around her mouth, a blindfold over her eyes. Who else could it be but Hanna Liora? I closed the door behind me quietly, pulled out my pocket knife and cut the rope away from her hands. I stripped off the blindfold, and signaled her to follow me. We crawled back along the hall to the door, and when we breached that opening, we ran like crazy.

"Out in the little forest across from my father's home, I helped Hanna Liora remove the tape from her mouth. We sprinted a good distance, then walked into Mevaseret. Being Shabbat, the shopping center and main streets stood empty, with just a bit of traffic. I called for a taxi. One came over from Abu Ghosh, and here we are.

"And you know what, Mr. and Mrs. King? I still don't have that textbook I need."

The kid displayed a sense of humor, and we all laughed. "Don't you worry, Yonatan. You'll have it by tomorrow night, word of the King of Israel."

Dina said, "Yonatan, you *are* a hero. The whole people will know it. We'll make sure of that."

"No, please, I don't want a big fuss made," Yonatan demurred. "I don't like being singled out. In my high school, it's best to keep your head low."

I said, "That's something we can talk about with you and your mother. In the meantime, we'll keep your name to ourselves, as you want."

The Shin Bet man arrived, we introduced Yonatan, and the official immediately took him aside for questioning. Shin Bet dispatched the police to the home of Orev Lev, Yonatan's father. All the kidnappers had evaporated into the night when they discovered Hanna Liora's disappearance. Eventually they found Orev Lev, along with all his accomplices, a coterie of higher-ups in their ministries who abhorred my advocacy to change policies toward the ultra-Orthodox. They felt their positions would be threatened if the usual government coalitions with religious parties collapsed in the face of stronger involvement by Haredim in general society. They occupied jobs well situated for the bribes they received over many years and fretted over possible loss of income. Now they should worry about their day in court.

Before Shin Bet questioned Hanna Liora, she told us of her ordeal: pushed to the floorboard and held down continuously so as not to be seen in the van, in the minibus, and finally in an ordinary back seat of a small sedan. She was blindfolded, gagged, and tied up the entire time. Her captors humiliated her with the few toilet breaks they permitted, standing over her as she went. They fed her nothing, not even a glass of water for fear that with her mouth uncovered, she'd scream and be detected by neighbors in the vicinity. Nonetheless, our daughter survived the hours in captivity without harm, and we thank God for that.

The Prime Minister walked over from his nearby residence to our palace to meet Yonatan and speak with Hanna Liora. He told us of his delight that he could make this personal visit to celebrate the end of the day-long ordeal. He congratulated Yonatan for his bravery and quick thinking, gave Hanna Liora a two-cheek kiss, and extolled her valor for enduring a fearful and threatening day.

We waited while Hanna Liora met with the investigator. When he emerged, he commented on the situation, saying, "*Melech*, if you check the failed and successful plots in the Middle East and elsewhere, you'll find it's not the generals who constitute the danger to the public order. It's not the big fish. It's the colonels who do the plotting and the overthrowing, and this group of sub-ministers, from the point of view of their position in the government, they're like the colonels. Now we in Israel are learning, these are the ones we have to watch."

After his departure, we all sipped some chamomile tea together as Hanna Liora shed more light on her captivity. She heard the perpetrators conversing, their Hebrew giving away the fact of their Israeli background, but they let slip no reason for their motive in kidnapping her.

"They wanted my abdication of the crown of Israel by tomorrow night," I told her.

"Would you have done it?"

"Without question. To get our daughter back? Absolutely."

Hanna Liora wiped the nascent tears from the corners of her eyes.

I reached across and lifted up her chin, causing her to look directly at me. "What else would any parent do?" She took my hand and kissed it.

Suddenly a wave of exhaustion seemed to burst over Hanna Liora. She begged to be excused for bed, ready to talk more in the morning. After thankful clasps of one another, we all looked forward to a long and peaceful night's sleep. I invited Yonatan to follow me to a guest bedroom and told him along the way that we would respect his need for privacy regarding involvement in the rescue, if that's what he preferred. "Have a good night's rest, Yonatan, and thank you again. Shabbat shalom."

"Shabbat shalom," he said, and collapsed on his bed.

CHAPTER FORTY-EIGHT

The next evening after Havdalah, I commiserated with Yonatan about the fact that his father faced the penalties of law, but there could be no other way. Yonatan reiterated that no loving relationship existed between him and his dad, and that his father deserved whatever sentence the law meted out to him.

"We'll have to wait and see what the court says," I said. "One thing we know for sure, Yonatan. You're not like him. You've got a moral compass. You know which way is up, thank heaven. Now have a good week."

Yonatan nodded. "You, too, Mr. King. And thanks for the hospitality."

I made sure that Yonatan had a ride home to Mevaseret Zion via his father's place, and plenty of protection and help to pick up the book he needed.

A late-evening phone call came from Kol Yisrael news to ask Hanna Liora for a live interview the next day, Sunday, which she gave from her shared apartment in Tel Aviv, her army life already back to normal, though her guard will multiply.

Dina, David, and I watched the interview on TV. Hanna Liora impressed the nation with her poise and directness. The interviewer asked if she was scared, and she said, "Scared? Of course, but that doesn't mean I revealed the fact to my captors. I made it my central task to live each second of my captivity concentrated on something other than my helplessness, and maybe even occasional hopelessness."

"What did you do?"

"In my head, I said some Psalms I'd memorized, staying conscious of my breath as I did. At the appropriate hours, I went through the morning service. Later I sang the Kabbalat Shabbat service in my mind to draw some uplift from the prayers."

"How did you do? Did you recall those prayers all right?"

"Naturally. They're a part of who I am, and I could lead a service by heart, if required."

"What else did you do?"

"I started to think about kidnapping in a logical way. What's the negative commandment involved in it, the commandment that forbids it? Did you know it's one of the Ten Commandments? Since Leviticus 19 also forbids theft, when Rashi sees 'You shall not steal' in Exodus, he immediately connects it to stealing persons: don't kidnap. Why? Because it's part of the top ten commandments, the ones that came from Sinai, and they've got heavy penalties attached. Among thefts, all are recompensable except kidnapping. It's a capital crime, so the Ten Commandments must forbid stealing persons. I wondered if these men had any idea how seriously they violated Jewish traditional law, how wrong they were, and I wondered if someone put their planned crime to them in that way, would they have committed it? I played out a courtroom scene in my head.

"I also thought about what to do if they attacked me. I'm a woman. I was bound to a chair, gagged, and blindfolded. I planned my physical response if they should attack, and that required some detailed imaginings. They left me untouched, but if they had not, I knew how to respond from army training.

"The rest of the time I spent walking the streets of Jerusalem, Jaffa, Tel Aviv's White City, and Haifa."

The interviewer looked puzzled. "What do you mean?"

"I mean, I walked those cities in my head, reproducing the cityscape in my mind. We have distinctive, unusual, and attractive cityscapes in Israel. Not everywhere, mind you, but I love those four cities, I love walking their older streets. It calmed me to imagine myself there. Do you know that computer game where you build your own city? I played it in my head, as well, taking the best of Israel's cities and expanding it in my imagination, something I think we should do in real life, too. All that kept me engaged in my own Israeli world, not the kidnapper's world. They couldn't own my mind. I wouldn't let them. I'm an Israeli soldier, and in war, we have to be prepared for the worst. Being taken prisoner is one of those worst-case scenarios. I was a prisoner of war, only it wasn't the enemy we usually expect."

At that point, Dina and I looked at each other with pride glowing from our faces. What a daughter we have, deeper and more capable than ever we expected. I turned to David. "Quite a sister you've got there, buddy. Yes, she could be Israel's queen someday."

CHAPTER FORTY-NINE

I, Nachum, was king over Israel in Jerusalem. By means of wisdom, I planned a thorough investigation of all that is done under heaven, for there are troublesome problems that God has given humanity to resolve . . .

But in much wisdom there is much grief; and whoever increases knowledge increases sorrow.

I should have known: the crooked cannot be made straight; those who lack integrity cannot be counted upon.[91]

12 Tishri 5788 – Wednesday, 13 October 2027

After a year and a half as King Nachum, I began to take a day off. Wednesday made a good mid-week break. With Hanna Liora already in Tsahal, sometimes we used Wednesday to visit her in Tel Aviv, where our nearby "palace" made it easy to enjoy dinner together. Dina and I would also spend time with wider family, check up on parents, and so forth.

The Wednesday between Yom Kippur and Sukkot provided an opportunity to get away completely. While David was in school, Dina and I drove – scratch that, were driven out to the Jerusalem Forest, the trunk of the car packed with a complete picnic lunch in a large knapsack. We walked a trail for a while, absorbing the quiet, listening for birds, peering downhill at the views while pebbles crunched under our feet with each step. When we chose a place for lunch, the bodyguard who ported the backpack helped us spread a blanket under a tree in the shade. Then all the guards seemed to disappear, though that was an impossibility.

Dina trolled in the bag for the day's lunch and withdrew jars and plastic containers filled with food, a fresh loaf of bread, plastic cutlery and plates, water bottles, wine, and more. Spread before us on the blanket we saw a feast. Looking at each other, we felt the urgency of this moment alone together away from almost everything.

Dina asked, "Do you think they listen to what we say?"

"Listen? No. Hear, yes. I suppose one of them could write a book about us in a couple years, like that butler to the Queen of England some time back."

"Do we have to pass notes to each other?"

I laughed, "Is it about the future of the nation? What's on your mind?"

Dina chuckled, "If you really want to know, it's what's on my head. It's this damned sheitel. The sun's too hot for wearing a wig."

"Take it off. Maybe just a bandana would do. What do you think?"

"I'll try it." She searched in her backpack-style purse until she found a kerchief, pulled off the wig, tucked it in the purse, and wrapped the cloth around her head.

"Better," she said.

"What else is going through your mind?"

"Your next Throne Speech to Knesset: you need to do some marketing, Nachum. If you keep playing the social justice prophet, you'll lose your audience just like the prophets did. People can't handle a lot of jeremiads and bellyaching. They turn off."

"You don't think I should point to another area of weakness in the Land? I've considered following up on Hanna Liora's theme. Did you know, if you take away the Negev, Israel's population density approximates that of Bangladesh? No wonder the cost of housing is climbing sky-high in central Israel. Millions of people are competing for space, all in the same little area."

"Nachum, don't go there. If you must, talk about it another time. Besides, if we open up the Negev beyond Beersheba and make it easier to travel from the Galil to Haifa, what's to keep people from moving there? Then you can cut your density figures in half. No, you need to say something that speaks to the soul, the soul of the country, the soul of our disparate groups, the soul of each individual. Even if what you say is an impossible dream, it doesn't matter. The King should make the throne stand for regal hopes. This time, be a king and a rebbe both."

"OK, marketing consultant. What should be my theme?"

"That's your call," she said. Generous words from Dina, but obviously she had an opinion.

I said, "Pretend you're standing in my shoes before Knesset. What's my theme? How should I say it?"

"For two years you told Knesset that you were unburdening your soul to them. Maybe you unburdened the soul of prophetic teaching to them, but you didn't really share with them your heart, your feelings, your personal questioning, your *neshama*. Give them a piece of your innermost self, not a piece of your mind. Then tell them how good you think they can be and give them a lesson in Torah that they can take home to ponder."

"I like it."

My wife grinned. "I knew you'd like it. Or else," she said, and winked.

I gave Dina a big kiss, followed by a warm hug. Then propriety and hunger overtook both of us. We settled down to our gourmet lunch and a chance to talk about the family.

CHAPTER FIFTY

You have loved justice and hated wickedness, therefore your God anointed you with the oil of gladness beyond your peers (Ps. 45:8). Rabbi Azariah said in the name of Rabbi Aha, "This verse refers to our patriarch Abraham."

God said, "Abraham, 'You loved justice,' which means you loved to vindicate My creatures; and 'you hated wickedness' means you refused to hold them guilty.

"What do I mean by 'beyond your peers'? From Noah to Abraham there were ten generations, and among all those generations, Abraham, you're the only one with whom I ever held a real dialogue."[92]

13 Tishri 5788 – Wednesday evening, 13 October 2027

After evening services, I worked on my address to Knesset, keeping Dina's admonitions in mind. So many years of focusing on issues, first among the Hasidim as their Rebbe and now as King, made it difficult for me to talk about myself, about what's roiling inside my emotions. I started a couple of talks, read them through, but simply filed them away. Scanning my bookshelves, my eyes landed upon *Orchot Tsaddikim, The Ways of the Righteous*. I pulled it down and perused it. The book is 500 years old and sourced from works even older.

The unknown author of *Orchot Tsaddikim* had a sixth sense portending Dina's exhortation in the forest because he speaks of many emotions while getting at higher values. I began to read, and his section on love moved me forward.

I spent a couple of hours developing my talk for Knesset, reviewed it on screen and printed two copies double spaced so that later I could readily mark corrections and additions, and Dina could, too. It was time to call it a night. I left the two copies on my desk and repaired to our bedroom.

13 Tishri 5788 – Thursday morning, 2 AM, 14 October 2027

The history of the Sukkot War is written in the chronicles of the King of Israel and all the press of the Jewish state: how the ALA, Aramean Liberation Army, poured across the Golan Heights from Syria, as well as down from Lebanon, seeking to take back territory lost in the Six Day War and to occupy Israel; how missiles from Lebanon fell in grand number upon cities as far south as Haifa and Tel Aviv; how Jewish soldiers fearing poison gas and biological warfare donned their masks and fought back.

When King Nachum was awakened and learned of the attacks, he hastily donned his uniform, kissed his wife Dina good-bye, and went down from Jerusalem in his own automobile. He was followed in another vehicle by a contingent of surprised guards who could not deter his rash, audacious, and abrupt departure.

Along the way Nachum heard the rumble of fighter jets roaring across the sky. As he drove into the north he saw flashes where rockets hit the earth, followed by thunderclap explosions that assaulted his ears. Above him, intercepts by Iron Dome flared closer with every kilometer he traveled nearer the war zone. Undaunted, the King drove on, adjudging the enemy in possession of too many missiles, reckoning Israel's Iron Dome insufficient to destroy them all.

When the King at last arrived at Ma'alot Giv'at Rabin high in the Galil, he reached his goal: a small station of *Tsahal* troops drafted from Kfar Rachel, all Borisover Hasidim. He parked his car and announced his presence to the guard on duty, who identified the King and saluted. King Nachum proceeded to the commanding officer, again introduced himself and said, "I have come to lead *Shacharit* morning services for our troops."

Gathered as a congregation of Borisover Hasidim ready to defend the town, the soldiers wrapped themselves in their taleisim and tefillin and stood facing south toward Jerusalem and an outdoor ark containing a small, nearly weightless Torah given by the people of Kfar Rachel. The King in his *Tsahal* uniform led services from a rickety and battered Ikea bookcase abandoned to the street.

As he reached the end of the *Aleinu* and chanted the words *Bayom hahu*, "on that day, there will be one God, and God's name shall be One," a rocket launched by the ALA smashed directly into the troops, exploded with cruel force, and killed every soldier in the group, every royal bodyguard, and Nachum, the first Davidic King of Israel in more than two millennia.

So Nachum Steinitz, the servant of God and of the people of Israel, died there in the north of the Galilee. Following tradition, the remaining parts of all bodies were identified by their DNA as speedily as possible, then sent for burial to their respective cemeteries.

Because of the circumstances of identification and wartime exigencies, they interred King Nachum on Mt. Herzl during Chol HaMo'ed Sukkot in the presence of the Knesset, the Israel Supreme Court, the Chief Rabbis, and the King's family. At his funeral, the Gaon of Kfar Rachel read Nachum's *Notes for the Throne Speech in Knesset, 5788*, words found lying upon Nachum's desk on the morning of his death. The Gaon did not call the words a *hesped*, for they were not a eulogy, but instead he asked all to listen to Nachum's *tsava*, his ethical will.

Notes for the Throne Speech in Knesset, 5788

The Effects of Love
I. Introduction

I, Nachum son of David, am *Ha-melech Ha-mashiach*, the anointed King of all Israel – old and young, men and women, city dwellers and country folk, the religious and the secular, Jew and Arab. Therefore I take seriously this single annual opportunity to address the nation in Knesset.

As King Nachum I have discovered a major difference between the former presidency and the throne of Israel. It is the concept of mutual service. In our ancient past, the sovereign head that wore the crown asked the people to pay taxes and give service to the King. Today, Knesset exacts the taxes, but the King can still ask the people, including the Knesset, to freely serve the nation – like *Terumah*, a freewill offering. In turn, the monarch must render a lifetime of service to the people. In our day, this requires a mutual relationship beyond loyalty. It is a relationship of love. That concept caused me to examine the many facets of love in our tradition.

II. Love in Jewish tradition

Our morning prayers speak of *Ahava Raba*, great love. Our evening prayers speak of *Ahavat Olam*, eternal love. These prayers teach that God loved the people of Israel by giving us the Torah, and there is the expectation of a loving response on our part. A book called *The Ways of the Righteous, Orchot Tsaddikim*, teaches that our greatest love and our eternal love must be the love of God.

III. The ways that love can lead us astray

I am fascinated that the *Orchot Tsaddikim* deprecates human love. He criticizes the many loves that can lead us astray. Some of those loves appear on the surface to be generous, even selfless, but *Orchot Tsaddikim* demonstrates their dangers. He caused me to review the history of love in my own family, a powerful and compelling history.

A. Sexual love

I reflected on my great-grandfather Emanuel Davidson, the late Borisover Rebbe. He loved two women in his lifetime. The woman he married, Rachel, daughter of the Borisover Rebbe, and Hannalora Steinitz, my great-grandmother. Were his motivations so pure?

Rachel and Emanuel loved the joys of this world: to dance, to laugh, to partake of the secular offerings of modern life. Rachel used to leave her family home to spend the night with friends. There she changed into non-Hasidic clothing to meet Emanuel, whose beard looked more like Freud's than a Hasid's. They enjoyed Warsaw's night life together, and in her great love for him, she gave Emanuel permission to leave the yeshiva in order to study engineering in Berlin.

Alone in Berlin, he encountered a woman, Hannalora Steinitz, a deeply committed Zionist planning to leave for her greatest love, Israel, then Palestine. Emanuel, without Rachel's presence and perhaps finding in Hannalora the woman whose physical and emotional touch he required at that moment, fell into bed with her. Did he fall in love with her, too? Maybe. But not enough to stay with her and be physically present as father to her child in Palestine. She therefore wanted no part of him ever again. The passion, the sexual love of Emanuel and Hannalora vectored the course of their years, yet it is the source of my very life.

Emanuel returned to Warsaw and married Rachel, never forgetting that he owed Hannalora a debt of child support, which he secretly undertook to fulfill. While Emanuel and Rachel never had children of their own, they made the Borisovers their children, and the loving commitments of Emanuel and Rachel are the source of my life's work.

B. The love of power and money

Did love of power, love of money bring about Emanuel's love of Torah? Indeed, was his love of Rachel brought about by her connection to a powerful and wealthy Hasidic dynasty? How are we to know these things?

I weighed the facts. The existence of Kfar Rachel, which Emanuel first promoted, makes me wonder whether Emanuel was truly anti- or non-Zionist. Was his refusal to go with Hannalora out of ideology, or did he love Rachel more? Or was he in love with the idea of a future that promised more than a pioneer could obtain in Eretz Yisrael? My guess is, at least at the outset, Rachel's family connections attracted Emanuel to her. Is that so unusual, so terrible?

Originally Emanuel might have represented a powerful freedom from Hasidic life for Rachel, while for Emanuel, Rachel may have meant wealth and influence. Often couples who marry for ulterior motives like power and money eventually arrive at a deep and abiding love for one another. That certainly happened with Emanuel and Rachel, considering all they accomplished together for Jewish Warsaw before the Shoah and their constructive work in Brooklyn and in Israel. I don't think their eternal love began *lishmah*, for its own sake, but how can anyone know?

Then I turn to the altar of my own heart, and despite my efforts to purify it, I wonder if I made sacrifices there to the love of power and the need for wherewithal to provide the good life for my family. So, who am I to judge my forebears? To judge anyone?

C. The love of pleasure and of honor

Orchot Tsaddikim speaks of the love of pleasure and of honor, and I am caused to examine myself more closely. I freely admit to you my love of Torah. Study of Torah gives me pleasure. Immersing myself in its questions, its answers, its possibilities for teaching the good life, the godly life. All these give me immense pleasure. Making connection to great thinkers like Maimonides in the past or our own Gaon of Kfar Rachel has illuminated my days.

My study of Torah – is it *lishmah*, for its own sake, or for the sake of my own enjoyment? Accepting honors that came my way because of Torah and the vagaries of chance, the Borisover Rebbe-ship, the kingship of Israel – did I accept these out of a desire to serve, or did honor and glory motivate me? How can I be sure? I love this country, I love its people, I have something to add through leadership, but who does not love honor, at least at some hidden level of their being?

D. The love of close relatives

I love my parents, my family. As you know, I grew up in a secular home. Was it my respect for parents and their attitudes that influenced the direction I sent the Borisover Hasidim, opening the group to employable learning and national service? Or was it a clear and logical assessment of the needs of our country and our Hasidim? I want to believe it was for the good of Borisov and of our country, but how am I to know my own motivations with a certainty?

I think, then, of my closest family, our daughter Hanna Liora, who, according to the Basic Law of the Monarchy, should follow me on the throne, God willing. A brighter, more beautiful heir apparent to the Davidic throne you'll never find. The last Queen of Israel, Salome Alexandra, or Shlomtzion, the final ruler of our independent kingdom from 76 to 67 BCE, proved herself a superb monarch. Rabbis are present here today in part because Shlomtzion elevated the Pharisees to high national position. Rabbis are the heirs of the Pharisees.

My wife Dina and I try to shape Hanna Liora's attitudes and provide her an education to meet her future tasks. Some day she will help make decisions as difficult as Queen Shlomtzion once shouldered. Recent events tell me that she will have that ability, but still, I can only hope that we, her parents, inclined her heart to do what is right and what is just for the great decisions she is yet to make. That is a hope we may never live to see in its fulfillment, which causes us to ponder almost daily whether our choices for our daughter serve the national welfare or simply the love of our close family.

And there's our son David, who loves his Torah study perhaps more than I do, if that's imaginable. Is he the next Borisover Rebbe? Quite possibly, and if we tell him like most parents to do what makes him happy, shall we have failed to form his person with discipline sufficient to his needs and, I might add, sufficient to the needs of the Borisovers and of all Jews? The *Orchot Tsaddikim* warns us against such laxness. It is a fault of parents who love their children.

E. Love of long life

Finally, *Orchot Tsaddikim* speaks in a startling way about the love of long life. Our age extols long life. While they lived, we honored survivors of the Shoah. We introduce our young to veteran survivors of Israel's many wars to illuminate for youth the story of our country. But *Orchot Tsaddikim* frets over those who love long life. When the time comes to make the ultimate sacrifice, to give up their life for something higher than themselves, will they do it?

The walls of every high school in Israel tell of those who sacrificed their lives for the nation. We know they would rather have lived long lives, so is *Orchot Tsaddikim* wrong, or is his comment not on the young, who think they'll live forever and so take risks, but on the middle-aged and old, who know they won't live forever, but who crave as much life as God can possibly afford them? Have I now become one who dons his uniform gussied up with gold braid and ribbons, but who cannot imagine sacrificing his life for a higher cause? Again, I do not have the answer.

IV. What God wants

With all this doubt about the purity of love, what does the *Orchot Tsaddikim* say is expected of us? In his discussion of truth, he points to the siddur, a prayer for Shabbat and festivals: *V'taher libenu l'ovdecha be'emet*, purify our hearts that we may serve You in truth.93

Looking over the history of my own family, I suggest that we do not read it as, *V'taher libenu*. Instead read it, *V'tohar libenu l'ovdecha be'emet*, the center of our hearts, the altar of our hearts must serve You in truth. How do we know what is at the center of our hearts? Only by our own self-examination.

All week long we struggle to earn a living, capitulating to much that is beyond our control. Only on Shabbat have we the liberty to scrutinize the state of our own souls and to purify our hearts to their very core. Each week new temptations and diversions arise to twist our intentions and bend our resolution, demanding we spend part of each Shabbat searching our souls for ulterior motives and mistaken steps. That prayer, *V'taher libenu*, grabs us by both shoulders, shakes us, and says, "Look inside. Read your motives. Cast off the kinds of love which on their surface seem so ethical, so benevolent, but divert you from the Highest."

I, your King, come before you today to confess: though I seek to serve truly, I must question whether I have purified my heart sufficiently for true service, not just to the nation and its people, but to God. When I appeal for your service to the King, I do not ask you to serve me, the King of Israel. I ask, instead, that you serve the King of all the Kings of the Kings, the Holy One of Israel. What shall that service be? Let Knesset join me in my dubiety; walk with me into this chamber in humility, skeptical of our own rectitude. Paradoxically, only when we doubt our motivations, only when we doubt our righteousness can we give others the benefit of the doubt and find our way together.

The benefit of the doubt: a strange phrase because it is not the other person whom we doubt, but ourselves. To doubt our own certitude, purity of heart, and righteousness leads to a certain humility that benefits others. That humility may bring us to a higher love. In this tough corner of the Middle East, can we Israelis learn to love those made in God's image sufficiently well to end the mistrust, the jealousy, the haughtiness, the absurd certainty, the self-righteous chutzpah that separates Jew from Jew and one Israeli from the other?

Knesset is a place where Israel looks for answers. The genius of the Jews taught monotheism, and the genius of monotheism teaches that all exists within the One God. All the answers are there. Elie Wiesel intimated that in our time we find God more in the questions we ask than in the answers we seek. Surely he meant that the answers we seek exist within God, but the God we seek exists within the questions we ask. May this year in Knesset, indeed, in all Israel, be one in which the first questions we ask are not put to our opponents, but rather to our souls, for who among us can be certain that they have entirely purified their heart?

Self-doubt is the gateway to change. It leads to a higher form of love for which our prayers have long yearned, not the welfare of one person or one group, but the welfare of all, shalom in this realm. That kind of higher love may finally permit each of us to give every citizen of the State of Israel and every stranger within her gates an equal share of the rights we claim for ourselves.

I, your *Melech Ha-mashiach*, pray that in these days we can call the days of the mashiach, the words of the prophet will come true, that God's law will be put in our minds and written on our hearts, for we shall all know the Eternal, from the least to the greatest of us (Jeremiah 31:33). This prayer, this hope I offer as your King. I invite you to make it your own. *Ken Yehi Ratson.* Be this God's will. Shalom.

The grave of King Nachum son of David is marked and known and lovingly visited till this day. Nachum was forty-five years old when he died; his eye was not dim, nor his natural force abated. And the people of Israel wept for Nachum across the Land for seven days following the end of Sukkot; and then the days of weeping and mourning for Nachum concluded, along with the mourning for all who died during the bloody war in the north, a war of short duration but of much destructive power. When each side finished counting its dead, the Third Temple still stood, with nary a square cubit nor a *dunam* of land gained or lost, but *Tsahal* battered the Aramean Liberation Army and its dwelling places until their followers turned on the ALA leaders, hanging their bodies out to dry with vows to bring down the Third Temple at a later time.

There has not since arisen in Israel a King like Nachum, who desired to know the ways of the Eternal and of the Torah. Still, other monarchs may yet surpass even his greatness. Nachum took a strong hand to establish the deeds of love and kindness both awesome and small that will be expected of the Davidic House to be performed in the sight of all Israel.[94]

And Hanna Liora, daughter of Nachum Aviam and Dina, was full of the spirit of wisdom; for her parents guided well her formation; and the people of Israel were animated to contemplate her accession to the throne.

CHAPTER FIFTY-ONE

Rabbi Nehorai said, ". . . when the child of David arrives, elders will stand before the young."[95]

30 Tishri 5788 – Sunday, 31 October 2027

The Speaker of the Knesset, Tamara Yarkoni, called the Israeli parliament to order. Following the day's agenda, she asked the leader of the Etz Chaim Torah Party to speak.

"Madam Speaker, I rise to put before Knesset the need for an immediate change in the Basic Laws of the State. In our hurry to finish the Basic Laws we inadvisably included the possibility that a woman could become the monarch of Israel."

Jeering, cheering, table pounding, cries of approval and thundering disapproval poured forth.

The speaker smacked her gavel hard against the table. "Silence!"

The leader of Etz Chaim Torah continued, "Many of us here agree: we simply cannot suffer a woman to be sovereign over Israel. Before we take another step, I propose we review the Basic Law of the Monarchy . . . and change it. I have a motion to offer."

The speaker interrupted. "You realize that the coronation is tomorrow noon at the *Kotel*? Only a very large majority can change the Basic Laws, and we always need time to study such proposals. How can it be done in a day?"

The leader of the conservative Shurat HaDin Party rose to offer an amendment. "If we are going to study the Basic Law of the Monarchy and alter it for the future, then I suggest that today we install a Regent for the interregnum. We are about to have an 18-year-old as our queen. A mere 18!"

More jeering, cheering, and table pounding. Someone yelled, "18 is old enough to die for our country in *Tsahal!*"

The leader of Shurat HaDin added, "She would gain maturity by learning from a solid, long-time, perhaps retired leader of our country. I urge an interregnum and a Regent."

Another MK cried out, "18 was old enough for Queen Victoria to rule!"

Another MK squawked, "Someone new to rob us, a Regent!"

The Speaker responded, "Silence! If it be the will of Knesset to create an interregnum and install a Regent, then according to law, we must consider two factors: the age of the monarch and the mental competency of the monarch to serve. Would not these two factors also require some discussion and investigation? We are dreadfully short on time today."

The leader of the liberal Rodfei Tsedek Party then arose. "I propose a compromise. Tomorrow let us accomplish the coronation of Queen Hanna Liora, who will take the name Shlomtzion II. After the coronation and its festivities, we'll have plenty of time to consider whether we want to change the Basic Law of the Monarchy; whether she, at 18, is too young to rule; and whether she is mentally competent to do so. All this can be considered in Knesset with time for careful weighing of the issues. We made major changes in our law a few years ago. We can always fine tune those changes. Don't forget that the last president of Israel was constrained by law to sign a bill eliminating his own position."

The leaders of Etz Chaim Torah and of Shurat HaDin looked at each other, lifted their hands forward with palms up, and shrugged as if to say, "Why not?", and they sat down, nodding to the Speaker their approval of Rodfei Tsedek's plan.

The Speaker of the Knesset then rapped her gavel. "I take it that any motions on the matter will wait. We all have much to prepare before tomorrow's coronation ceremony, and I am among those who must rehearse the ceremony today. May I have a motion to adjourn?"

Mishnah: After the destruction of the Temple, Rabban Yochanan ben Zakkai ordained that the shofar should be blown on Shabbat in every place where there was a court.

Gemara: Our Rabbis taught that the New Year once fell on a Shabbat, and everyone went to Yavneh to hear representatives of the beth din blow the ram's horn.

Rabban Yochanan said to the B'nai Batira, "We're going to blow the shofar."

They said to him, "Let's discuss whether it is permitted or not."

Rabban Yochanan replied, "Let's blow the shofar, and afterward we'll discuss it." After they blew the shofar, the B'nai Batira said to Rabban Yochanan, "Let us now discuss the question."

He replied, "The shofar has been heard in Yavneh, and what has been done is no longer open to debate."[96]

דברי הימים של שלומציון ב'

THE CHRONICLES OF
SHLOMTZION II

Nachum was king over Israel. Nachum and Dina gave birth to Hanna Liora and David. After the death of Nachum at the hands of the Aramean Liberation Army, all Israel gathered in Jerusalem, saying to Hanna Liora, "Behold, you are our flesh and blood, the rightful heir to the throne, and we declare you today our sovereign." Hanna Liora was anointed Queen Shlomtzion II and led her people for many decades.

As her first officially recorded act, Shlomtzion II, *Ha-malkah Ha-meshichah*, the anointed queen, called a Royal Conference of Israeli Women – all women: secular and religious, Arab and Jewish, temporary workers, teachers and rabbis and students, straight and LGBTQ, and others – to address issues of pay equity, women's place in business and industry and professions, violence against women, labor rights, marriage rights, family planning, religious rights, child care, educational opportunity, housing and neighborhood improvement, problems of ageing.

More than any other cause after the completion of the Basic Laws, it was the extensive work of this annual conference stamped with the imprimatur of Queen Shlomtzion II that dramatically changed Israeli life and made it seem as if, indeed, the days of the *Meshichah* had arrived.

Hear, O Israel, the Eternal, our God, the Eternal is One. (Deut. 6:4)
Why say "our God"? Isn't it enough to say simply "the Eternal is One"? Why add "our God"? To teach that God's name rests in great measure upon us.[97]

Notes

The Mossad Messiah is fiction. Statistics will always be a tricky business, but the author sought accuracy insofar as possible using materials publicly available during 2016-17. Statistical sources include Israel government documents, newspapers and journals, internet sources, and reports of scholarly research. For the sake of accuracy, sources included everything from rabbinic responsa literature to 1930's train timetables, ocean liner brochures and old travel guides. Accuracy in these matters helps make fiction feel authentic, but it does not change the fact that no Borisover Rebbe, no Borisover Hasidim, and no Kfar Rachel exist. For full disclaimer, see the copyright page.

Spelling of English words generally follows the advice of https://www.dictionary.com, which accepts many Hebrew and Yiddish terms into the English language, with the result that many such words are not italicized in the novel.

In the main, only classical Jewish texts will be found cited in the body of the novel or the notes. Unless otherwise indicated, traditional texts are translated and elucidated by the author based on the sources cited. "Talmud" is the Babylonian Talmud. Rabbi Levi ben David v'Yehudit is not in the notes because his quotations are the author's own novellae.

---

[1] Seymour Hersh, *The Samson Option* (New York: Random House, 1991), 223.

[2] Talmud Berachot 28a. When the Sanhedrin deposed Rabban Gamaliel as its head, on that day [Bo BaYom] they added new seats and permitted other disciples to enter. Alarmed, Rabban Gamaliel fretted that he had blocked new wisdom from the people. In a dream he saw casks of worthless ashes, to him symbolic of those who occupied the new seats. But the dream was a meaningless diversion to assuage his spirit. In fact, fresh wisdom filled the new seats.

[3] Talmud Sanhedrin 73a.

[4] Mishnah Orla 3:9.

5 Talmud Rosh Hashana 18b.

6 Ecclesiastes/Kohelet 12:9.

7 Talmud Ketubot 62b. Rabbi Akiba was a shepherd for Ben Kalba Sabua, whose daughter Rachel noticed Akiba's modesty and nobility. She said to him, "If we decided to marry, would you go away to study Torah?" He agreed. They were secretly betrothed, and she sent him away to study.
When her father discovered the matter, he drove Rachel from his house and forswore from her any benefit of his estate. Akiba spent twelve years at the academy. Upon his return, he brought with him twelve thousand disciples. Then he overheard an old man say to Rachel, "How long will you live the life of a widow?"
"As far as I'm concerned," she replied, "he could spend another twelve years in study." Akiba thought, "So I have her consent to go again." Off he went for a dozen more years of study at the academy.

8 Talmud Chagiga 16a. Rav Elai the elder said: If a man feels his evil inclination overcoming him, let him go to a place where he is not known, dress in black garments, and let him do what his heart desires; but let him not profane the Name of Heaven publicly.

9 Midrash Genesis Rabbah 85:9.

10 Section based on Talmud Ketubot 63a. When Rabbi Akiba finally returned from his years of study, he brought along 24,000 disciples. His wife Rachel went to meet him. As she kissed his feet, Akiba's attendants ran to thrust her aside, but the rabbi cried, "Let her be! Whatever learning we have we owe to her, for it was she who inspired my studies."
Rachel's father heard that a great man had come to town. He went to Akiba and asked, "Can you invalidate my vow to forswear the benefit of my estate from my daughter?" Rabbi Akiba replied, "Would you have made your vow if you knew that he was a great man?" Rachel's father said," If the fellow knew even one chapter, even a single law, I would not have made the vow."
Akiba exclaimed, "I am the man." Immediately Rachel's father kissed Akiba's feet and also gave him half his wealth.

11 Zohar I, 91b. Before it enters the world, each soul consists of male and female elements united in one existence. When the soul descends to earth at birth, the two parts seperate and animate two different bodies. These two parts – each merely half of an entire soul – seek the half that will properly complete them. When a couple is truly worthy of one another, the Holy One unites them as they were before, one soul, the right and left side of one individual.

12 Infertility in Judaism, Ritualistic Traditions, http://www.mazornet.com/infertility/traditions.htm and Nina B. Cardin, *Tears of Sorrow, Seeds of Hope: A Spiritual Companion for Dealing with Infertility and Pregnancy Loss* (Woodstock, Vermont: Jewish Lights, 1998).

[13] Cardin, 59.
[14] Talmud Shabbat 66b.
[15] Cardin, *op. cit.*
[16] Talmud Bava Kama 82a.
[17] Midrash on Psalms, Ps. 118, section 17.
[18] Talmud Bava Batra 8a. During a year of scarcity, Rabbi Judah the Prince, the wealthy author of the Mishnah, opened his storehouse of victuals, proclaiming, "All who have studied words of Torah may enter. The ignorant are barred."
Rabbi Jonathan ben Amram pushed his way in and said, "Master, give me food."
"Have you learned Torah or Mishnah?"
Rabbi Judah said, "So how can I give you food?"
"Feed me as you would feed a dog or a raven."
Rabbi Judah gave him some food, but later his conscience gnawed at him: "I wish I had not given my bread to an unlearned man!"
His son Simeon suggested, "Maybe he was Jonathan ben Amram, your pupil, who lives by the principle never to derive material benefit from the honor paid to the Torah."
Rabbi Judah checked, and sure enough, his son was correct; then he said: "Anyone may now enter."
[19] Charity and Charitable Institutions, http://jewishencyclopedia.com/articles/12271-poor-relief-of.
[20] Moses Hess, *Rome and Jerusalem*, trans. Meyer Waxman, (New York: Bloch Publishing, 1918).
[21] Midrash Rabbah Kohelet I:4.
[22] Sifre, Piska 1. Rabbi Levi said in regard to the words "of gold" (*Di-Zahav*) (Deut. 1:1): This refers to the Golden Calf. There were two collections of gold. Aaron made one for the Golden Calf, and after that idolatry, a different collection funded the sacred tabernacle of the wilderness wanderings, the Mishkan.
Where did the Children of Israel obtain the gold to make the Golden Calf? From the Egyptians (Ex. 12:35, The Israelites did as Moses instructed and asked the Egyptians for articles of silver and gold . . .).
Where did the Children of Israel obtain the gold for the Mishkan? From their own horde of hidden treasure. Their great remorse for the sin of the Golden Calf induced them to offer all they had so laboriously saved during dangerous times in Egypt.
[23] Midrash Rabbah Kohelet I:3.
[24] Talmud Eruvin 13b.
[25] Talmud Bava Metzia 62a.
[26] Talmud Eruvin 53b. Rabbi Joshua ben Hananiah said, "While on a journey I noticed a little boy sitting at a crossroads. I asked him which road leads to the town. He pointed to one and said, 'This way is short but long, and the other is long but short.'
"I chose the short but long road. Approaching the town, I realized that

it was hedged in by gardens and orchards and impossible to enter. I returned to the crossroads and said to the boy, 'Didn't you say that this road was short?'"

He replied, "Didn't I also tell you: But long?"

I kissed his forehead and said, "Happy are you, O Israel, for you are all wise, both young and old."

27 Chaim ben Moshe ibn Attar, Ohr HaChaim commentary on the Torah.

28 Genesis 18:19.

29 Mishnah Pirkei Avot 2:15. Rabbi Tarfon said: The day is short, and the work great; and the workmen are lazy, but the reward is much; and the master of the house is urgent.

30 Midrash Tanhuma to Mikeitz, 6, Genesis 42:1. When, after many years, Joseph saw his brothers in Egypt, he recognized them immediately, but his brothers failed to recognize him, for they had not been merciful to their brother. Why did Joseph recognize them? Because he was merciful towards them.

31 Talmud Yevamot 9a, also Berachot 36b; Beitsa 11b. ("*Beit Shammai bimekom Beit Hillel einah Mishnah*").

32 Mishnah Yevamot 15:3.

33 Based on Bet Hillel and Bet Shammai, http://jwa.org/encyclopedia/article/bet-hillel-and-bet-shammai.

34 Mishnah Eduyot 1:5.

35 Based on Wrestling with Ethically Challenging Rabbinic Sources, https://prizmah.org/wrestling-ethically-challenging-rabbinic-sources.

36 Isaiah Horowitz (Shl'ah), Shavuot, chapter Ner Mitzvah 35.

37 Talmud Pesachim 50b.

38 Talmud Yevamot 62a.

39 Talmud Sanhedrin 5a Rabbi Hiyya said to Rabbi (Judah, editor of the Mishnah): My sister's son is going down to Babylon. Is he permitted to decide on matters of ritual law? (*Yoreh?*) He may. (*Yoreh!*) Is he permitted to decide on monetary cases? (*Yadin?*) He may. (*Yadin!*).

40 Mishnah Ketubot 13:11 All can be made to go up to the Land of Israel, but not compelled to leave; all can be made to go up to Jerusalem, but not compelled to leave.

41 Rashi on Gen. 33:2.

42 Birkat HaMazon, blessing after meals.

43 Talmud Shabbat 31a.

44 Nedarim 28a and other Talmudic sources.

45 Midrash Rabbah Numbers (Midreshei Agadah) 1:11.

46 Based on Pesikta d'Rav Kahana 5:3. In the Isaiah text, *chorvoteha*,"her ruined places," compare the reference to the name of the ruined synagogue, usually spelled in English "Hurva."

47 Talmud Bava Metzia 59a.

48 Maimonides, Introduction to *Moreh Nevuchim* (*The Guide of the Perplexed*).

49 Pesikta d'Rav Kahana 5:3.
50 Midrash Rabbah Genesis 98:4.
51 Talmud Berachot 27b.
52 Rabbi Herschel Schachter, Halachic Aspects of Family Planning, download.yutorah.org/1982/1053/735664.pdf.
53 Midrash Rabbah Ecclesiastes 7:20.
54 Soncino Midrash Rabbah Genesis 98:4, Davka Judaic Classics Software, compiled by David Kantrowitz (Davka,1991-2009).
55 Talmud Yevamot 90b.
56 Based on Samuel 1:12ff.
57 Isaiah 40 and Deuteronomy 16:19.
58 Mishnah Avot 4:5.
59 Mishnah Avot 3:17.
60 Berachot 35b.
61 Talmud Yoma 82a. See also Deut. 22:25-26.
62 Talmud Yevamot 45a.
63 Mishneh Torah, Kings and Wars 11:1.
64 Jer. 7: 22, 23, and Jer. quotes Lev. 26:12.
65 Moreh Nevuchim 3:32.
66 Biblical quotation: Hosea 6:6; Midrash: Avot deRabbi Nathan 4:5.
67 Talmud Berachot 55a.
68 Talmud Sanhedrin 98a.
69 Raphael Patai, *The Messiah Texts* (New York: Avon, 1979), 42-3.
70 Mishnah Avot 1:12.
71 Isaiah 56:7.
72 Gevurot HaShem, p. 114, chapter 29.
73 See Ashamnu Bagadnu Yom Kippur prayer Vidui Zuta.
74 Talmud Shabbat 31a.
75 Talmud Horayot 12a.
76 Talmud Keritot 5a.
77 Ibid.
78 Ibid.
79 Talmud Horayot 12a, Keritot 5b.
80 *Mishneh Torah, Hilchot Melachim* 11:3.
81 II Samuel 6.
82 Ecclesiastes/Kohelet 1.
83 Talmud Kiddushin 71a.
84 NGO (non-governmental organization) = Hiddush, World Map of Marriage Freedom, http://marriage.hiddush.org/.
85 Elie Kaplan Spitz, Mamzerut, https://www.rabbinicalassembly.org/sites/default/files/assets/public/halakhah/teshuvot/19912000/spitz_mamzerut.pdf.
86 Talmud Pesachim 66a.
87 Ecclesiastes/Kohelet 1.
88 II Samuel 12:23.

[89] Based on Yom Kippur Machzor, *Mipnei chata'einu galinu mei'artzeinu v'nitrachaknu mei'al admateinu*, Because of our sins we were exiled from our country and banished from our land.

[90] Midrash Ruth Rabbah, prologue 7.

[91] Ecclesiastes/Kohelet 1.

[92] Midrash Rabbah Genesis, 39:6, 49:9.

[93] Based on *Orchot Tsaddikim*, Gate 5 - Love, Gate 23 - Truth; Gate 28 - Awe of Heaven.

[94] Deuteronomy 34.

[95] Derech Eretz Zuta 10.

[96] Talmud Rosh Hashanah 29b.

[97] Sifre, Parshat Vaetchanan, Piska 6.

Made in the USA
Middletown, DE
18 December 2021